Design for Aging Review

AIA Design for Aging Knowledge Community

Design for Aging Review 10

AIA Design for Aging Knowledge Community

THE AMERICAN INSTITUTE OF ARCHITECTS

Published in Australia in 2011 by
The Images Publishing Group Pty Ltd
ABN 89 059 734 431
6 Bastow Place, Mulgrave, Victoria 3170, Australia
Tel: +61 3 9561 5544 Fax: +61 3 9561 4860
books@imagespublishing.com
www.imagespublishing.com

The Images Publishing Group Reference Number: 912

National Library of Australia Cataloguing-in-Publication entry:

Title:	Design for aging review / AIA Design for Aging Knowledge Community.
Edition:	10th ed.
ISBN:	9781864703917 (hbk.)
Notes:	Previous ed.: 2008.
Subjects:	Older people—Dwellings—United States—Design and construction.
	Old age homes—United States—Design and construction.
	Barrier-free design for older people—United States.
	Architecture—Awards—United States.
Other Authors/Contributors:	American Institute of Architects Design for Aging Center.
Dewey Number:	725.560222

Production by The Graphic Image Studio Pty Ltd, Mulgrave, Australia
www.tgis.com.au

Pre-publishing services by Mission Productions Limited, Hong Kong

Printed on 140gsm GoldEast Matt Art by Everbest Printing Co. Ltd., in Hong Kong/China

IMAGES has included on its website a page for special notices in relation to this and its other publications. Please visit www.imagespublishing.com.

CONTENTS

AIA Foreword

The projects that have been chosen as award winners in this Design for Aging Review competition celebrate design excellence and show why design matters for our aging population. It is gratifying to see the continued success of the competition. This 10th cycle represents 20 years of collaboration between designers and care providers to promote a competition that seeks to identify and document quality in the design of life-enhancing environments for older adults.

While going 'gray' may not be as desirable as going 'green,' the increase in the aging population nationally and globally cannot be ignored. Twenty percent of the population in the United States will be over the age of 65 by 2030.

In a survey of the top 10 concerns for older Americans, financial security took first place followed by improvements to Medicare and health insurance, avoidance of isolation or loneliness, and in fifth place, concerns about the affordability of housing and services.

As the national rate for skilled nursing care in a private room exceeds $77,000 per year and with only 46 percent of nursing home and home care costs being paid through Medicaid, there is great cause for concern. Previous assumptions that fostered the design and delivery of facilities for our aging population are being reevaluated in response to our current economic climate. This recession may have 'right sized' the industry and promoted the concept that bigger is not necessarily better. A smaller, well-designed, and appropriately appointed apartment can be more livable, comfortable, and more importantly, a supportive environment for older adults.

Within this collection of award-winning projects, the issue of affordability is clearly addressed, demonstrating that quality environments can be achieved within budget constraints. Designers and care providers also raised the bar on wellness, encompassing a more holistic approach to spiritual, mental, and physical well-being while other projects focused on the care, compassion, and unique environments required when addressing end-of-life issues.

Above all, this 10th cycle of the *Design for Aging Review* confirms that the profession is thinking 'outside the box' and continues to address the important challenges of an aging society.

George H. Miller, FAIA, 2010 AIA President.

AAHSA Foreword

Although capital is tight, the demand for healthy and health-fostering environments is on the rise. I believe we are on the precipice of an environmental transformation in the senior communities we create. This is already evident in the beautifully designed environments I have seen on visits to AAHSA-member communities across the country.

The very best communities function as what I like to call 'centers for healthy aging.' Our challenge is to develop more of these healthy environments, in which some people live, some visit, and others work. In such environments, all are finding community, solace, fun, comfort, new opportunities, and programs that encourage health and well-being.

I visit many, many member communities. One can see, feel, smell, and experience centers for healthy aging. These are welcoming places that invite choices. They offer variety in décor and venues for interaction and activity. They use technology to foster community within and outside their walls. There are planned wellness programs and, often, spa-like services. There are programs for reflection and remembrance, as well as new experiences and opportunities for active learning.

Increasingly, there is an emphasis on green living and stewardship of the environment. Clinical expertise and the technology to support it are present but camouflaged.

Sensitive design is also evident in lighting, with neither shadowy wall sconces nor glaring lights from sterile ceilings. Armrests, tables, and chair seats are the right height. Attention to detail is apparent inside and out. Garden spaces are attractive, accessible, and safe. Digging, planting, and nurturing are encouraged as much as just looking. Wandering is enabled and made safe because security is strong, but subtle.

Yes, our job is transforming artificial, institutional environments into natural, healthy, welcoming communities. Places to call home.

In *Design for Aging Review 10*, the AAHSA and AIA's Design for Aging Knowledge Community celebrate advances in creative design for seniors. The new volume features fine examples of transformation and reinvention to support frail elders and maximize opportunities for all who live, visit, and work in these centers for healthy aging. The AAHSA and AIA also celebrate a new collaboration to publish *Trends in Design* featuring evidence-based, award-winning design projects that illustrate the best in design for aging projects.

In both publications, readers will find examples of the finest re-imagining of design solutions for senior-living environments.

William L. (Larry) Minnix, Jr.,
President and Chief Executive Officer

The Jury

Jeff Los, AIA, LEED AP is an architect and managing principal at Ankrom Moisan Architects in Portland, Oregon. His 35-year career encompasses master planning and design of all levels of care for senior housing developments throughout the country. He is a published author of articles about trends in design for senior living and building design considerations, and has spoken at a variety of regional and national senior-care conferences. Jeff Los was the principal architect for Mirabella Portland, a 30-story urban Continuing Care Retirement Community that achieved LEED Platinum certification and opened in August 2010. Jeff Los also serves on a council sponsored by Oregon Health and Sciences University that focuses on research and development of technology to promote independent aging.

D. Scott Crabtree is president and chief executive officer of Broadway Services, Inc., a New Orleans-based management company. Broadway Services, Inc. is the operator of Lambeth House, an urban Continuing Care Retirement Community. Scott Crabtree has worked in healthcare administration since 1982, and in senior living management specifically since 1992. He is a licensed nursing facility administrator and a board member of the Louisiana Board of Examiners for Nursing Home Administrators. He is also an appointed member of the Louisiana Emergency Preparedness Review Committee. He is currently a board member and past president of the Gulf States Association of Homes and Services for Aging. He has been active at the national level with AAHSA and serves on the House of Delegates and the Educational Committee. Scott Crabtree has been involved in numerous senior living and healthcare construction projects over the past two decades, and served on non-profit boards for organizations related to education, senior services and disabilities in the New Orleans community. He also serves as a preceptor for the Tulane University Master's of Health Administration program.

Diana Kissil, AIA, LEED AP is an architect and principal at SmithGroup, specializing in interior architecture and design of senior housing. Her material selection and design concepts have helped establish her as an acclaimed senior living and healthcare interior designer, credited with innovative spaces across the United States. Her award-winning projects, which focus on sustainable design and integrated delivery processes, have been recognized in publications like *Interiors*, *Health Facilities Management Magazine*, and the AIA's *Architecture California*. In addition, she has taught various interior design courses at the University of California, Berkeley.

Larry Mabry serves as Chief Executive Officer for Collington Episcopal Life Care Community in Mitchellville, Maryland. He is a licensed nursing home and residential care administrator. He serves as an evaluator for the Post Occupancy Review Project with the AIA and AAHSA. He is a past president of the Presbyterian Association for Homes and Services for the Aging, past member of the AAHSA House of Delegates and a two-term member of the AAHSA Board of Directors. Larry Mabry is active in his community with the Presbyterian Church, Rotary, and various chambers of commerce in the metropolitan Washington, DC area.

Jury Statement - Architects' Perspective

The Process

Have you heard the story about the two architects and two senior housing executives that walk into a room and talk about 92 senior housing projects? No, I didn't think so.

That's because, regardless of the Jury's years of experience, and the hundreds of times architects and owners meet to review a specific project, it is unique to review the full spectrum of current design thinking about senior housing in one sitting. But in August, 2009 that is just what we did, although truthfully, it began two weeks before when we were the first Design for Aging Review Jury to receive all the submitted projects electronically. This allowed each individual Jury member to evaluate every submittal in detail (reportedly a 40–60-hour effort), and arrive at the formal Jury ready to compare notes. What followed was an energetic and productive discussion. In most cases, it showed that high-quality aesthetic and functional design resonated with the architects and providers equally. The Jury selected 14 projects for overall merit, 3 for special recognition, and 21 other notable projects for inclusion in this publication.

The process yielded lively discussion, some debate, but mostly affirmation of how thoughtful design and creativity, when balanced with operational needs, can contribute meaningfully to senior housing and services. The array of submittals demonstrates how diversified service models for seniors have become in size, context, specialized services, and market focus. The term 'senior housing' includes a collection of buildings ranging from a one-story house for 10 hospice residents to a high-rise, urban Continuing Care Retirement Community (CCRC). And yet, design sensitivity, imagery, innovation, and social responsibility are the common themes that distinguished projects selected by the Jury.

The Projects

The projects submitted covered the full spectrum geographically, financially, and in the scale and scope of the services offered. For the first time, there was a category for affordable developments, and it was gratifying to see the creative solutions and quality environments that emerged on limited budgets. Adaptive reuse, revitalization of older facilities with new centers, and increased attention to sustainable design principles shared the spotlight with upscale high-rise urban and suburban CCRC housing. The projects continue to demonstrate the broad range of senior housing options that the public needs, and the multiple ways in which they can be delivered. Interestingly, design for new or remodeled skilled nursing facilities, despite a 'culture change' service philosophy, remains generally uninspired, perhaps because the buildings are physically restrictive, or because financial reimbursement simply won't support more significant renovation. With the large number of older existing facilities, this remains a significant challenge for both providers and the design community.

The Trends

Building designs and resident programs that promote integration with the greater community, as opposed to isolation from it, seem to be the impetus for many projects. Older campuses look to adapt to the changing expectations of the market. An emphasis on health and wellness continues to grow, as does the prevalence of resort-style amenities. An emerging trend appears to be affordable senior housing as a component of the revitalization of urban and semi-urban neighborhoods. Smaller-scale projects for hospice, collaborative housing, and multi-generational projects and services indicate a desire to diversify options beyond traditional senior housing models. Innovation and adaption to a more discerning and informed senior market seem to be at the root of all of these trends. With the extended timelines required to take a project from concept to occupancy, providers and architects will need to be ahead of the curve to align building designs and market demands.

While there was heightened attention to sustainable design principles, green design is just beginning to mature for senior housing. Several projects embraced LEED certification and adaptive reuse strategies as part of project design criteria. Given the long-term benefits of energy savings, improved indoor air quality, and the socially responsible aspects of green design, it is anticipated that future developments will attach increasing emphasis to this issue.

The Jury wishes to congratulate all of the teams that are recognized in this publication, and thank everyone who submitted projects for consideration. The projects are the end result of creative and collaborative efforts by designers and providers who seek to improve environments and services for seniors.

Jeff Los, AIA, LEED AP
Jury Chair

Jury Statement - Providers' Perspective

Every two years, two architects and two providers receive a call from the AIA's Design for Aging Knowledge Community and the American Association of Homes and Services for the Aging (AAHSA). It is the collective affirmative response of those individuals that begins the process of reviewing outstanding designs for aging. However, the process has begun in earnest well before this call comes. Architects, providers, consumers, and countless other people have been integrally involved in designing and building these environments for our aging consumers. These people are to be commended for their dedication to energetic designs and built environments for seniors. As the reader will find when studying *Design for Aging Review 10*, the most successful designs are indeed those that were a collaboration of the stakeholders in the project. It is critical for our industry's future to continue the AIA/AAHSA relationship. By combining both architects and providers on this Jury, we have the ability to fully evaluate and reward functional and leading-edge design for seniors.

A little more about this call from the AIA – as a provider in the senior living industry and healthcare industry since 1982, I was a bit reluctant when the request was made for me to participate in the Design for Aging Review (DFAR). Having been involved in a number of design and construction projects, on one hand I was eager to bring this experience to the review process, but on the other hand, I wondered if I could commit the time. Once the submittals were made available to the Jury, just the sheer number of projects was daunting. Having not yet met any of the Jury, and having only had a teleconference with the Jury and AIA staff, one might quickly ask why they agreed to serve on the DFAR. Yet, these concerns instantly dissipate with the review of only a few of the submittals (easily verifiable by my executive staff whose offices are next to mine – as I was overhead multiple times speaking to my computer with words like 'wow,' 'incredible,' and 'I want that building').

With the ability to review all projects via an online system, the review of the narratives as well as full series of color photography and renderings, much of the preliminary work was done over several weeks before convening in Washington, DC. After a lengthy but easily manageable process, the Jury then came together for two intense days of review of the projects and selection of the awards. This is the point when you realize that had you passed on the opportunity to serve, you would have regretted this for quite some time. The synergy that develops between the two extraordinary architects and two providers is immediate. The process is highly structured and guidelines and criteria for the review are precise. The decisions regarding the projects that deserve recognition and/or awards are sometimes easy to make and sometimes very difficult. However, the AIA facilitator and the Jury seemed to never lose focus during the review process. The results: 14 Award Recipients and 3 Special Recognition recipients.

For this cycle 92 projects were submitted for review – a surprisingly large number given the economic condition of the USA and the senior living industry over the past three years. Clearly, the majority of the projects were in the Building category with 47 projects. Most impressive, in my opinion, were the 13 submittals in the Affordable category. This is an area of service delivery that often results in the least expensive designs and construction with the least effort in quality and leading-edge design. This is clearly changing and one only needs to look at the DeVries Place Senior Apartment in Milpitas, California. This project was an Award of Merit honoree in both the Affordable and the Building categories and is truly one of the most outstanding projects in this cycle. Not only is the design significant, but the program and services will anchor this area of the city. DeVries shows how a city cares about its own future through the design, building, and operation of this senior-living setting. Also, Buena Vista in San Francisco was evidence of an adaptive reuse that creates a high-quality affordable living environment for seniors. It rivals many designs for even market-rate senior living (as does Sky 55 in Chicago, a stunning design and an example of combining market-rate, affordable, and low-income options into the same campus).

Repositioning was clearly evidenced in a number of submittals. This was not surprising given the age of many of our senior living communities and the demands of the new generation of consumers. One particular project that exemplifies a comprehensive repositioning is The Point at C.C. Young in Dallas, Texas. This holistic wellness center was thoughtfully designed and executed with special attention to opening the campus to intergenerational and community activities. The Jury chose the phrase 'heart and soul of the community' as significant descriptor of this project. As a provider who works in the CCRC sector of the industry, I was impressed by the focus of some organizations in designing and building hospice environments that place the resident and their families first. One example of this was Hospice of Lancaster County in Mount Joy, Pennsylvania. We hope that this trend will continue to be a primary focus in design.

As the reader reviews *Design for Aging Review 10*, I am certain that they will see consistent commitment from architects and providers to research, design, and build that reflects advancements in quality of life, care, and services. The continued focus on the whole person (designing for the body, mind, and spirit) is a trend that all of us will want to see continued. Innovation and enthusiasm will create great results. We are all stewards of the environment, and sustainability is an area that we are all challenged to implement in our projects. Each time I review a project, I simply ask myself, 'Will I want to live in that environment?'

The great architect Philip Johnson said, 'All architecture is shelter, all great architecture is the design of space that contains, cuddles, exalts, or stimulates the persons in that space.' A thorough review of the 38 projects in *Design for Aging Review 10* and one sees how far we have advanced in creating vibrant, compassionate, and stimulating spaces. Make a difference – be involved in any way you can in the future of design for aging.

D. Scott Crabtree
Jury Member

Projects & Awards

HKIT Architects

Buena Vista Terrace

San Francisco, California // Citizens Housing Corporation

Facility type: Independent Living
Target market: Low income/subsidized
Site location: Urban (city or town)

Capacity: 40 units; 47 people
Total project cost: $8.7 million
Date of completion: July 2007

Below: Front façade and entrance, Haight Street
Opposite: Aerial view, surrounding neighborhood

Overall Project Goals

The conversion of an abandoned church into 40 senior apartments preserves an important local landmark and provides new affordable housing; this innovative project achieved adaptive reuse with minimal changes to the historic exterior. The 1915 Romanesque Revival church is considered an architectural gem and is valued for its unchanging presence in the vibrant Haight-Ashbury community. From the time the site was identified, the team knew it would be a challenge to strengthen the unreinforced masonry church and fit a feasible number of units into the shell. Ultimately, the design team was able to create small but graceful apartments that highlight the church's unique qualities. The design and construction teams collaborated to retain as much of the existing structure as possible. Architectural details were carefully removed, catalogued, repaired, and reinstalled into the new work. Historic stained glass windows were retained despite stringent state energy efficiency standards by making the new windows far exceed code requirements. The gentrification of urban neighborhoods often results in loss of religious structures abandoned by a changing population. This project not only saved a historic church but provides operating income to maintain it in perpetuity. This unique solution allows the neighborhood to preserve affordable senior housing and its architectural heritage simultaneously.

Provider's Statement

Provider goals for marketing and sales

This project is specifically designed for the senior affordable rental market. With a high demand for affordable housing, approximately 1,500 people picked up applications to live at Buena Vista Terrace (BVT) prior to the opening. It was 100 percent leased on the day it opened.

How did the provider plan to improve the residents' quality of life?

First and foremost, BVT maintains a smoke-free environment, which benefits all people who enter the property. In addition, BVT's location provides residents with the advantages of living in a city as well as benefits that one may expect to find in a more rural setting. Located directly across from Buena Vista Park, residents have easy access to the type of rich urban park that San Francisco is known for. At the same time, the location allows for ease of access to public transportation and amenities. Combined with modern, environmentally sound units housed in an historic shell, BVT greatly enhances the quality of life of its residents at affordable rental rates.

Did the provider give specific direction about the style, materials, features, or other design aspects of the project? If so, what were those directives?

The project designers were given the monumental task of restoring and maintaining the original structure while still fitting enough units into the building to meet the financial goals of the development. In short, the challenge was to fit a feasible number of units into an historic shell without jeopardizing its architectural character. The new design preserves the outstanding Byzantine exterior of the church building, which has been a neighborhood landmark for many years. The church's existing stained glass windows were restored and the interior converted into private residences.

How did the provider's financial goals influence the project's organization, configuration, layout, or sizing of components?

The project is cost effective considering the multiple goals it achieved – preservation of an important historic landmark in the Haight-Ashbury community, complete seismic and systems upgrade, and the

Typical upper floor plan

1 Lobby
2 Office
3 Garbage/recycling
4 One-bedroom unit
5 Studio unit
6 Elevator

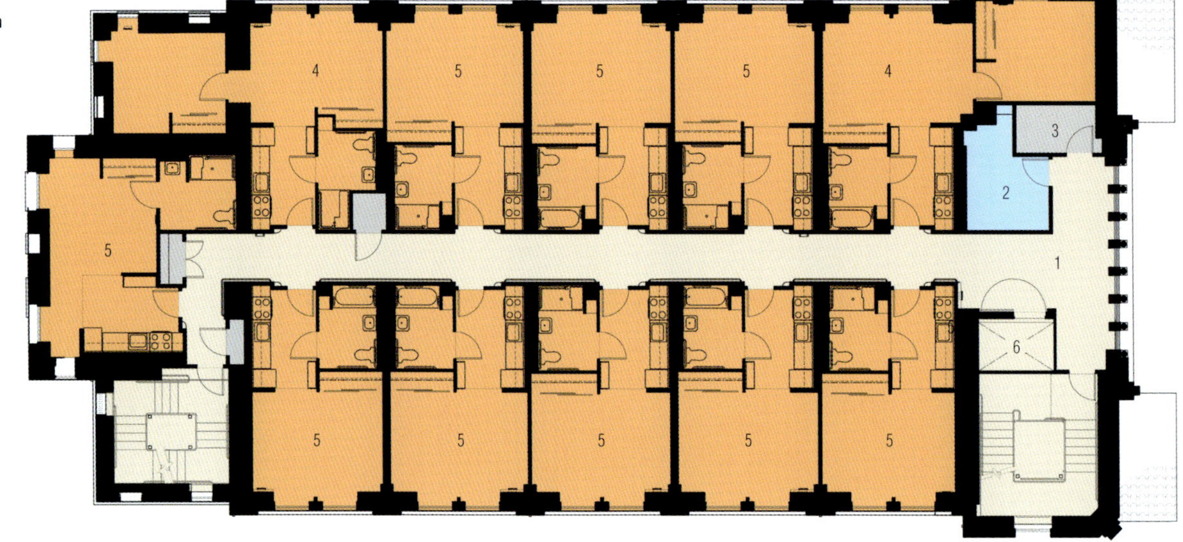

First floor plan

1 Lobby
2 Library
3 Office
4 Laundry
5 Mechanical
6 Studio
7 One-bedroom unit
8 Storage
9 Electrical
10 Community room
11 Elevator

creation of permanently affordable housing for low and very-low-income seniors. In addition, unlike other financing sources, the HUD Section 202 program provides an operating subsidy that allows for the provision of permanent housing for seniors with a very low income, through the allocation of a capital subsidy for the development.

Architect's Statement

Design goals

- Restore the building exterior to its 1915 state, making minimal interventions to adapt the building to its new use.
- Create small but livable apartments and shared spaces that highlight the church's unique qualities, using a very limited budget. Architectural details from the original sanctuary were carefully removed, catalogued, restored, and planned into the new work. These decorative elements – religious medallions, plasterwork, stained glass, and wall paneling in particular – were reinstalled in community spaces.
- Work collaboratively with neighbors and City Planning and Building department officials to overcome challenges unique to the project in order to succeed with this unusual adaptive reuse. Examples include: planning code requirements for parking, building code requirements for exiting and accessibility, and the reuse of architecturally significant entrance doors on the principal façade.

Challenges: What were the most difficult challenges in designing the project?

- The change of use from a single, grand sanctuary space to 40 small living units seemed an ill fit. The design of the apartments carefully accommodates the unique vertical sanctuary window locations. New energy-efficient windows, based on the historic designs, were fit into existing locations. The resulting apartments are flooded with natural daylight.
- The change of use from a church to housing required open space, parking, and significant revisions for accessibility, exiting, and safety. Working collaboratively with City Planning and Building department staff was the key to resolving each of these challenges as they arose.
- The need to provide 40 units necessitated four floors. This required the removal of the Sanctuary's embellished vaulted ceiling. It was a difficult compromise, but allowed the overall project to succeed and thus both provide housing and preserve the building's exterior architectural character.

Innovations: Does the project offer its users unique opportunities or new features not typically available in previous similar projects?

- The most obvious innovation was to convert a church to senior housing in the first place. It not only provided for the protection and seismic upgrade of a historic but vacant landmark, but also allowed a non-profit developer to realize extremely high-quality apartments, rich with architectural detail, for a reasonable cost.
- The design of the apartments carefully accommodated the unique sanctuary window locations. New energy-efficient windows, with glass etched to echo the designs on the historic windows, were fit into existing locations.
- The site sits at the base of a large hillside park – a destination for the whole city – and is visible for several blocks in multiple directions. The project is unique in its purist approach to the historic reuse. The new use is minimally announced on the building's exterior, but rather allowed to occur quietly within while the historic church continues to play its public architectural role in the neighborhood.

Form shapers: What factors had the most influence on the physical form of the project?

- The project provides independent-living apartments so most residents are relatively able. Despite this, all bathrooms are completely accessible, and sized for mobility needs. Kitchens are designed to be simple and easy to use.
- An easily accessed front stair connects all the elevator lobbies and incorporates historic architectural details. This is provided to encourage able residents to take the stairs when possible, rather than the elevator.
- The project designers and developers worked hard to make this building work on this site, as the proximity to public transit, amenities, and neighborhood retail made the location ideal for low-income seniors.

Top trends

- Integrating with the surrounding community: Keeping affordable housing integrated in market-rate neighborhoods.
- Responding to the site and local conditions: The project's central achievement is in saving a building that had outlived its original use. The 1915 Romanesque Revival Christian Science church was a neighborhood landmark, but had long been vacant. The developer explored removing the old building for new senior housing, but realized the opportunity in adaptive reuse. Initial neighborhood meetings made clear local affection for the church, the neighbors' determination to keep the building intact, and support for an innovative housing project.
- Being green/sustainable: The project's environmental approach was a simple one: reuse all that could be repaired. The design and construction team collaborated to minimize construction waste and design the building to retain as much of the existing structure as possible. Units were carefully designed to fit

Section AA – Removal
Existing – to remain
Existing – for removal
New floor level at street elevation

0 20ft

0 20ft

First floor plan – Removal
Existing – to remain
Existing – for removal
New floor level at street elevation

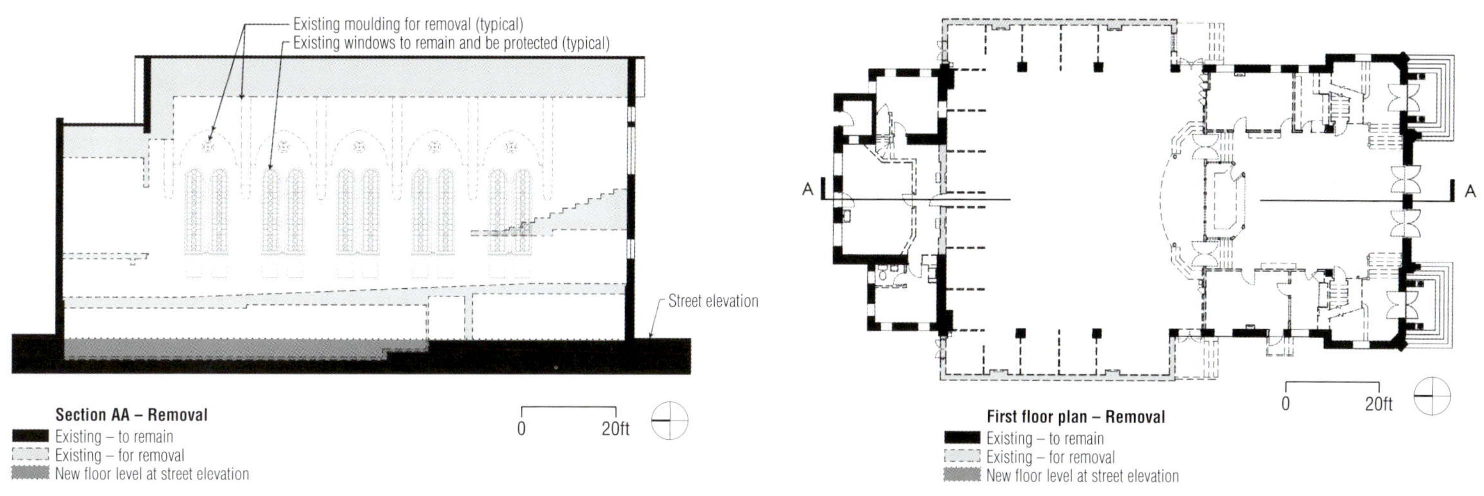

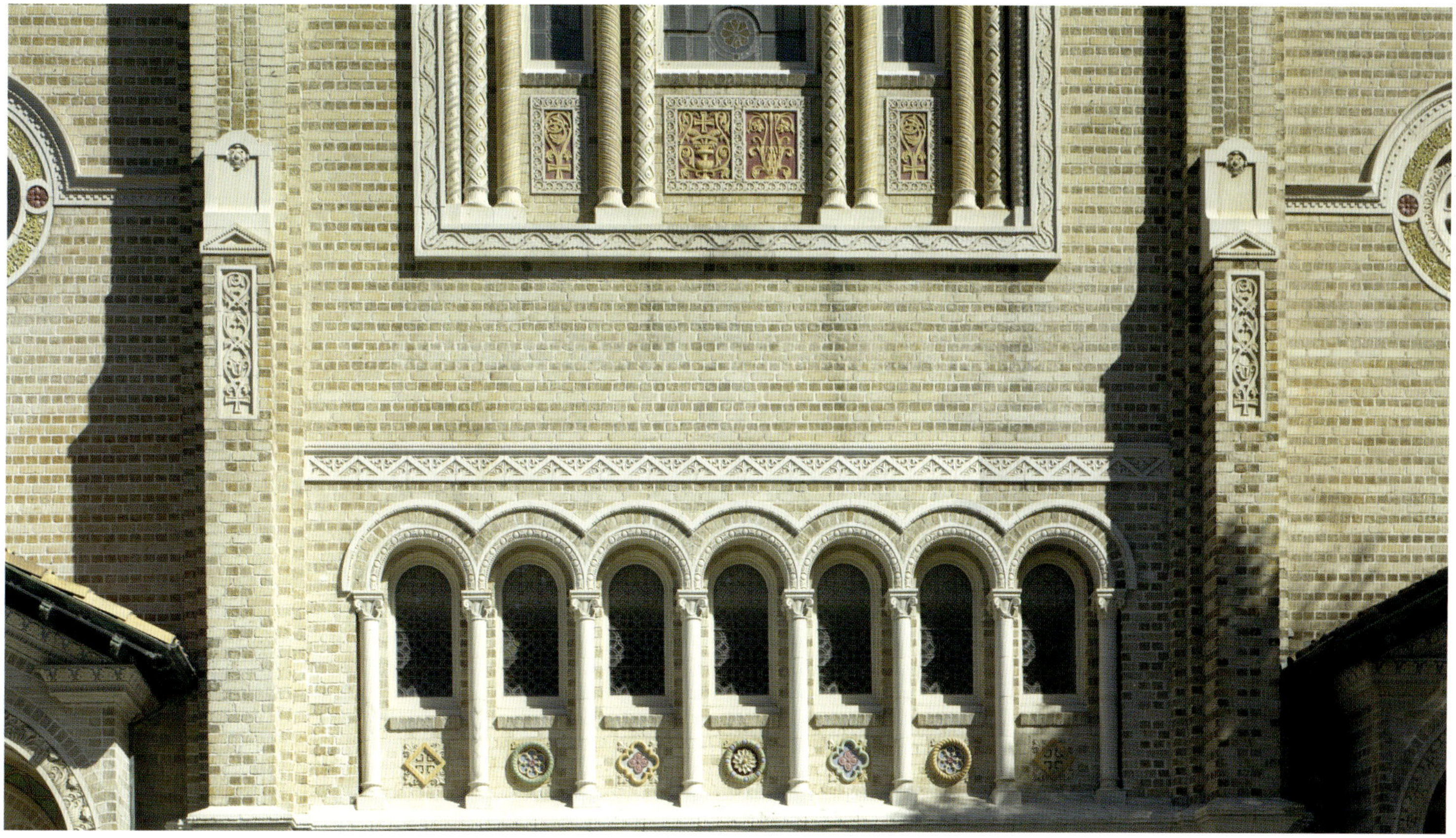

Opposite: Refurbished lead glass windows in common space
Above: Front façade, cleaned, tuckpointed, and restored

the unique windows. The resulting effect of small apartments with grand, oversized windows makes for exciting, bright, daylit interiors. New high-efficiency windows perform much better than required, allowing the overall envelope to meet energy code requirements even while maintaining the original, low-efficiency, historic stained glass windows on the street façade.

- Other: The project has been a great success in the community. A neighborhood landmark was saved. One thousand five hundred low-income seniors, many of them long-term residents of the neighborhood, applied for 40 apartments. The thoughtful reuse of a local landmark, combined with creating 40 affordable apartments for neighborhood seniors, has created a project of timeless value in this rapidly changing and gentrifying neighborhood.

Sustainability: Does the project conserve energy, water, and other natural resources? Does it reuse existing material or buildings, or include recycled building materials? How will the project improve indoor air quality in operation?

- The project reuses a vacant historic church that was slated for removal.
- By building in a centrally located, dense urban neighborhood, low-income residents can remain in this expensive neighborhood, as well as having ample access to public transit.
- Historic interior details (wall paneling, stained glass windows) were removed, restored, and reinstalled, while modern elements (insulated windows, efficient plumbing fixtures, lighting, equipment, and appliances) improve building performance.

Community: How does the project advance the sense of community for residents, staff, families, and neighbors?

- In addition to unique studio and one-bedroom apartments with full kitchens and private bathrooms, the project provides common spaces: a library/computer room, laundry, and two lobbies for gatherings and awaiting the mail.
- The historic entries to the church – no longer used due to floor level revisions – have been transformed into oversized windows looking on to the street. This creates a strong visual connection between interior public spaces and the exterior, linking seniors to the daily activities of the neighborhood. Similarly, the formal entrance stairs and porticoes have been transformed into 'front porches' where residents may overlook the adjacent park and interact with neighborhood activity.

Opposite left: Reused original wood wainscot in community room
Opposite right: Main entrance lobby
Top: One-bedroom apartment
Above: Library

Photography: Cesar Rubio

Target market: What specific features/services/amenities were incorporated into the overall project to attract your target market?

- Affordable rents are the principal feature for the targeted market: very-low-income seniors at or below 50 percent of median income. Rents are set at 30 percent of tenant's income; the range is from $15–1,013 per month. Thus, low-income seniors are able to remain integrated in this desirable, centrally located neighborhood, where rents continue to increase.
- An on-site resident manager is available to assist residents to access community services that help the seniors to remain independent. This, combined with easy access to public transportation, allows this low-income senior population to remain connected to the city's supportive services.

Jury Comments

An excellent example of adaptive reuse that reflects optimism about existing possibilities rather than limitations of constraints. It broadens our understanding of how existing buildings can serve new uses, and accomplishes its goals in a sustainable manner. The sensitive design retains much of the fabric and spirit of the original building, and where original architectural elements could not be retained, they were reused elsewhere in the project. A remarkable amount of program was accommodated through efficient and well-organized planning. The interior design acknowledges the original architecture and has a level of detail unusual in affordable housing.

MERIT AWARD AFFORDABLE

MERIT AWARD BUILDING

HKIT Architects

DeVries Place Senior Apartments

Milpitas, California // Mid-Peninsula Housing Coalition

Facility type: Independent Living

Target market: Low income/subsidized

Site location: Urban (city or town)

Capacity: 103 units

Total project cost: $18.7 million (new); $2 million (restoration)

Date of completion: August 2008

Below: Modern 'Prairie Style' building design elements surround podium courtyard allowing residents to enjoy the morning sun

Photography: Misha Bruk Studio

Opposite: Careful project siting emphasizes relocated historic house and creates appropriate street scale and complementary design between the two building elements

Photography: Steve Proehl

Overall Project Goals

This $18.7 million senior housing community is part of a larger planning effort by the City of Milpitas to revitalize the North Main Street downtown area. The vision was to integrate affordable senior housing into a transit-oriented city project that included a new library and county medical center. On-site goals were to develop 103 affordable apartments for independent seniors and to relocate and restore the site's existing 1915 Prairie Style historic single-family residence into a civic amenity. Key elements of the site design were to maintain walkability between building entrances and neighborhood paths and to balance the varied scale of the site's two buildings. Key elements of the architectural design were to wed the historic and new structures by reinterpreting the residence's strong Prairie Style architecture into a modern architectural language suited for a multifamily mid-rise building.

The resulting residential community includes amenities such as a game room, arts and crafts room, exercise room, a movie theater, laundries on each floor, two large roof terraces, gardens, and a dining room in the historic residence. Further, the historic house provides a public meeting facility that can be used for civic functions or rented by the public. The rich and multilayered mix of spaces and uses – well connected to existing and developing civic elements in the neighborhood – makes this senior housing project a supportive and enriching place to dwell and thrive.

Provider's Statement

Provider goals for marketing and sales

This project was specifically designed for the senior affordable rental market. With a high demand for affordable housing, there will likely always be a waiting list. It was fully leased very quickly and met the provider's goals.

How did the provider plan to improve the residents' quality of life?

The apartments were designed spaciously with floor-to-ceiling windows allowing plenty of natural light, and each unit has its own patio. Every floor has a laundry room and the hallways are wide and spacious. In addition, there are many on-site amenities that add to residents' experience and positive well-being: a fitness center, a theater, a community room, an arts and crafts room, and a computer lab. The service staff coordinates on-site health and wellness programs, special events, and computer training, and helps residents access community referrals. There are many off-site amenities within walking distance or easily accessible via local transit, including a new library across the street and a new medical center next door. Finally, the common areas were designed to foster community and along with the caring, on-site staff this helps to create a true community and sense of home.

How did the provider want to improve workplace quality for employees?

The office in the rehabbed DeVries House is beautifully designed and spacious. Separate office space for services and property management are equipped with state-of-the-art office equipment. All employees are trained on Bostonpost software, which makes them more efficient and productive.

Did the provider have specific goals for the project's staffing quantities, training, or distribution?

There are 3.5 full-time employees at DeVries Place: A community manager, an associate community manager, a maintenance manager and a part-time services manager. All property management staff is trained on Bostonpost, the cutting edge property management software the developer uses in all of their nearly 100 communities.

Did the provider give specific direction about the style, materials, features, or other design aspects of the project? If so, what were those directives?

The designers were asked very intentionally to create a livable community for seniors to address the needs of an aging population. All amenities were designed to be appropriate for this population (fitness center, arts and crafts room, computer room, community center, and so on) and the architect was instructed to design common spaces where community would organically flourish. In terms of materials, instruction was given to make the community environmentally friendly, hence the use of green-labeled carpets, low-VOC paint, dual flush toilets, solar panels, and energy star appliances.

How did the provider's financial goals influence the project's organization, configuration, layout, or sizing of components?

The developer positions all properties to have long-term financial sustainability and viability. DeVries Place meets these objectives. One specific contributing factor was the substantial contribution by the City, which allowed the developer to take on minimal conventional loan debt.

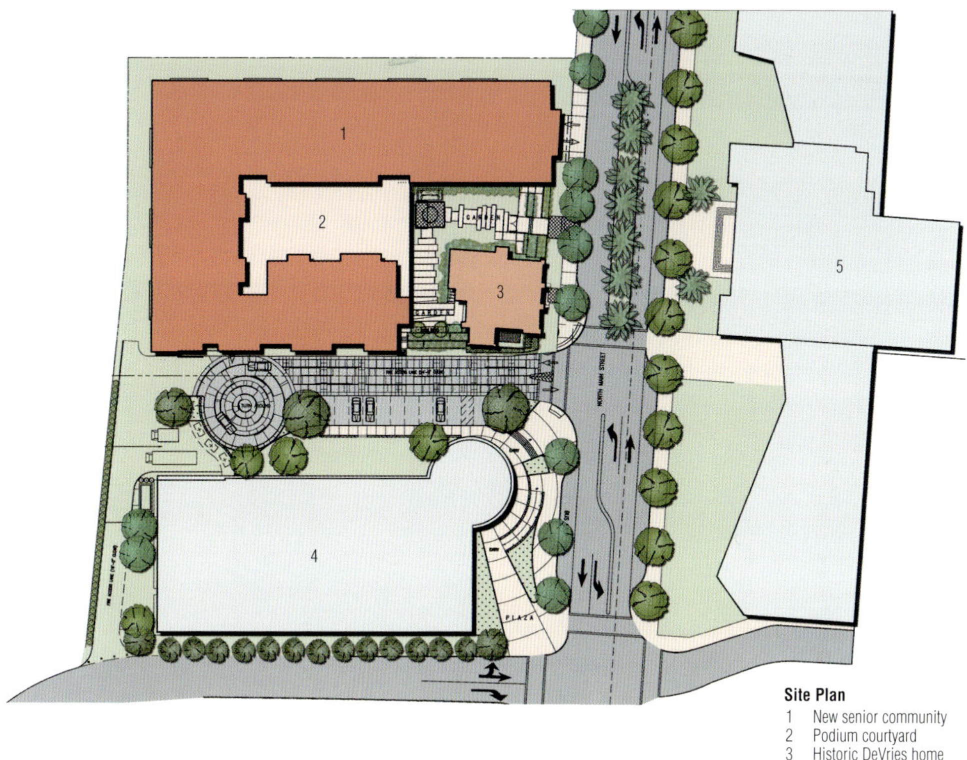

Site Plan
1 New senior community
2 Podium courtyard
3 Historic DeVries home
4 Country health center
5 Public library

0 60ft

Architect's Statement

Design goals

- Relate stylistically to the site's historic house: The 1915 Prairie Style residence was renovated to provide community rooms for residents and meeting space for City and local events, as well as three rental apartments. The design of the apartment building draws from the architectural themes of the historic house and is massed to address the difference in scale. For example, the larger building has a prominent entry colonnade with broad columns of similar proportions to the house's pilasters; further, apartment bays are capped with deep aluminum sunshades at the top floor to evoke the Prairie Style roof overhangs. The overall project illustrates how a clean, modern building can peacefully coexist with a historic residence.
- Provide public open spaces and community rooms on multiple levels: This project might be mistaken for high-end senior housing based on the community amenities provided. The developer made a commitment early on to provide ample on-site community spaces so that residents could have the opportunity to age in their own home. The design organizes the shared spaces to create a lively zone of community uses on the main floor, and then intersperses the remaining uses on upper floors. Thus, seniors are encouraged to interact and circulate as they enjoy the gardens, roof decks, game rooms, movie theater, exercise room, and sitting areas of their home.
- The building form was inspired by the architectural influences of the Prairie Style house and the design created an efficient roof form, keeping HVAC equipment organized to free up space, maximizing area for photovoltaic solar panels, creating roof decks for residential open space – a difficult challenge in urban multifamily infill projects – and using artful shading devices to minimize heat gain and glare in interior spaces.

Opposite: Entry courtyard provides shared community space for relocated historic house and senior residents

Photography: Misha Bruk Studio

First floor plan

- Parking
- Circulation
- Community, support
- Residential

Second floor plan (third and fourth plans similar)

- Circulation
- Community, support
- Residential

Left: Community space on every floor such as this A/V theater is included for the enjoyment of DeVries residents

Photography: Misha Bruk Studio

Challenges: What were the most difficult challenges in designing the project?

- From the developer's perspective, the greatest challenge was to keep the sustainable features that the team had committed to. Many of the green elements of the project added costs beyond what would have been a typical project. The team remained steadfast during the design and value engineering process to preserve these elements in order to address long-term costs and energy use. Selected examples include: photovoltaic solar panels, high-quality low-VOC paints throughout, recycled-content flooring, and dual-flush toilets.
- From the designer's perspective, the greatest challenge was to design a mid-rise, modern, multifamily housing building that was compatible with the historic residence. Balance had to be found between highlighting the historic building on the prominent corner, with the apartment building as a backdrop, and conceiving of the two buildings as compatible, but independent, neighbors. The design team gracefully found a bit of both. Further, the design preserved the smaller scale, pedestrian landscape, despite a huge increase in site density. On the architectural side, the project designers worked to find common architectural elements in the Prairie Style architecture and in their vision for a modern building.
- From the operator's perspective, the greatest challenge was to create a sense of community and social life within the development, given the high-density nature of the project. Architectural elements – such as community spaces on each floor and the cluster of community spaces on the first floor – assist in providing spaces for residents to connect. The primary solution, however, was in artful programming that surveyed and then addressed the specific interests and needs of this group of seniors.

Above: A landscaped roof terrace provides residents with spectacular views of surrounding California landscapes
Photography: Misha Bruk Studio

Innovations: Does the project offer its users unique opportunities or new features not typically available in previous similar projects?

- The most obvious innovation was to save and relocate the historic house, using it as the inspiration for the project's look and connection to the neighborhood. It not only restored a landmark building, but also allowed a non-profit developer to realize extremely high-quality spaces, rich with architectural detail, for a reasonable cost. This strategy was a green one, and created a rich connection to the district's past. This site will always be a part of civic activities, enlivening the seniors' experience of living there.
- The way that the design addresses parking illustrates the project's commitment to being a good civic neighbor. The building has 70 parking spaces, all tucked under the building and hidden from view. Pedestrian paths to the street are emphasized, consistent with a focus on senior health. A group of community rooms comprise the remainder of the first floor, creating opportunities for seniors to interact on their way to and from their apartments. On the second floor, the large podium courtyard created by the parking garage becomes a secure, protected outdoor seating area. This court is accessed from the main elevator lobby, further encouraging seniors to connect with each other in daily activities.
- The nature of a 103-unit mid-rise building requires long corridors. To mitigate the effect of these spaces, the designers made a conscious effort to modulate the space at residential 'front doors' and to open the corridors to daylight as often as possible. The main corridor opens into gracious sitting areas at four different points along its length, creating opportunities for rest or chance encounters. Three other locations allow for natural daylight in the corridor, marking entrances to community spaces.

Form shapers: What factors had the most influence on the physical form of the project?

- The project provides Independent Living apartments, so most residents are quite able. Despite this, all bathrooms are completely accessible and sized for mobility needs. Kitchens are designed to be simple and provide ease of use.
- As stated earlier, seniors are able to remain integrated in the larger community due to their location at the heart of this downtown neighborhood. Easy access to public transportation, health services, and civic amenities such as the public library gives them the freedom to make the best choices for their lives.

All Photography this page: Misha Bruk Studio

Top trends

- Responding to the site and local conditions: The project's central achievement is in saving a building that had outlived its original use and in integrating that residence with both a modern building and the surrounding urban fabric. The doctor's office and residence had been a neighborhood landmark. The developer explored removing the old building, but realized the opportunity in adaptive reuse. Initial meetings made clear local affection for the house and support for an innovative senior housing and preservation project.

- Integrating with the surrounding community: In all the ways stated previously – working as a part of a larger redevelopment effort, designing affordable housing on a transit corridor, being a good neighbor in site planning and building massing, strengthening pedestrian connections, and restoring a local landmark building – this project places a priority on connecting the seniors to the larger community.

- Being green/sustainable: The senior housing community was a part of a larger effort to revitalize the city's downtown area and bring civic services together. By including senior housing, the project both allows seniors to age in place, supported by local resources and services, and ensures that the use of these amenities will occur with a minimal number of vehicle trips. Further, multifamily housing is an inherently sustainable building type, beautifully suited for urban seniors. Initial material use is more efficient than in multiple single-family dwellings, long-term energy use is kept to a minimum, and seniors benefit from the social connections of group life and shared on-site services.

Sustainability: Does the project conserve energy, water, and other natural resources? Does it reuse existing material or buildings, or include recycled building materials?

How will the project improve indoor air quality in operation?

- The senior housing community was a part of a larger effort to revitalize the city's downtown and unite civic services along the public transit corridor. The project allows seniors to access local resources on foot or using transit.

- The project included the relocation and restoration of a historic house. The city retained a piece of its historic architecture and created a civic space, simply by imagining how the existing resource might be repurposed.

- A smart roof: the design organized equipment to minimize space use, installed the maximum number of photovoltaic panels, and created roof decks for seniors.

Community: How does the project advance the sense of community for residents, staff, families, and neighbors?

- Public spaces are an essential part of the project, despite the need to include as many units as possible. These spaces allow residents opportunities to interact and enjoy group activities. Spaces include a lobby area to await the mail, small seating areas throughout, laundries on each floor, an exercise room, a movie theater, a game room, roof decks and gardens, and the dining room created in the adjacent historic house.

- In order to understand what types of services and programs were most needed by residents, the services team surveyed the community and used the responses to develop the project's events programming.

- The project offers ESL classes to residents, most of whom have a first language that is not English. A recent survey of ESL class participants indicated there had been 90 percent improvement in residents' ability to have conversations with staff members. This is a great example of how the on-site team uses a creative feedback-loop method to provide effective services. Improving communication between residents and staff will circle back yet again to allow those services to be best understood by residents, and allow residents to be able to communicate what additional services and programming would meet their needs.

Target market: What specific features/services/amenities were incorporated into the overall project to attract your target market?

- Affordable rents are the principal draw for the targeted markets, which are low- and very low-income seniors. Thus, low-income seniors are able to remain integrated in this centrally located downtown neighborhood.

- An on-site resident manager is available to assist residents to access community services, helping the seniors remain independent. This, combined with easy access to public transportation, allows this low-income senior population to remain connected to the City's supportive services.

Jury Comments

An exceptional design solution that combines historic preservation with affordability and sustainability, this project illustrates the importance of integration with the surrounding civic resources in the community for an active senior lifestyle. It proves the value of synergy to revitalize an urban area. Exterior and interior design show sensitivity to the architectural context while feeling contemporary and residential. The proportion, articulation, and scale of the façade work handsomely. Exterior spaces create outdoor living spaces that reflect the accommodating climate. Preserving the existing home provides both a context and human scale to the development. Each enhances the other. The project design addresses a full array of issues that affect the quality of life for seniors and succeeds on all counts. Well done.

McCamant & Durrett Architects

Silver Sage Village Senior Cohousing

Boulder, Colorado

Facility type: Independent Living (common house with shared facilities and common open space; provision for caretaker unit if required)

Target market: Mixed income

Site location: Urban (city or town)

Capacity: 16 units

Total project cost: $3.9 million

Date of completion: October 2007

Below: Outdoor spaces are framed by a contemporary design that fits its urban and mountain context

Photography: Ben Tremper Photography

Opposite: The building front enlivens the city street, marking a community and defining the street within the larger Boulder community

Photography: Charles Durrett

Overall Project Goals

The project is a 16-unit senior cohousing community in Boulder, Colorado completed in 2007. It includes all ownership units, six of which are permanently affordable (80 percent of the area's median income [AMI] as per the City of Boulder Affordable Housing Program). The community is a small, custom neighborhood designed to provide support for its senior residents, not with institutionalized care, but by cooperative, caring neighbors – more like a traditional town. As per the resident group's mission statement, its purpose is 'nurturing and encouraging people's desire to keep learning, growing, and participating.' The architecture is designed, in cooperation with the residents, to provide a place to achieve these goals and to age in place, in community. Individual units are grouped around shared open spaces and a 3900-square-foot Common House with kitchen, dining area, living room, crafts and performance areas, guest rooms, and provision for a caretaker unit when needed. The Common House is used frequently for common dinners, lectures, films, concerts, reading groups, meetings, fitness, mail delivery, postings, and informal daily interaction. Individual units include porches to provide 'soft edges' and places of interaction between public and private space. The site has a clear point of entry marked by visible architectural forms that are discernable from the street, thereby engaging the community with the surrounding neighborhood.

Provider's Statement

Provider goals for marketing and sales

All units were sold within 12 months of project completion; 90 percent were sold within 8 months of completion.

How did the provider plan to improve the residents' quality of life?

The wonderful views from the building, the mixed-use neighborhood, the common facilities managed by the residents, and the garden all serve to improve quality of life.

Did the provider give specific direction about the style, materials, features, or other design aspects of the project? If so, what were those directives?

The design was to be energy efficient, accessible, attractive, and contemporary.

How did the provider's financial goals influence the project's organization, configuration, layout, or sizing of components?

The project was developed under Wonderland Hill Development Company's unique streamlined cohousing model in which residents participated by investing in the project and sharing the risk with the developer.

Architect's Statement

Design goals

- Community: Silver Sage Village Cohousing succeeds as a community by providing support to residents, particularly low-income residents, by virtue of residents who support, mentor, and lead each other. Shared facilities and resources facilitate relationships and cooperation.
- Participatory design and self-management: Fully involving the residents in the planning and design of the community produced a responsive environment and common facilities. Shared facilities are not only a supplement to the house,

Second floor plan

1 Podium deck
2 Elevator
3 Bedroom
4 Master bedroom
5 Living
6 Dining
7 Kitchen
8 Study
9 Deck
10 Roof below

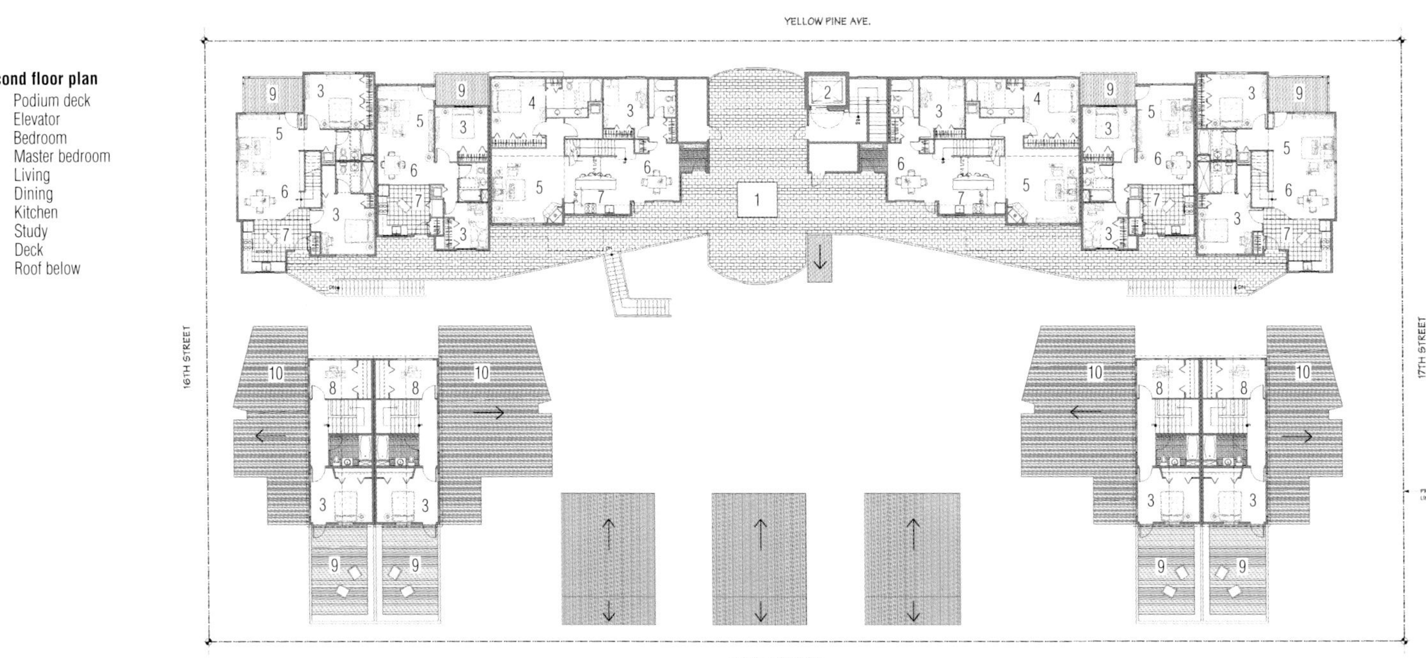

First floor plan

1 Common house foyer
2 Elevator
3 Common dining
4 Common kitchen
5 Common styling room
6 Common crafts room
7 Common laundry
8 Common exercise room
9 Bedroom
10 Living
11 Dining
12 Kitchen
13 Study
14 Bicycle storage
15 Arts and crafts
16 Garbage/recycling
17 Garage
18 Electrical

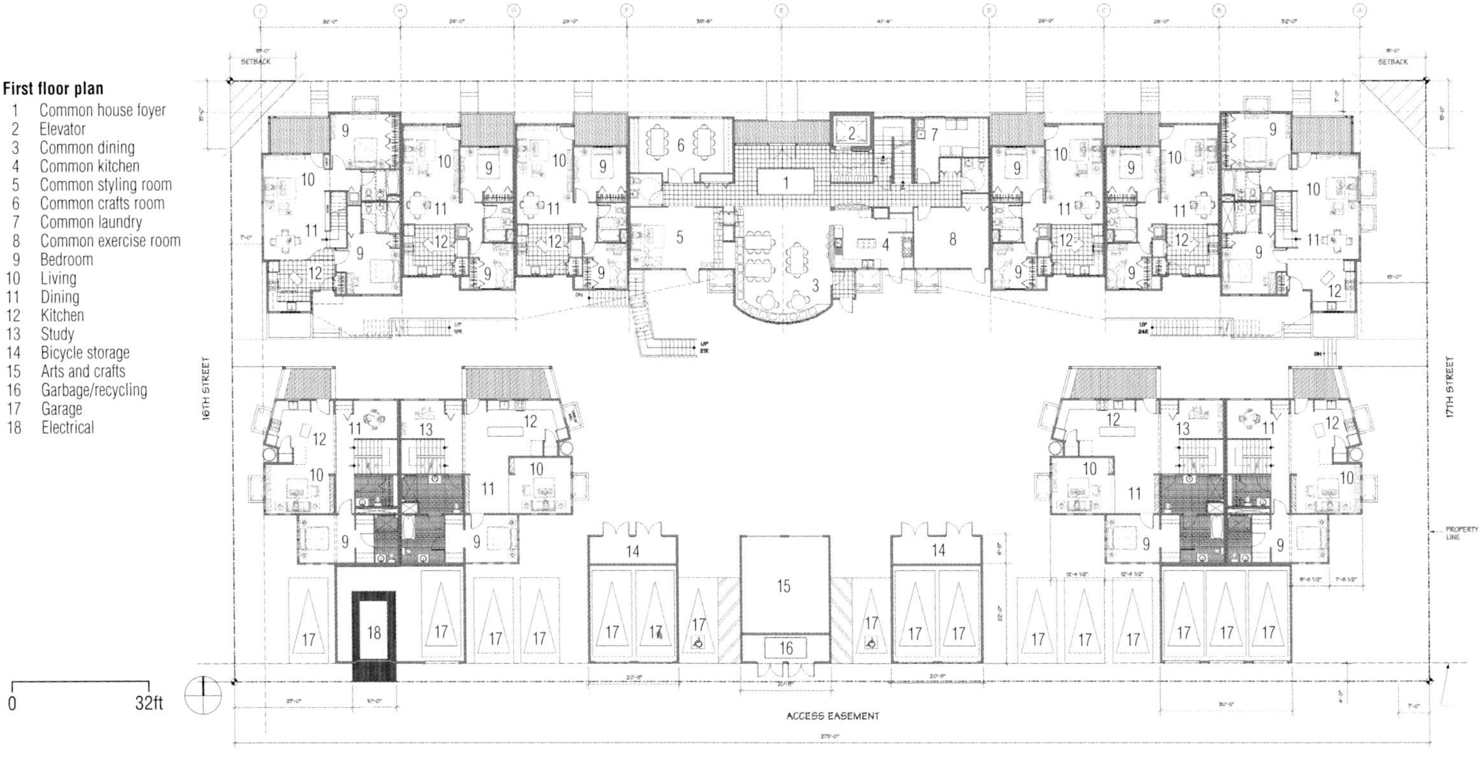

SETBACK
16TH STREET
17TH STREET
PROPERTY LINE
ACCESS EASEMENT

0 32ft

North (street) elevation

but also a place to be with other residents to discuss the issues of the day. The physical design facilitates communication and therefore cooperation – when people see and talk to each other they also find ways to cooperate to make each other's lives more practical, more economical, more convenient, more interesting, and more fun. By virtue of self-management, everyone is in the loop. This is not housing for people – this is housing with people.

- Sustainability: The project includes a long list of sustainability measures, including:

a) responsible use of resources and materials: advanced framing to reduce lumber use, minimal use of asphalt, sustainable lumber, linoleum flooring, low-VOC materials and finishes, and indigenous plantings

b) passive heating and cooling, high-value insulation, radiant barriers, high-performance windows, fans and cross ventilation, and maximum daylighting

c) reduced sprawl and increased density: a density of 19 dwelling units (DU) per acre, an urban infill site, one parking space per DU, a car-free living environment, services within walking distance, shared resources (cars, tools, gear), and small unit sizes (800-square-foot two-bedroom units) offset by shared facilities.

Challenges: What were the most difficult challenges in designing the project?

- Working with future residents during the design process to address their needs and interests while keeping the project within budget.
- Designing small, two-bedroom units (of 800 square feet) that feel large.
- Designing the project to be sustainable while keeping it affordable: to use little or no air conditioning; to use little energy to heat; and to achieve as many other green and sustainable architectural features as possible, such as low-formaldehyde and low-VOC materials and finishes, maximum natural light, high-quality insulations and windows, and so on.

Innovations: Does the project offer its users unique opportunities or new features not typically available in previous similar projects?

- Infill site: The location is a tight urban infill site that was still able to accommodate common facilities and shared car-free open space within close proximity to services and amenities including community gardens, bike trails, artists' studios, pedestrian walkways, a new public library, and other residential neighborhoods.
- Natural surrounding: A view of the natural surroundings including the Flatirons (rock formations that are symbolic of the City of Boulder).
- Contextual urban design: The design of the site, common house and private houses enabled the community to fit within the existing neighborhood (for example there are no setbacks on street façades) while also including open space and a common house for the residents on the interior of the site. These community elements were combined with private, individual units that include 'soft spaces' such as narrow yards and porches that serve as intermediaries between public and private spaces. Parking is kept on the periphery of the site.

Form shapers: What factors had the most influence on the physical form of the project?

- Shared facilities: Shared facilities encourage cooperation and shared activities.
- Design features: Common facilities are all American Disabilities Act (ADA) compliant, and all private dwelling units are readily adaptable, with universal design features incorporated throughout.

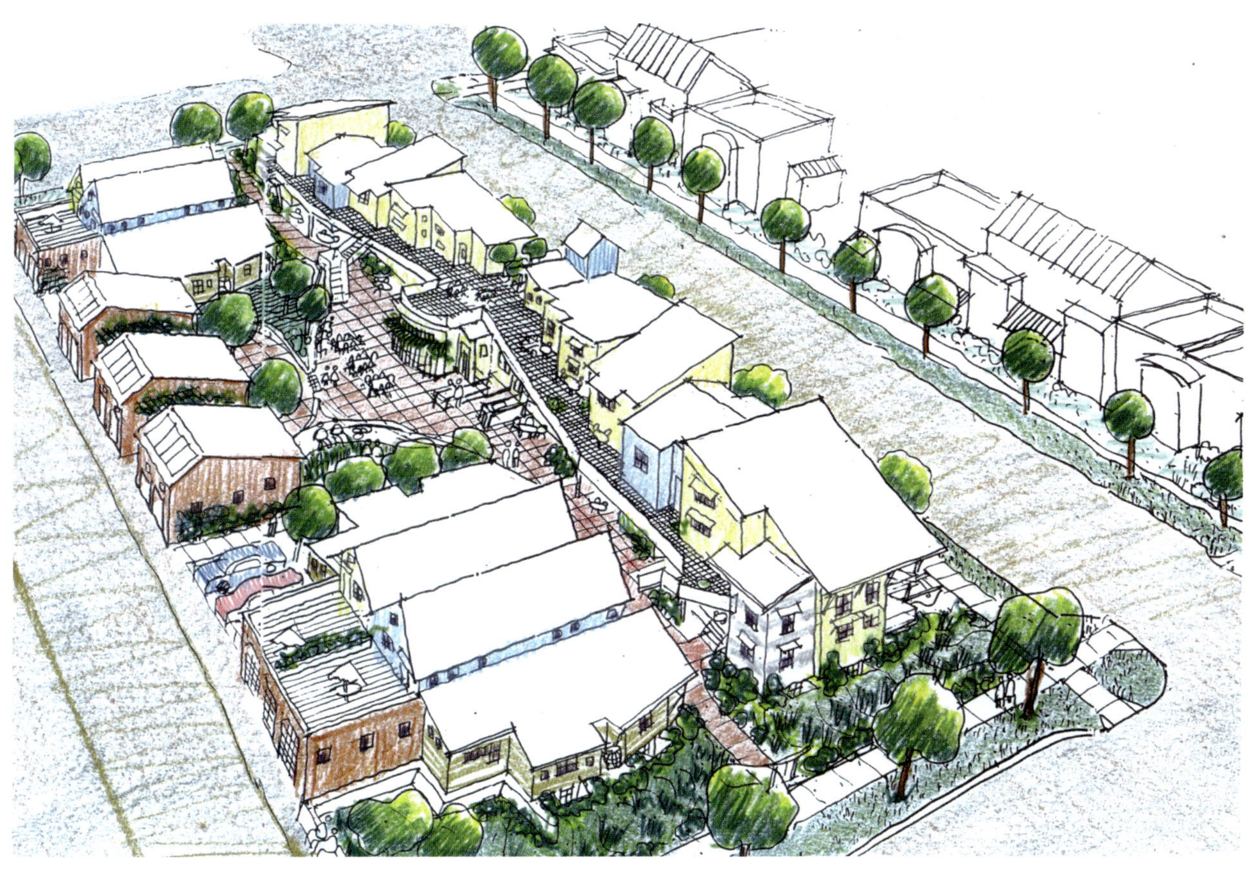

Opposite: The front porch – the soft edge – plays an important role in facilitating community over time

Photography: Bryan Bowen

Above: Aerial perspective view: The outdoor common spaces – the courtyard and upper deck – form internal streets that hold the community together

Drawing: McCamant & Durrett Architects

- Pedestrian features: The design of the site aims to facilitate pedestrian activities and to reduce dependency on cars. Design features include a car-free zone with parking on the periphery of the site and attention to site design that ensures easy mobility for senior residents in pedestrian areas.

Top trends

- Helping aging adults stay in their homes longer: Providing both private, individual dwellings and common facilities, the cohousing community enables adults to find support within the community rather than having to go outside the community. For this reason, senior cohousing allows adults to age independent of institutions or Assisted Living facilities.
- Being green/sustainable: The project includes a long list of green building materials and sustainable design features.
- Shared, common facilities to facilitate cooperation and mutual support enabling a choice between privacy and community: The cohousing movement, imported to the US from Denmark, encourages and enables cooperative living combined with private, individual residences. Senior cohousing offers this opportunity to adults aged 55 and over who wish to experience the advantages of cohousing with a community of other seniors.

Sustainability: Does the project conserve energy, water, and other natural resources? Does it reuse existing material or buildings, or include recycled building materials? How will the project improve indoor air quality in operation?

- Materials and resource conservation: Minimal use of asphalt, sustainable lumber, advanced framing to reduce lumber use; linoleum flooring, low-VOC materials and finishes, and indigenous plantings.
- Passive heating and cooling: Tight building envelope, high-value insulation, radiant barriers, high-performance windows, fans and cross ventilation, and maximum daylighting.
- Reduced sprawl and increased density: Density of 19 DU per acre, urban infill site, one parking space per DU, car-free living environment, services within walking distance, shared resources (cars, tools, gear), smaller unit sizes offset by shared facilities.

Community: How does the project advance the sense of community for residents, staff, families, and neighbors?

- Community design features: The final design is inspired by a village, where interrelations and interdependence are intertwined indiscernibly, and people can act out goals that they can only achieve together.
- Choice: The community functions towards choice. The choice, everyday, is between as much privacy as you want or as much community as you want. This scenario is in contrast with typical neighborhoods where you can have as much privacy as you want or as much privacy as you want.
- Resident involvement: Future residents were involved in the design of the site, common facilities, and private houses to combine the interests and needs of the resident group, instill a sense of cooperation and collaboration, and build confidence among residents leading to successful self-management once the project was complete.

Target market: What specific features/services/amenities were incorporated into the overall project to attract your target market?

- Common facilities: The project incorporates common facilities and a pedestrian-oriented environment.
- Design for seniors: The compact and efficient, yet spacious private houses are easy to maintain, with front porches to promote frequent informal connections with neighbors.
- Caretaker's unit: A provisional caretaker's unit is included in the Common House to accommodate the future need for an on-site caretaker for one or more of the residents.

Jury Comments

We value the opportunities for residents with a range of financial means, which create a meaningful impact on the community. This is a very interesting concept that could be translated to a larger scale if required. The premise of watchful oversight of neighbors is a strong concept, but will need to bear testing when a resident experiences significant physical or cognitive decline. The internal focus of common areas between buildings has an interesting relationship with how the building addresses the street in a semi-urban context. These are interesting contemporary buildings that mirror the unique approach to a community-based lifestyle.

Opposite top: Affordable unit, with open plan, generous natural light, and sustainable materials

Photography: Charles Durrett

Opposite bottom: Extensive common areas facilitate community and supplement the smaller spaces in the private houses

Photography: Bryan Bowen

Solomon Cordwell Buenz

SKY55

Chicago, Illinois // Forest City Residential Group

Facility type: Senior Community Center
Target market: Mixed income
Site location: Urban (city or town)
Capacity: 411 units
Date of completion: April 2006

Below: Front entry façade
Opposite: Aerial view of Central Station development

Overall Project Goals

SKY55 was developed to create a high-quality urban living environment for people at many different income levels within one comprehensive project. SKY55 incorporates three major residential components: senior living apartments, market-rate apartments, and affordable apartments. The 411-unit, 40-story tower has both market-rate and affordable units for a variety of incomes and the affordable units are mixed throughout the tower. The 91-unit, 10-story senior residential building is intended for lower-income residents. Overall, a total of 176 units (35 percent of the entire project) are classified as affordable. Parking for the project is completely screened from the street by the senior and rental buildings. The senior living component is seamlessly knitted into the project, sharing services and amenities such as the expansive recreation deck. The site is located at the south end of Chicago's Grant Park and commands views of the park, the city, and Lake Michigan. SKY55 is ideally located near work and recreation opportunities, minimizing the need for residents to use cars and optimizing the use of public transportation.

Architect's Statement

Design goals

- A goal of the project was to create a strong urban edge to the design. To achieve this, the 40-story tower was located along the south edge of the site and it punctuates the corner at Michigan Avenue and 13th Street. The Michigan Avenue frontage, traditionally a lower-scale street with a well-defined street wall, is occupied by the 11-story senior living building thus creating an environment that is scaled to the pedestrian.

- A goal of SKY55 was to create a dialogue between the lower senior building and the taller apartment building by cladding each structure in distinct materials. The senior building is clad in warm-toned brick detailed in a modern and sophisticated way, while the tower is clad in blue glass and crisply detailed concrete. This breaks down the scale of the project and creates a strong sense of identity for each part.

- A goal of the project was to completely screen the parking facility from the street. This was achieved by wrapping the parking garage with single-loaded apartments: senior apartments on the Michigan Avenue frontage and market rental apartments on the 13th Street frontage.

Challenges: What were the most difficult challenges in designing the project?

- To start out on the right financial footing, the initial design decisions ensured an economical basis on which other decisions could be made safely. For example, the movement of the residential components to the edges of the site created a large internal pad that was very efficient for a parking facility. In turn, this allowed the structural systems for the residential buildings to be designed in the most cost-effective manner.

- Maintaining operational efficiency between all of the parts was critical. The various components are arranged to share back-of-house staffing, parking, and functional spaces. For example, the leasing center is located between the senior building lobby and the apartment building lobby so that it can serve both communities seamlessly.

- The requirements for affordable senior units drove the arrangement of the senior building into a separate and efficient low-scale wing, which also helped fulfill urban design goals for a pedestrian scale along Michigan Avenue.

Innovations: Does the project offer its users unique opportunities or new features not typically available in previous similar projects?

- SKY55 is located on a site with unusually good views of the skyline of Chicago, Grant Park, and Lake Michigan. The apartment tower is shaped to optimize those views.

Form shapers: What factors had the most influence on the physical form of the project?

- All kitchens and bathrooms in the senior facility were designed to meet and exceed code requirements to ensure that residents can occupy any unit type or size with equal comfort and safety.
- Floor colors and carpet patterns were chosen to help aging residents identify their location in the building and assist with wayfinding.

Top trends

- Responding to the site and local conditions: SKY55 is designed to fit its site intimately, responding to the range of scales from the street to the skyline.
- Integrating with the surrounding community: SKY55 fills a gap in the community by addressing a variety of housing needs within one project.
- Offering choice through a diversity of housing options: SKY55 offers market-rate apartments, affordable-rate apartments, and affordable senior apartments. This creates a truly diverse community within the similarly diverse city of Chicago.

Left: View from Grant Park

Site plan

1. Pool
2. Multifunction room
3. Office
4. Library
5. Laundry
6. Card room
7. Health club
8. Locker room
9. Hospitality room
10. Theater

Left: SKY55 complex in context

Sustainability: Does the project conserve energy, water, and other natural resources? Does it reuse existing material or buildings, or include recycled building materials? How will the project improve indoor air quality in operation?

- The project occupies a brownfield site that was formerly occupied by rail yards and obsolete industrial buildings. The site is now an asset to the city rather than an environmental hazard.

- The project has over 17,000 square feet of green roof area for heat-island reduction, drainage run-off control, and recreation to enhance the environment for the residents.

- SKY55 is part of Central Station, an 80-acre development that reunites a formerly abandoned rail yard with central Chicago, creating a walkable neighborhood that is well served by public transportation and reduces the need for cars.

Community: How does the project advance the sense of community for residents, staff, families, and neighbors?

- The senior building and the apartment building share the large recreation deck that tops the parking facility. This large green space is extensively landscaped and provides opportunities for community interaction through a diverse range of options such as outdoor dining, reading on a park bench, or simply meeting neighbors for a leisurely stroll.

- The senior residents share a series of community rooms and activity spaces off the recreation deck that can be used for informal gatherings or organized activities. The warm residential atmosphere promotes a sense of expanding residents' living space beyond their own apartments.

Right: The 10-story senior residential building
Opposite: The soaring 40-story tower

Target market: What specific features/services/amenities were incorporated into the overall project to attract your target market?

- SKY55 created a high market standard for finishes and amenities that other projects aspire to. Amenities such as the recreation deck and fitness facilities are designed to a condominium level of quality.

- Natural light and views were considered amenities and every portion of the project is designed to maximize these advantages.

Jury Comments

SKY55 is a stunning design aesthetically, and a bold model of senior living. This project could be a national urban planning model for mixed-income housing that combines low-income senior housing, affordable, and market-rate housing in one project. Although the campus does not address a continuum of care, it clearly provides a 'high quality urban living environment for people at varied income levels.' The project has two buildings: a 10-story, 91-unit low-income senior living building, and a 40-story, 411-unit tower at market rate with affordable units mixed throughout the building. The owners and architects were able to design a setting where amenities and services are shared with all residents. The use of green-roof technology and the creation of visually stimulating, expansive, and highly functional rooftop landscaping and gardens allow seniors access to the outdoors, and an intergenerational connection. Aging in place is accomplished in the senior facility by designing all kitchens and bathrooms ensuring that residents can occupy any unit type with equal comfort and safety. The quality level appears to be of high-end construction, yet the facility was constructed on a very reasonable budget.

RLPS Architects

Hospice of Lancaster County

Mount Joy, Pennsylvania // Hospice of Lancaster County

Facility type: Hospice
Target market: Mixed income
Site location: Rural
Capacity: 24 units; 24 inpatients
Total project cost: $12.5 million
Date of completion: October 2008

Below: Exterior view of typical inpatient neighborhood
Opposite: Main entrance to inpatient care

Overall Project Goals

In 1996, Essa Flory Hospice Center began offering inpatient hospice and palliative care. It was the first freestanding facility of its kind in Pennsylvania. The need for inpatient care has increasingly exceeded the center's capacity, leading the owner to challenge the architect to design a facility that has twice the number of beds and maintains the homelike atmosphere of the original design while expanding on connections with nature to help address families' emotional needs through an end-of-life experience. The resulting $17 million, 52,700-square-foot care center focuses on the celebration of life to the very last breath. Three independent inpatient neighborhoods of eight rooms each are accessed through a central gallery, which also connects to administrative offices and a grief-support center.

Provider's Statement

Provider goals for marketing and sales

Before the completion of this project Hospice of Lancaster County had 12 inpatient beds available for its nearly 500 home-hospice patients. Throughout its history, the organization found that approximately 6 percent of its patients need a higher level of care than can be provided in the home. With the opening of the new center, Hospice of Lancaster County was immediately able to meet this very important need.

How did the provider plan to improve the residents' quality of life?

Patient rooms, dining rooms, living rooms and the newly designed screened-in porches were all designed with patient comfort in mind.

How did the provider want to improve workplace quality for employees?

While employee productivity and morale are important for any healthcare facility, Hospice of Lancaster County feels it is truly the most important part of its service to the community. Hospice of Lancaster County prides itself on consistently being one of the 100 Best Places to Work in the entire Commonwealth of Pennsylvania and it was extremely important that this facility be designed with employees in mind. Nursing care bases and documentation areas were specifically designed with the staff's input. Hospice of Lancaster County even had a mock documentation area created so staff could test it to see what configuration would work best for them.

Did the provider have specific goals for the project's staffing quantities, training, or distribution?

Hospice of Lancaster County began working on staffing the facility more than a year before completion. While the current nursing shortage certainly presented many challenges, all were met and the new facility was fully staffed with every staff member completing a lengthy and detailed orientation process prior to the facility's opening on October 1, 2008.

Did the provider give specific direction about the style, materials, features, or other design aspects of the project? If so, what were those directives?

The project's designers became very familiar with hospice services during the completion of Hospice of Lancaster County's first Inpatient Center in 1996. While hospice may be similar to other healthcare facilities, and of course must meet all applicable codes, the designer was given direction to make this facility look, act, and feel just like a patient's home and not another healthcare facility.

How did the provider's financial goals influence the project's organization, configuration, layout, or sizing of components?

This facility was built to meet the growing needs of patients and upon its opening this need has clearly been met. During the first 10 months of operation the facility is also ahead of financial forecasts.

Below: Typical inpatient room with abundant outdoor connections and space for family and friends

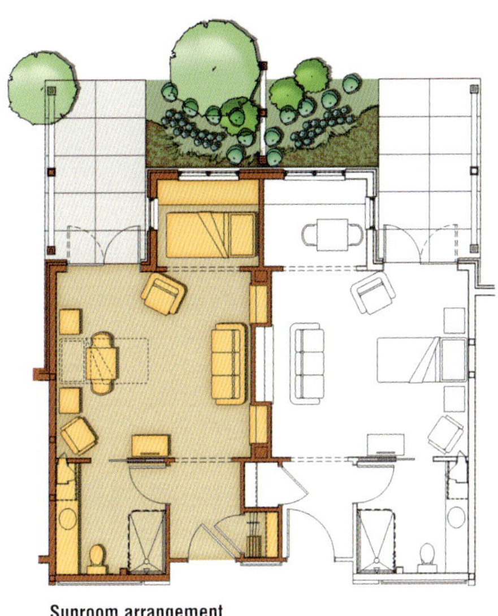
Sunroom arrangement

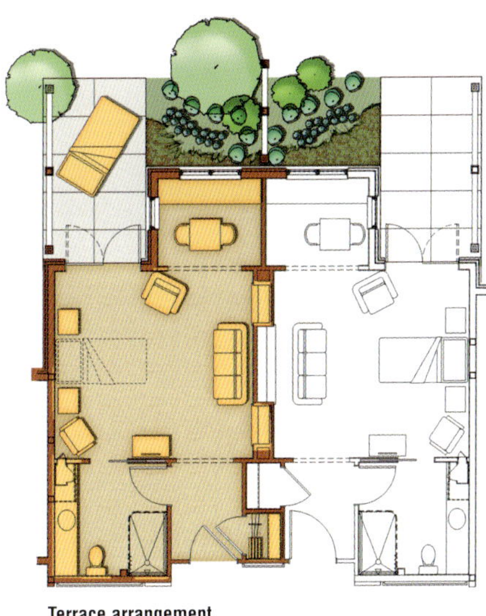
Terrace arrangement

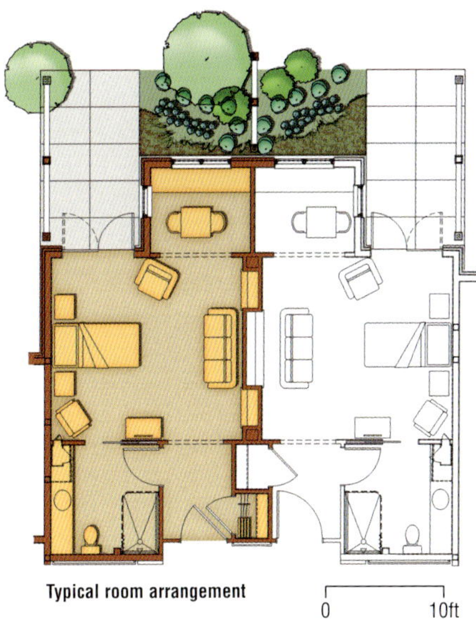

Typical room arrangement

Architect's Statement

Design goals

- Provide care and comfort in a non-intrusive, thoughtful environment that preserves individual dignity and allows for personal privacy: three inpatient households are accessed from a common gallery. The households are physically and visually separated from the public areas and function independently. The entry sequence into patient rooms emphasizes privacy. Doorways are carefully positioned not to be directly across from one another and the beds cannot be viewed from the corridor. An entry vestibule further supports privacy while offering an access point to the bathroom for staff cleaning or restocking without disturbing the patient or family members.
- The goal to provide an inviting, comforting residence that 'looks like, acts like, feels like home' was achieved through carefully designed 'guest' rooms of more than 450 square feet allowing patients to be surrounded by loved ones at all times and designed to allow for personalization and rearrangement to suit individual patient preferences. Family spaces in each neighborhood are varied and intimate with limited capacity to help maintain the residential scale and qualities. All services and implements of care are kept 'out of sight and out of mind' while nature takes center stage, with each patient wing surrounded by public and private courtyards.
- To maximize connections to daylight and nature, the three inpatient neighborhoods radiate like peninsulas from a central circulation gallery so all patient rooms and common areas have courtyard views. Each room has a private patio with access to courtyards, a solarium, and a window seat, which converts to a bed for overnight guests. The patient bed is typically positioned to provide a view to French patio doors, but can be moved to the solarium or even outside on the private patio depending on patient preferences. A family room and screened sun porch at the end of each wing are lined with windows overlooking landscaped courtyards and a natural wooded area to provide positive distractions for family members and patients utilizing these areas.

Challenges: What were the most difficult challenges in designing the project?

- The first 12-bed hospice center, constructed 12 years ago, was hugely successful in part because of the intimate scale of the environment. Doubling the census to 24 in the new hospice center posed a significant design challenge of maintaining the same intimacy with twice the floor area. Following several planning and staffing scenarios to provide efficiency without loss of patient dignity, the team of owner, contractor and architect settled on three households of eight beds each. Each household is autonomous with regard to support and operations, but tethered back to a central core via an open gallery. Household corridors are shortened by clustering the eight rooms in two blocks of four organized around a care base and country kitchen.

- Providing each inpatient room with meaningful access to daylight in the new household configuration posed another challenge. The original 12-bed hospice oriented all rooms directly south for maximum daylight exposure. Doubling from 12 to 24 beds rendered a duplicate solution inefficient for walking distances and staffing economies. Post-occupancy review of the 1997 design supported consideration of softer daylight access, especially in patient rooms where glare was problematic. The final solution orients the three neighborhoods of eight to the south providing each primary courtyard with direct southern exposure and each resident room with softer daylight access via south, east, and west orientations. By design, no rooms face north.

- Maintaining separation of back-of-house services from the private life of patients, families, and friends was a high priority and challenge for the design team. Assuring patient dignity throughout their stay was of utmost importance in all design decisions. All mechanical systems for inpatient rooms are accessed from a dedicated attic space allowing replacement, annual maintenance, and servicing to be accomplished without intrusion to the inpatient rooms or public areas. Likewise ample storage and supply rooms were included to keep medical equipment and supplies 'out of sight and out of mind.'

Innovations: Does the project offer its users unique opportunities or new features not typically available in previous similar projects?

- The layout of the inpatient neighborhood wings maximizes exposure to courtyards and sunlight. All rooms overlook gardens oriented south to receive the benefits of sunlight year-round. Common areas at the end of each wing take advantage of a previously existing wooded area for added natural appeal and variety.

- All inpatient rooms include a solarium and private patio for outdoor connections and a private bath with European shower for patient dignity.

- The three-season porches located at the end of each neighborhood are elevated several feet above the natural grade. Building codes require porch rails with a height of 42 inches and a picket balustrade with 4-inch spacing to ensure occupant safety. The use of this traditional means of safety was deemed intrusive to viewing the woods and meadows beyond. The agreed-upon solution installed fixed Lexan® panels in front of the screening below the rail and removable Lexan® panels above the rail for flexibility during seasonal changes. The panels are stored conveniently next door when not in use.

Form shapers: What factors had the most influence on the physical form of the project?

- An inpatient hospice care center must be prepared to support the needs of patients and family members of any age and physical ability. The private bathroom in each patient room includes a tiled roll-in shower allowing easy accessibility for all guests, including family members that may stay through the night.

- Wider beds that stand lower than a hospital bed were specified to provide side rails for those that need them, which can alternately be tucked underneath to feel like a normal residential bed for patients who don't need the extra security of side rails.

- Patient charting is carried out in each inpatient room by using a system and casework custom-designed by the owner. This high-tech computer center permits accurate record keeping and accounting at the point of service.

Top trends

- Addressing a holistic sense of wellness: End-of-life environments tend to embrace a holistic sense of wellness by the very nature of their timing in a person's life. The physical environment has to evoke a positive spiritual and emotional response in the individuals experiencing this final passage of life. Although the goal of hospice is to allow terminally ill patients to remain in their own homes, that is not always possible. The inpatient hospice care center provides an alternative to a hospital setting, which is often ill equipped to meet the unique emotional needs of dying patients and their families.

- Integrating with the surrounding community: The site was selected based on its proximity to the target population, easy accessibility and most importantly its natural amenities in a tranquil setting. The one- and two-story building scale blends into the rural setting where the natural surroundings are the focus of a facility designed to celebrate life.

Sustainability: Does the project conserve energy, water, and other natural resources? Does it reuse existing material or buildings, or include recycled building materials? How will the project improve indoor air quality in operation?

- The building incorporates automatic lighting controls and automatic low-flow faucets.

- Access to daylighting and outdoor views was a key design consideration.

Site plan

1 Main entry
2 Patient wings
3 Counseling center
4 Service entry

Typical household plan

1 Care base
2 Team leader
3 Electrical
4 Office
5 Counselors
6 Lounge
7 Soiled utilities
8 Clean utilities
9 Pantry
10 Dining
11 Family kitchen
12 Counsel room
13 Three season porch
14 Family room

Top: Each neighborhood includes a fully stocked country kitchen
Above: Private bathrooms include a nurse servery with owner-designed charting and casework
Opposite: Typical three-season porch at the end of each neighborhood wing

Above: Typical family room, adjacent to the three-season porch, at the end of each neighborhood wing

Photography: Larry Lefever Photography

- Instead of a traditional irrigation system, a surface well was tied into the creek running through the property.

Community: How does the project advance the sense of community for residents, staff, families, and neighbors?

- Common areas in each neighborhood, including a fully stocked residential kitchen, were carefully scaled to provide comfortable spaces for family members. The varied and multiple spaces allow for privacy while the familiar scale and finishes of a family kitchen or family room promote positive interactions with other families facing similar challenges.
- The bereavement center provides support to more than 8,000 people per year who have experienced the loss of a loved one. The multi-purpose room, smaller conference and meditation rooms and outdoor courtyard spaces accommodate a wide range of programs to help members of the community deal with grief and loss. In addition, these spaces are also used by community civic groups for meetings and special events.
- Each household is provided with a large family room and three-season porch for extended use into fall and early spring. Two of the three family rooms are subdivided into smaller social zones by a fireplace feature allowing for greater use and flexibility. The three-season porches are made possible by the use of removable Lexan® inserts.

Target market: What specific features/services/amenities were incorporated into the overall project to attract your target market?

- To meet the growing need for end-of-life care beds in the county, the new facility was defined to provide patients with a higher level of care than could be provided in their homes in the most homelike environment possible. This is exemplified through the care bases in each neighborhood, which feature public and private areas to provide family members with ready access to care professionals in a personalized, non-institutional setting. The open, public area is equipped with a furniture desk and bookshelves while the adjacent service areas are equipped to respond quickly to changes in a patient's condition but keep medical equipment and activities 'out of sight and out of mind.'
- To encourage families to take advantage of the inpatient care center when needed, accommodations are made to allow family members to comfortably remain by their loved one's side during a difficult transition period. This ranges from oversized rooms with ample seating and sleeping accommodations to a well-appointed kitchen for meals.
- Because the original center was so well known in the community, care was taken to assure the target market that the new center would embrace and expand upon the successes of the original. The new Grief and Loss Center is designed to meet the diverse needs of all age groups with designated spaces for children, pre-teens, teens, and adults.

Jury Comments

Individual rooms have a very nice layout with visual connection and access to personal outdoor space. Imagery provides tranquil and simple rooms with generous space for families to provide support to the resident. Providing only eight rooms per wing and abundant natural light to shared areas makes the interior and exterior scale of the building seem more approachable and private. Landscaping is carefully integrated and visually connected to the interior spaces. Furnishings are thoughtfully selected to relate to the interior architecture. Overall, a carefully considered design that functionally and aesthetically places the resident and their family as the highest priority.

THW Design

Lenbrook

Atlanta, Georgia // Lenbrook Square Foundation, Inc.

Facility type: Independent Living, Assisted Living, Skilled Nursing, Dementia/Memory Support Unit, Wellness/Fitness Center, Senior Community Center

Target market: Middle/upper middle

Site location: Urban (city or town)

Capacity: 142 Independent Living units, 16 Assisted Living units, 60 Skilled Care units

Total project cost: $107 million

Date of completion: 2010

Below: Entry court

Photography: Kim Sargent

Opposite: South aerial

Photography: Michael Chase Eayton

Overall Project Goals

Lenbrook offers the city-dwelling 50-plus population a variety of distinguished upscale living choices, complete with lifestyle packages geared to entice the most discerning of consumers. Yet the client knew that to remain viable, they needed to engage in a renovation and expansion program to meet the significant and growing demand for in-town living opportunities. Lenbrook's $109 million expansion consists of a 25-story tower with sweeping views of downtown. This project hosts 163 Independent Living, 16 Assisted Living, and 60 Skilled Care units. Among the amenities on the campus is an elegant garden court building, which overlooks a 38,000-square-foot tranquil landscaped plaza. This plaza serves as the social hub for multi-generational social connectivity. Three upscale dining venues were added, a 5,000-square-foot multipurpose room, and a state-of-the-art video theater. Additionally, a 10,700-square-foot fully equipped wellness center and spa, and glass-enclosed natatorium complete with heated pool are available for resident indulgence. This urban mixed-use development not only serves the needs of seniors seeking fashionable in-town community living, but also provides a platform for assorted social confluence opportunities in the heart of Atlanta's prestigious Buckhead community. Lenbrook is Atlanta's only nationally accredited Continuing Care Retirement Community (CCRC).

Provider's Statement

Provider goals for marketing and sales

This project provides an attractive and welcoming space that is well poised for current and future generations. These are well-thought-out residential designs with plenty of open and closed space.

How did the provider plan to improve the residents' quality of life?

The project includes plaza gardens, a wellness center, gathering spaces, and dining venues.

How did the provider want to improve workplace quality for employees?

Staff members are very proud of the design and have an increased level of enthusiasm about their surroundings.

Architect's Statement

Design goals

The client desired to add state-of-the-art modifications to this CCRC. Comprising just some of the newly added components are a 5,000-square-foot multipurpose room, billiards room, two-tiered video theater, postal center, convenience store, full service bank, resident business center, fully equipped 10,700-square-foot wellness center, day spa, and glass-enclosed natatorium with heated swimming pool. Three new dining venues were also added to offer even more resident choice options. Lenbrook wanted the residents who chose to live there to feel as though within their community home they are offered service packages similar to that of a resort. In addition to the many amenities the community offers, concierge service is abundant throughout.

A philosophy and value system that the design team understood was the imperative need to create multiple social hubs, because happy and engaged residents are also healthier ones. In addition to the various internal common space renovations and additions, the design fashioned outdoor rooms created specifically for resident wellness. Intergenerational connectivity opportunities are abundant within the socially engaging Wellness Plaza. This plaza is the true epicenter of community activity. A plethora of activities can be held here, such as marshmallow roasts on the fire pit on crisp fall evenings, wine and hors d'oeuvres by the outdoor kitchen, peaceful strolls in the plaza garden, and outdoor sporting events.

Falling in the urbanism category, Lenbrook is a Mecca for innovation in senior living. Contemporary

design elements are thoughtfully blended with existing traditional structures, and the design team needed to create a smooth and cohesive mix between the varying styles. In addition to the glass-enclosed natatorium, the residential tower has a sleek, modern flair with glass and concrete structuring, and other elements have a more traditional appeal. Common space interiors present a comfortable and inviting setting with elegant furnishings, reflecting timeless sensibility.

Challenges: What were the most difficult challenges in designing the project?

- Meeting very restrictive zoning height and setback limitations that would satisfy the building integration requirement: From the rear of the existing building tower to the beginning of the new expansion tower, a 120-foot gap had to be created to link the differing floor heights of the two buildings. Removal of the first four bays of the existing parking structure was thus administered. The remaining parking structure was then extended to the west, which doubled the size to accommodate more parking. Atop the western side of the parking structure is a three-story Garden Court wing, tailored to fit within the allocated narrow plot. Now the parking is improved, and the buildings are properly and seamlessly connected.
- To create a new high-rise structure that would not impede on the views that the existing homeowners were already enjoying in the existing tower: The new tower was oriented east and west, slightly behind the old tower to preserve existing resident views with the smallest dimension facing the adjacent neighborhood to mitigate their view impact concerns. It was important to Lenbrook that the existing residents maintain their views of the city skyline and Stone Mountain.
- To unify the existing campus residents with the new residents: In order for existing Lenbrook residents to truly feel at home, they needed to feel comfortable with the community's physical and programming changes, as well as with their new neighbors. A younger resident needing little or no assistance has vastly different lifestyle necessities than an older resident requiring more care. New social confluence opportunities were essential. The new entry point became a centralized location for every resident. This way, each resident can cross paths with new neighbors daily and become better acquainted. Existing residents are able to teach the community's history, while newer residents can help pioneer the way towards shaping the future.

Innovations: Does the project offer its users unique opportunities or new features not typically available in previous similar projects?

- Outdoor rooms were created by taking advantage of the new Wellness Plaza and implementing eight three-story Garden Court flats to frame it. The flats are situated atop the west perimeter of the parking structure, and they will house two floors of Independent

Opposite: North elevation

Photography: Kim Sargent

Above: Natatorium exterior

Photography: Kim Sargent

Living residences over a main floor of common amenity spaces. The intentional framing allows for residents to have visible sight lines to the courtyard below while inside.

- The new entrance to the site is strategically located to take advantage of the existing curb cut. It curves gently to the west and extends along the property line, following the natural grade to provide access to the two levels of parking. This new entrance now serves as primary access for all residents and visitors. The existing entrance to the east (once shared by residents and service traffic) now provides service access only to the newly constructed loading dock. The owner wanted the residents and guests to feel as though they are arriving at a welcoming home, not an institutional workplace where the main entrance is shared by delivery persons and other personnel.

Form shapers: What factors had the most influence on the physical form of the project?

- There are a total of 367 Independent Living apartments that are adaptable to changing resident needs. Roll-in showers are available so that residents do not have to be moved down a continuum of care as their mobility level decreases with time.
- The owner challenged the design team to create living accommodations that would allow all residents to have a comfortable amount of space and amenities, regardless of the level of care that the respective resident requires. In many CCRCs the Independent Living quarters are much more spacious and accommodating than the spaces allotted for Assisted Living or Skilled Care residents. The design team complied, and many of the Assisted Living homes have been designed for couples to remain together, despite having differing healthcare needs, which diminishes the trauma a resident may feel when being separated from his or her spouse.

Top trends

- Responding to the site and local conditions: Due to the prestigious location of this CCRC, design innovation was a must to attract the target market. Today's 50-plus resident who desires urban living is often drawn to the more modern, sleek design, versus traditional buildings that may appear dated or not befitting of the city lifestyle. Lenbrook offers residents high-rise living options within a stately concrete-and-glass building tower. A lush ambiance was created within the common space interiors to complement the streamlined architecture and evoke a warm and welcoming feel. In addition, a glass-enclosed natatorium adds a fresh, modern twist to the wellness component, adding an element of the unexpected.
- Addressing a holistic sense of wellness: Resident wellness is at the top of this client's mission. For any community to be successful in today's 50-plus market (and beyond), it must employ wellness components. Providing venues for residents to enjoy dining experiences while ensuring that respective nutritional needs are met, providing ample green space for residents to feel the sunlight and be amid nature, creating multiple 'spaces and places' for residents to connect with one another socially, and hosting services and programming geared toward resident health, are all key components. Lenbrook prides itself on the commitment made to resident wellness, and has garnered significantly more residents as a result.

Sustainability: Does the project conserve energy, water, and other natural resources? Does it reuse existing material or buildings, or include recycled building materials? How will the project improve indoor air quality in operation?

- This project is not yet LEED Certified, but the renovation and expansion of Lenbrook was designed with sustainability in mind. One such example is on-site storm-water collection.

Penthouse

1. Tuxedo
2. Chatham
3. Habersham
4. Ansley

Typical floor plan

1. Windsor
2. Ivy
3. Wieuca
4. Cherokee
5. Andrews
6. Wesley
7. Stratford

Typical Skilled Care floor plan

1. Residences
2. Staff commons
3. Living
4. Dining
5. Activities
6. Lounge
7. Resident commons

0 25ft

- The owner chose high-performance glazing for this project, which has significant benefits. Not only does it achieve lower energy bills, it also cuts out 92 percent of the sun's UV rays while eliminating the blazing heat of the Atlanta summer sun.
- This project has extensive natural landscaping and green roofs. Sustainability, resident comfort and protecting the environment are core principles for both the owner and the commissioned architect.

Community: How does the project advance the sense of community for residents, staff, families, and neighbors?

- The new dining additions provide an immediate sense of community, as each is continually thriving with guests keeping residents socially engaged with one another. One restaurant in particular is a popular gathering spot. When friends want to chat about the latest reality television show or hit the highlights of the latest baseball game, they come to The Bistro. This relaxed and inviting dining locale features flat-screen televisions for guests' enjoyment, and offers take out for convenience. The al fresco appeal is persuasive to residents on a warm summer evenings as cold beverages can be enjoyed among friends. Residents from each level of care frequent this site and are engaged socially.
- Community connectivity is abundantly apparent here, particularly in regard to the Wellness Plaza. Residents, guests, families, and friends, are able to enjoy activities together in all seasons. Varying outdoor performances and activities are observed around the grounds, all of which entice community gatherings. Outdoor performances such as theatrical plays or musical performances are frequently held here for resident enjoyment. Lawn sports such as bowling or croquet are the perfect way for grandparents to reconnect with grandchildren. Whether a resident desires to read a book and enjoy quiet reflection, or is using the space to gather around the fire pit with friends, they are never far from others.
- This community hosts amenities that make it a metropolis within a metropolis. Lenbrook features a Starbucks-like coffee service bar within a quaint on-site library. After a lovely meal with friends in the private dining room, residents may wish to walk to get a cup of gourmet coffee after dessert, and the library is just the spot. When residents have places where they enjoy being, their presence invites other residents, and so forth. Billiards and card rooms serve as additional spots for social connectivity, as the residents of this community are offered a surplus of social outlets.

Target market: What specific features/services/amenities were incorporated into the overall project to attract your target market?

- Within a city known for a vast array of upscale dining choices, the owner understood that today's senior is looking to live in a community that affords them the types of dining experiences to which they are accustomed. The creation of The Bistro, The Grill Room, and the Main Dining Room was the design response to meet consumer demands. The Bistro features a popular al fresco dining area and hosts an informal self-service atmosphere, while the Grill Room offers a more formal dining experience with an exciting display kitchen. The Main Dining Room is a pleasure for residents looking to enjoy a sophisticated dining experience, as here they can dine in an idyllic atmosphere complete with marble fireplace and white linens.
- An all-inclusive Wellness Center, Natatorium, and Wellness Plaza were incorporated into the design of Lenbrook to entice residents who are drawn to the types of lifestyle amenities that they may otherwise only frequent while on vacations. Within the Wellness Center and Natatorium, a broad range of services are included, such as a styling salon, heated indoor pool, whirlpool spa, exercise room, aerobics room, and meditation room. Residents are able to live comfortably while nurturing their minds, bodies, and spirits, as pampering and luxury are offered to them at Lenbrook. The Wellness Plaza with fire pit, kitchen, lovely water features, and shaded seating provides a unique, expansive lawn area for outdoor activities and special events.
- The on-site healthcare component at Lenbrook is particularly appealing to prospective residents. The owner's goal was to offer private rooms for all healthcare residents. The Health Care Center is exceptionally convenient. Each floor will have 20 private rooms, a large community living room and dining room, and outdoor areas for gathering. The 60-room Health Center will offer skilled rehabilitative services, dementia care, and long-term medical support. Two-room suites with private baths and kitchenettes (some have balconies and terraces) will provide spacious living accommodations for residents who need some assistance, but do not require medical support.

Jury Comments

This upscale urban high-rise CCRC highlights an important trend in senior housing of accommodating to the needs of seniors who find dense urban settings appealing. Interestingly, this expanded a high-rise project that started in 1983 – adapting and repositioning it to meet new expectations from residents. The exterior and interior images are appealing. Floor plans show the challenges of incorporating healthcare components into tower footprints, but also illustrate how these components can be appropriately anonymous on a CCRC campus. On a tight site, the building planning created outdoor spaces that bring borrowed light into many areas.

Left: Grill Room
Top and Above: Fine dining room
Photography: Kim Sargent

Perkins Eastman

NewBridge on the Charles

Dedham, Massachusetts // Hebrew SeniorLife

Facility type: Independent Living, Assisted Living, Skilled Nursing, Dementia/Memory Support Unit, Wellness/Fitness Center, Senior Community Center, Chronic Care Hospital, Rashi School

Target market: Mixed income

Site location: Suburban

Capacity: 182 apartments, 24 villas, 50 cottages, 51 Assisted Living units, 40 special care/dementia units, 268 skilled nursing beds

Total project cost: $244 million

Date of completion: July 2009

Below: Courtyard preserves open space with 235 parking spaces beneath the building and green roof
Opposite: Active adult neighborhood offers freestanding cluster homes for privacy and independence

Overall Project Goals

The campus was created by the sponsor to reduce their financial dependence on revenue from regulated sources and to house 268 relocated long-term care residents to facilitate the downsizing of the sponsor's original campus. The project's goals included:

a. develop a campus that brings multiple generations together

b. create an optimal living environment for elders at all points of the aging continuum

c. provide a rich array of choices for elders in the form of housing options, lifestyles, engaging activity, and dining venues

d. preserve the spectacular site and provide views and access to it.

The new campus, located on 152 acres of environmentally fragile land along the Charles River in a community west of Boston, is becoming the home of approximately 750 aging adults. The site also provided a setting for 450 students in the Rashi School and associated play and athletic fields. The living accommodations include 50 cottages, 24 villa apartments, 182 apartments, 51 traditional Assisted Living apartments, 40 Memory Support rooms, and a 268-resident healthcare center with 220 long-term care residents and 48 sub-acute patients. The campus is equipped with a full array of programs to integrate the physical, emotional, and spiritual dimensions of aging.

Provider's Statement

Provider goals for marketing and sales

All sales goals were exceeded during a challenging financial time.

How did the provider plan to improve the residents' quality of life?

The community was built as one of the most comprehensive and thoughtful campuses in the nation where seniors have abundant choices in living environments, meaningful activities, dining venues, and supportive and medical services; where residents age in place, and couples with different service needs can remain on one campus together; where isolation can be combated via a strong community; and children can bring vitality to everyday life.

The community was planned with the highest standards of sustainable design practices. The site design protects environmentally sensitive areas, controls storm water, maintains native landscape materials and integrates the Northeast's largest geothermal system to serve more than 1 million square feet of enclosed conditioned space. This system utilizes 400 heat transfer wells with projected gas savings of 50 percent and a 34 percent CO_2 emissions reduction equating to about 18 million pounds per year. Other key green design elements include:

- Material and finish selections that incorporate recycled products were assessed for their impact on indoor air quality and overall reduction of CO_2 emissions.

- Natural resource management and sustainable site design that integrates existing trees and dense vegetation, preserves open space with underground parking, and uses green design principles like storm water capture for limited irrigation along with xeriscaping.
- Integrated architecture and interior design that distributes over-sized windows providing abundant natural light, utilizes energy efficient lighting, specifies long-lasting and easily maintained floor coverings, and utilizes recycled materials.

There was also a strong desire from the beginning to maximize the residents' connection to the always-changing natural environment and the way that it marks the passage of time. This was accomplished through the selection of natural materials, naturally occurring colors and patterns, and the utilization of oversized windows throughout the campus to maximize natural light and to connect residents to the natural environment. Opportunities to connect to the outdoors abound, as the design team ensured that nearly every space in the building has a view into the natural environment.

How did the provider want to improve workplace quality for employees?

The direct-care staff was at the center of the decision-making process for the design of the Health Center. The care-giving community contained a richly experienced interdisciplinary team with direct, valuable knowledge to contribute. The team's work had a profound impact on program, policy, and design of the physical environment as well as on staff morale.

The healthcare center households have a warm and comfortable residential feel to reduce the stress levels of residents and staff and result in more healthy environments and interactions. The households have kitchens, living rooms, and dining rooms at the center with resident rooms wrapped around the kitchen space to create a tightly knit community of residents and caregivers with the shortest possible walking distances between them. This approach was also in sync with the desire to provide autonomy to the household staff members, who are best suited to address the needs of the residents.

An overhead lift system is installed in 36 resident rooms, with infrastructure so that lifts can be installed in all of the resident rooms in the future. These lifts eliminate the use of wheeled lifts and allow a single caregiver to safely lift a resident from reclined to seated or standing positions without the risk of injury to staff.

Did the provider give specific direction about the style, materials, features, or other design aspects of the project? If so, what were those directives?

Haimish was the single word that the client offered to direct the interior design. A group of synonyms was developed for this Yiddish term: domestic, familiar, approachable, responsible, sustainable, simple, genuine, elegant; informal, intimate, honest, warm, timeless, enduring – these terms were utilized in programming, planning, and design, and material selections. Simple, elemental, and connected forms combined with richly colored and textured natural materials respond to the local New England vernacular and the natural setting. The simple and unpretentious nature of the vernacular was easily reinterpreted with oversized and mulled windows providing increased daylight, while playing a role in making an architecture and interior design that is refreshingly of the 21st century. The interior design that resulted is fresh and comfortable; it has received remarkable acclaim from those who live and work on the campus.

How did the provider's financial goals influence the project's organization, configuration, layout, or sizing of components?

The project was completed under budget and move-ins are occurring ahead of schedule.

Architect's Statement

Design goals

- To complete a remarkable campus plan and design that provides the broadest continuum of supportive, wellness, and healthcare services to integrate the physical, emotional, and spiritual dimensions of aging. Preserve as much of the spectacular site as possible and make the natural environment an integral part of the resident's lives.
- To build the most comprehensive and thoughtful campus in the nation where seniors have abundant choices in living environments, meaningful activities, dining venues, and supportive and medical services; where residents age in place, and couples with different service needs can remain on one campus together; where isolation can be combated via a strong community; and children can bring vitality to everyday life.
- The community was planned with the highest standards of sustainable design practices. The site design protects environmentally sensitive areas, controls storm water, maintains native landscape materials and integrates the Northeast's largest geothermal system to serve more than 1 million square feet of enclosed conditioned space. Material and finish selections incorporate recycled products and focus on their impact on indoor air quality and overall reduction of CO_2 emissions.

Challenges: What were the most difficult challenges in designing the project?

- The land was environmentally sensitive with extensive frontage on the Charles River – so

managing this process while moving the design process forward thoughtfully was a challenge. The owner, architect, and landscape architect/civil engineer collaborated in an iterative design process that flexibly responded to new opportunities and obstacles as they arose. The site design and buildings that resulted were shaped and crafted to carefully fit into the landscape.

- Also challenging was the process of designing, presenting, specifying, procuring, and installing furniture, finishes, and art work for the million square feet of space. An integrated team of interior designers and architects worked together with a client team to select furniture and finishes that maintained a fresh, non-repetitive feel throughout the campus. The interior environment accommodates over 800 pieces of original art acquired by volunteers.
- Making value decisions about construction costs, buyer expectations, and sales prices during the lengthy and extensive land use approval and the following marketing pre-sales period when the construction market experienced extensive cost escalation was a further complication. The value and cost of resulting site work and buildings were carefully managed to maximize the value for monies expended.

Above: The community center is the intergenerational gathering place for learning, living, eating, and sharing

Innovations: Does the project offer its users unique opportunities or new features not typically available in previous similar projects?

- The community was planned with the highest standards of sustainable design practices. The site design protects environmentally sensitive areas, controls storm water, maintains native landscape materials, and integrates the Northeast's largest geothermal system to serve more than 1 million square feet of enclosed conditioned space. Material and finish selections incorporate recycled products and were assessed for their impact on indoor air quality and overall reduction of CO_2 emissions. A state-of-the-art building automation system allows energy consumption to be monitored and for heat energy to be shifted from one portion of the campus to another via the geothermal system.

- The 'declining balance' or 'country club style' payment plan was selected, rather than the '30 meals a month' approach in order to provide residents with infinite flexibility in food choices. This approach allows for the creation of broad menus with many price points that can be adjusted to respond to demand.

- The next generation of consumers is especially sensitive to compromising their existing lifestyle, and the design team ensured that the dining experiences at NewBridge on the Charles echo those of the local cafés and restaurants the target market currently enjoys. The design of vibrant brands for each environment took that solution a step further, creating names for each venue such as 'Nosh' and 'Centro', adding a dose of personality to each space.

Opposite, top and bottom: NewBridge meets lifestyle needs with diverse living and dining accommodations

Form shapers: What factors had the most influence on the physical form of the project?

- An adaptable system for providing and locating the lavatories, grab bars and other devices was provided in the resident room bathrooms in the healthcare center. Occupational therapists will meet with each resident when they move in to locate the lavatory and grab bars to best support each resident's abilities. Further adjustments can be made as abilities change.

- An overhead lift system will be installed in 36 resident rooms. The infrastructure has been provided for the lifts to be installed in the future in all of the resident rooms. These lifts will eliminate the use of wheeled lifts and will allow a single caregiver to safely lift a resident from reclined to seated or standing positions without the risk of injury to staff.

- A system of state-of-the-art electronic infrastructure was put in place to support an electronic medical record system and to flexibly grant staff access to it from any location. The termination of the centralized paper medical record eliminated the need for a centralized organizational system and the accompanying nurses' station. This infrastructure will provide the sponsor's staff the support that it needs to use new technologies to monitor residents and document their conditions to support new research initiatives.

Top trends

- Responding to the site and local conditions: The design team planned the campus to preserve the natural landscape and utilized mature trees as a way to break up the campus into smaller-scaled elements with individual entrances for each component. Extensive blasting was needed to carve buildings and roads into the site. The rock was then used to build retaining walls and crushed for the compacted base for roads. Derived from the

Above: The household has a working kitchen at its center and a dining room and living room
Opposite top and opposite bottom: Independent Living includes cottages, villas and apartments

New England vernacular, the architecture is composed of simple, elemental and connected forms. The simple and unpretentious nature of the vernacular was easily reinterpreted with oversized and mulled windows providing increased daylight, while playing a role in making an architecture that is refreshingly of the 21st century.

- Addressing a holistic sense of wellness: There was a strong desire from the beginning to maximize the residents' connection to the always changing natural environment and the way it marks the passage of time. This was accomplished through the selection of natural materials, naturally occurring colors and patterns and through the utilization of oversized windows throughout the campus to maximize natural light and to connect residents to the natural environment. Based on the belief that intergenerational interactions can have positive impacts, the Community Center was created to encourage and support interaction between residents, staff, and visitors of all ages. Accommodations were made to encourage access by parents and children from the Rashi School throughout the day.

- Offering choice through a diversity of housing options: The living accommodations include 50 cottages, 24 villa apartments, 182 apartments, 51 traditional Assisted Living apartments, 40 Memory Support rooms, and a 268-resident healthcare center with 220 long-term care residents and 48 sub-acute patients. Within each building, there are multiple floor plans to select from and the residents were allowed to customize units to further fit their needs.

Sustainability: Does the project conserve energy, water, and other natural resources? Does it reuse existing material or buildings, or include recycled building materials? How will the project improve indoor air quality in operation?

- Natural resource management/sustainable site design: integrate existing trees and dense vegetation, preserve open space with underground parking, and using green design principles like storm water capture for limited irrigation along with xeriscaping.

- Integrated architecture and interior design to distribute numerous over-sized windows providing abundant natural light, utilized energy-efficient lighting, specified long lasting and easily maintained floor coverings, and utilized recycled materials.

- Development of New England's largest closed-loop geothermal heating and cooling system, which utilizes 400 heat transfer wells with projected gas savings of 50 percent and a 34 percent CO_2 emissions reduction equating to about 18 million pounds per year.

Community: How does the project advance the sense of community for residents, staff, families, and neighbors?

- Building social interactions around food is an intuitive human practice. The Nosh deli and coffee shop is centrally located in the Community Center where residents, visitors,

and staff can enjoy breakfast, lunch, or a mid-afternoon snack. Kosher food is available for those residents who desire it. An expansive floor-to-ceiling window wall opens onto an outdoor patio and meadow with a preserved 100-year-old beech tree, making it a great place to visit with family and friends or serve as a pre-function space for lectures, movies, and other events. Soft seating and bistro tables make this a comfortable, inviting place to gather before or after fitness classes, people watch, or play a quick game of pool.

- The architecture and interior design of each of the housing options on the campus has a strong residential quality and a degree of separation and autonomy. These elements share certain architectural elements that tie the campus together, but are intended for the occupants of each building to feel a sense of ownership over them. The architecture of the Community Center, which lies at the center, strives for a more public feel that does not promote ownership by any group in order to provide cues to residents, visitors, and especially students from the adjacent school that this is an environment where everyone is welcome and encouraged to interact.
- The hospitality design aesthetic is a major contributor to the sense of community. It creates the experience of being at a luxury resort, not a retirement home. The success of this concept can be attributed to the fact that it is embodied not only in a visual manner – from forms and colors to materials and furnishings – but also programmatically. It is both the lively exterior and interior design and exciting amenities of the community center that draws residents from their apartments and brings them together with staff, parents and children, family and friends, and visitors.

Target market: What specific features/services/amenities were incorporated into the overall project to attract your target market?

- Numerous options have been created for those residents who are looking for an independent, but supportive living environment. There are 50 cluster cottages nestled on the hillside overlooking the main campus. There are 24 villa apartments, which are detached except for an underground tunnel connection. There are 150 apartments that are physically connected to the Community Center and there are 32 apartments that are located in the Community Center. Within each building, there are multiple floor plans to select from and the residents were allowed to customize units to further suit their needs. Service offerings are also flexibly designed to provide the desired level of service to each resident.
- The Assisted Living program was divided to provide traditional Assisted Living services with a separate program that focuses on accommodating the needs of residents who require memory support. The modular design of the healthcare center allows the sponsor to offer flexible niche programs at the household increment level. All areas were designed to be 'dementia ready' so that an individual or group with dementia may be flexibly accommodated. One group of households is set up as a rehab/short-term stay program to address that market.

Jury Comments

From the planning to the final design execution, this project sets a new standard of excellence. The planning reflects a commitment to retaining open space and sustainability. Socially it is a multi-generational community that offers residents an outstanding array of choices. It promotes wellness by providing an abundance of natural light, stimulating programs, and a wide variety of common spaces. The simple, strong architectural design sits lightly on the land and relates well to the New England vernacular. The interior design is handsome and an extension of the exterior design. Overall the project avoids becoming too complex. A high level of quality and attention to detail is maintained from the front door through the entire continuum of care. The design is appealing from both contemporary and traditional points of view and was achieved by engaging both caregivers and residents in the process.

Opposite left, opposite right and below: Community center amenities support an active lifestyle focused on wellness

Photography: Chris Cooper Photography

BAR Architects

Sun City Palace Tsukaguchi

Itami, Hyōgo Prefecture, Japan // Half Century More

Facility type: Independent Living, Assisted Living, Skilled Nursing, Dementia/Memory Support Unit, Wellness/Fitness Center

Target market: Upper

Site location: Suburban

Capacity: 760 units; 1,000 persons

Total project cost: $15 million

Date of completion: March 2008

Below: Central courtyard
Opposite: Exterior entry to community

Overall Project Goals

Set on 5 acres, the site plan consists of three 13-story buildings in triangular arrangement to provide residents with highly valued unobstructed southerly views. All three towers are connected by a garden-level promenade providing residents easy access to community amenities along a short and walkable circulation loop. Promenade lounge spaces overlap the circulation loop and offer both garden views and seating areas to rest and/or socialize. The 650,000-square-foot building includes numerous dining and social amenities to encourage and support physical and social activities for residents.

Provider's Statement

Provider goals for marketing and sales

A larger number of small units (when compared with other Sun City facilities) were desired in order to expand the sales target in the Kansai area in western Japan.

How did the provider plan to improve the residents' quality of life?

Sun City Hall and its public spaces such as the exercise room and the 'Billiard,' 'Mah Jong,' and 'Spa' rooms give the residents great opportunities to enjoy cultural and physical activities every day. Sun City Tsukaguchi residents are also invited to attend jazz and classical music concerts as well as various cultural events in Sun City Hall.

How did the provider want to improve workplace quality for employees?

Employees are provided with significant 'back-of-house' areas for daily meetings, group consultations, and training. Additionally, Tsukaguchi staff members are also given high-quality dining facilities as well as a large break room area to encourage and facilitate morale, team building and collaboration, improved productivity and overall staff retention.

Did the provider have specific goals for the project's staffing quantities, training, or distribution?

At the time of writing the occupancy level was about 20 percent, therefore goals for the project's staffing are not yet finalized.

Did the provider give specific direction about the style, materials, features, or other design aspects of the project? If so, what were those directives?

The provider issued the 'Sun City Standard' as a reference, which indicates all requirements and specifications regarding interior and architectural materials, features, and equipment for Sun City facilities.

How did the provider's financial goals influence the project's organization, configuration, layout, or sizing of components?

With 600 Independent Living units, this is the largest senior community that the provider has ever planned. Providing sufficient services and amenities such as an onsen (a hot spring public bath) in order to make this facility attractive was paramount.

Architect's Statement

Design goals

- Integration of architecture, interiors, and landscape architecture: The collaborative design process lead to a project with very integrated interior and exterior spaces. The space planning of the building yields two large garden courtyards and three perimeter gardens. The location of common spaces within the space plan allows for cross-axial spatial relationships, which provide the greatest amount of common spaces with multiple garden views.

Ground floor plan

1 Porte cochère
2 Reception
3 Lobby
4 Administration
5 Circulation promenade
6 Restaurant
7 Dining
8 Grill
9 Back of house
10 Activities
11 Salon
12 Lounge
13 Service
14 Kitchen
15 Cafe
16 Pool
17 Aerobics
18 Library
19 Exercise
20 Tea room
21 Performance hall
22 Ofuro
23 Cross axial garden views

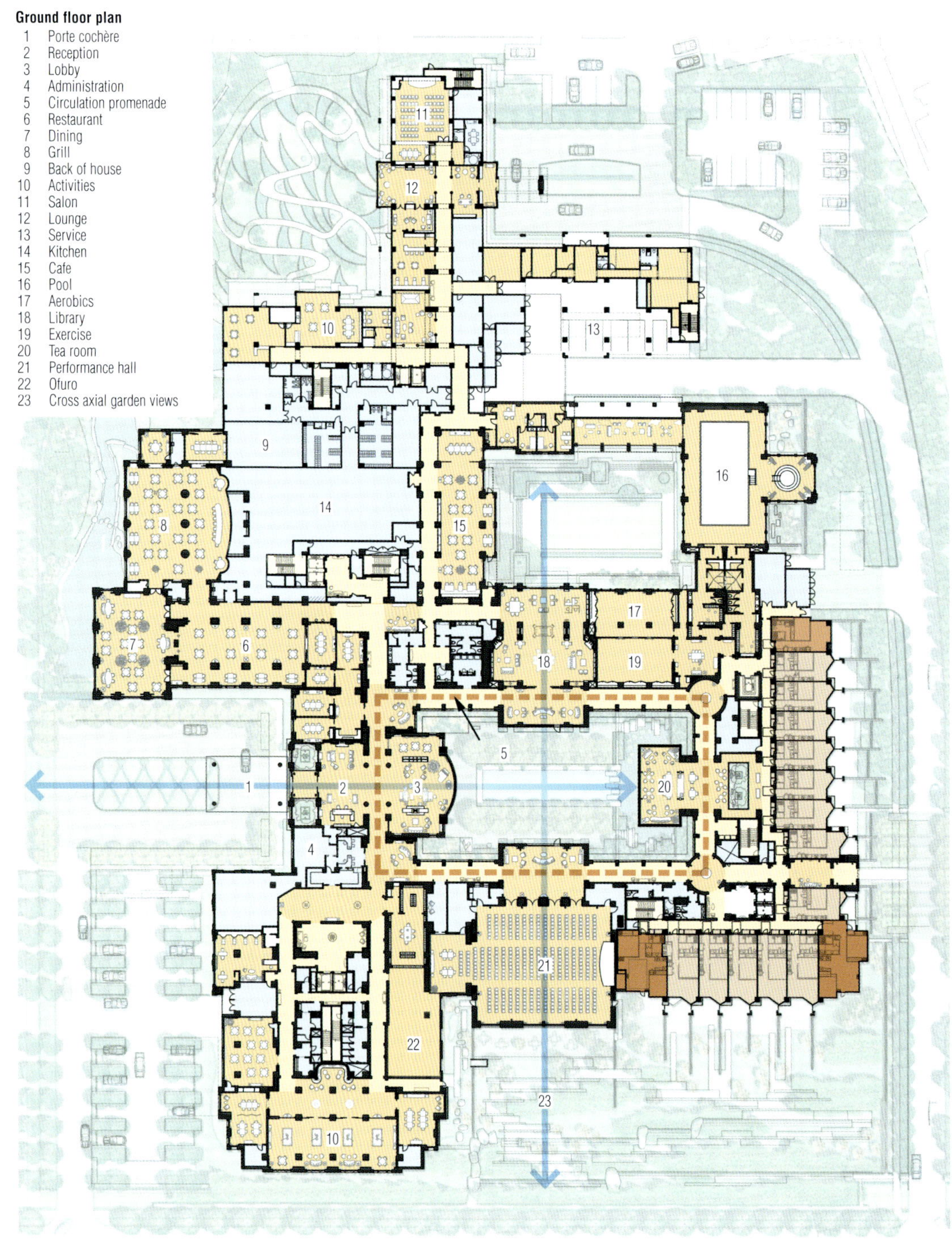

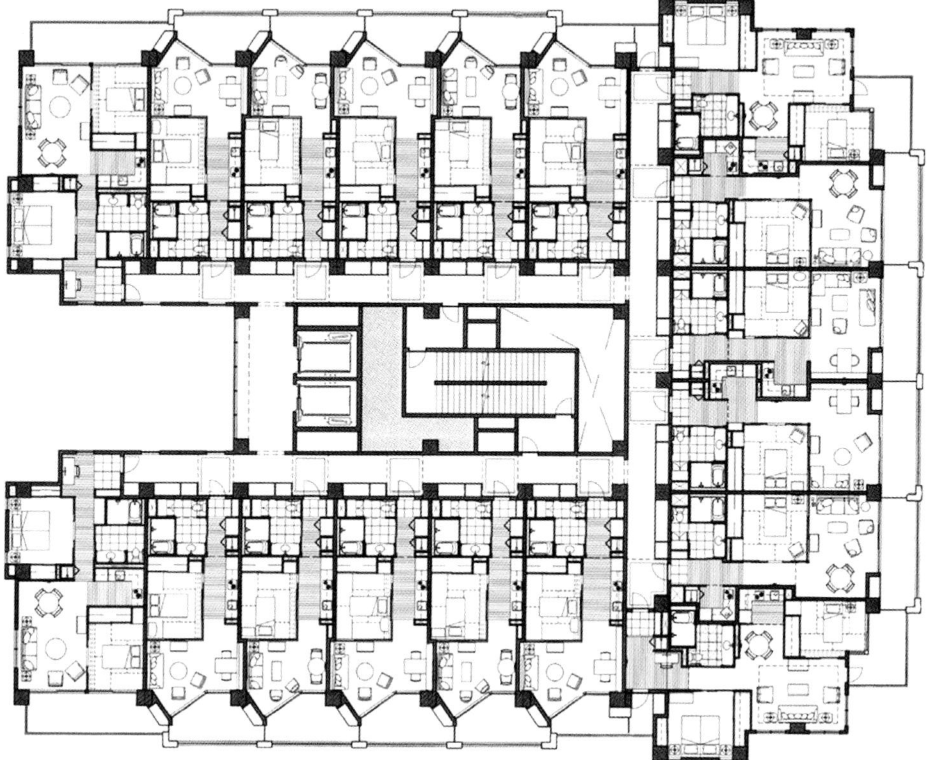

Typical floor plan

- Quantity and diversity of common space: Due to the scale of the project (760 units) and the client's target market (high-net-worth seniors) a vast amount of common space is provided (15 percent of the gross building area). The perception of both the quantity and diversity of common space is particularly strong due to the initial impression of openness one has when walking into the reception pavilion. Multiple dining rooms and lounges give residents daily choices while breaking down the scale of these program elements to give the project a very warm, non-institutional, residential feeling.
- Quality of common space: The quality and circulation flow of the interiors is similar to that of a five-star hotel. The reception and lobby lounge are exquisitely appointed with custom, woven silk carpets; contemporary furniture, lighting, and accessories; and modern art. All other lounges and dining rooms are similarly appointed. The main circulation promenade has limestone floors and a combination of plaster and oak wood paneled walls. The performance hall has oak parquet floors, fabric-covered acoustical walls and handmade light fixtures from Venice, Italy. The spa, swimming pool, and ofuro bath areas have marble counters and glass mosaic walls. These are all long-lasting materials that are easy to maintain.

Challenges: What were the most difficult challenges in designing the project?

- The greatest challenge for the project was to control and focus views within the project. This design challenge was addressed with an axial layering of courtyard and exterior perimeter gardens. This strategy brings a lot of daylight into the public spaces while focusing views within the site (neighboring mid-rise condominiums, a hospital and neighboring two-story single-family homes).
- The second challenge was to maximize south-facing units. This was accomplished by creating as many south-facing units as possible, and also by creating unit plans that provide angled living room windows and by allowing living room furniture to be positioned to focus views in a southerly direction.
- The third challenge was to create one-bedroom, two-bedroom, and two-bedroom-plus-den units that range from 400 to 900 square feet. This required much more meticulous unit planning compared with standard US unit sizes, but was achieved through judicious prioritization of program area while meeting all of the cultural factors that need to be considered for Japanese home buyers.

Innovations: Does the project offer its users unique opportunities or new features not typically available in previous similar projects?

- Locating the main entry drive along the edge of the park, about halfway into the site, enabled it to be lined on both sides with a double row of mature trees, reinforcing the park entry concept. The arrival court and reception pavilion are located far off the street, immersed in a park setting. Three Independent Living gardens and one Nursing Care 'walking' garden are strategically located to benefit the project's major common spaces. Building planning and design embraces an adjacent city park used by children in the surrounding community.
- While meeting the required number of units (and the city's maximum floor area ratio, or

FAR), the number of units with south-facing views was maximized, a very important marketing requirement in the Japanese market. Designing three towers located in a triangular pattern on the site connected by ground-floor common amenities allows the majority of units to have unobstructed southerly views and meet the unit count and mix.

- The overall design philosophy was to achieve the client's significant site density goals while creating a very 'walkable,' amenity-rich senior community. This was achieved by providing a circulation loop around a central landscaped courtyard that connects the elevator cores of all three towers. This promenade provides access to all of the project's amenities, which are located at garden level.

Form shapers: What factors had the most influence on the physical form of the project?

- This amenity- and service-rich project is completely resident oriented and is tailored to encourage residents to be physically active and engage in social interaction. For example: the performance hall is intensively programmed with a range of activities (concerts, plays, and dancing nights, among others) to embrace a variety of interests.
- Efficient and thoughtful space planning was utilized to enable ease of use and wayfinding. The Nursing Care wing is separate, but also directly connected to Independent Living so that if one spouse is moved into Nursing Care, it is easy to visit their partner without going outside the building. This arrangement also allows the family to enter the project through the main Independent Living reception area, even though Nursing Care does have its own nicely decorated entry.

Right: Floating tea pavilion
Opposite: Interior amenities

- State-of-the-art monitoring systems are in place to ensure the safety and well-being of the residents, alerting staff if a resident has not been moving around in their unit for a period of time or missing meals.

Top trends

- Helping aging adults stay in their homes longer: Client sponsor provides a very high level of care in Independent Living, which allows residents to remain in their apartments for longer than most senior living facilities before transferring into Skilled Nursing.
- Addressing a holistic sense of wellness: The high level of services provided to the residents by staff combined with the quantity and quality of shared amenities immersed in landscaped garden courtyards provide a pleasurable place to live and age gracefully and with dignity.
- Offering choice through a diversity of housing options: The CCRC provides multiple options for Independent Living units at a variety of price points. Assisted Living and Skilled Nursing allows residents to age-in-place by providing a range of support for daily living activities based on individual resident needs.

Opposite: Common facilities
Above: Lobby lounge

Sustainability: Does the project conserve energy, water, and other natural resources? Does it reuse existing material or buildings, or include recycled building materials? How will the project improve indoor air quality in operation?

- This is a high-density project on transit hub including two city bus lines and train and taxi points. The provider offers an hourly daytime shuttle to cultural and commercial areas and nearby train station. Resident parking is limited to 0.25 spaces per unit.
- Several water conservation techniques have been employed. Permeable pavement was used to lessen run-off, while rainwater from roofs is collected in underground storage tanks. Natural wells have been used where irrigation is necessary.
- Local materials have been used when possible, particularly for the stone watercourse and the new trees and plantings added to the site.

Community: How does the project advance the sense of community for residents, staff, families, and neighbors?

- Community plays a vital role in a holistic sense of wellness. A focus on the communal activities outside potentially isolating Independent Living units helps foster this sense of community. Clustering social amenities on the ground floor helps integrate functions from dining to mahjong into a community of active seniors.
- The project sponsor programs daily activities promoting both physical activities (dancing, yoga) and social activities (garden club, flower arranging) and performing arts events (music, dance, theater) for residents, thereby fostering a sense of community.

- Residents have casual and formal dining options at each meal, the ability to relax or socialize in different lounges at various times of the day, and a diversity of activities in which to participate – all supporting their overall health and well-being, encouraging them to remain active and enjoy their lives.

Target market: What specific features/services/amenities were incorporated into the overall project to attract your target market?

- The project amenities are of the quality, variety, and scale of a luxury five-star hotel. The arrival court has a nicely scaled porte cochère that leads into a reception pavilion consisting of the reception area and lobby lounge. The entry provides an axial view through the lobby lounge to a floating tea pavilion at the end of a central garden. This design strategy creates a stunning first impression for visitors and a sense of the scale of the project's amenities.
- Independent Living has four dining areas, each designed with a unique interior design and garden view. The largest dining room has an exhibition cooking counter open to preparation of Japanese specialties. One main kitchen prepares all of the food. Nursing Care has dining rooms on each of its five residential floors. The primary goals are giving residents daily choice, diversity, and high-quality service.
- Other amenities include a library, a spa with a swimming pool, ofuros (with Japanese soaking tubs), exercise and aerobics spaces, a tea lounge, a performance hall, and an activities area. The administrative office backs on to the reception desk and the project supports a concierge office and shop for sundries.

Jury Comments

Excellent example of the recently emerging trend of high-density, high-rise urban senior housing. Particularly unique is the skill with which the planning turns the building inward and integrates the exterior landscape into interior spaces. The common areas are located around a series of courtyards, and large windows offer an abundance of natural light and views.

Above: Dining area
Opposite: Loggia

Photography: Steve Hall, Hedrich Blessing

Perkins Eastman

The Point at C.C. Young

Dallas, Texas // C.C. Young

Facility type: Wellness/Fitness Center, Senior Community Center

Target market: Mixed income

Site location: Suburban

Total project cost: $5.1 million

Date of completion: September 2007

Below: Exterior of library at dusk

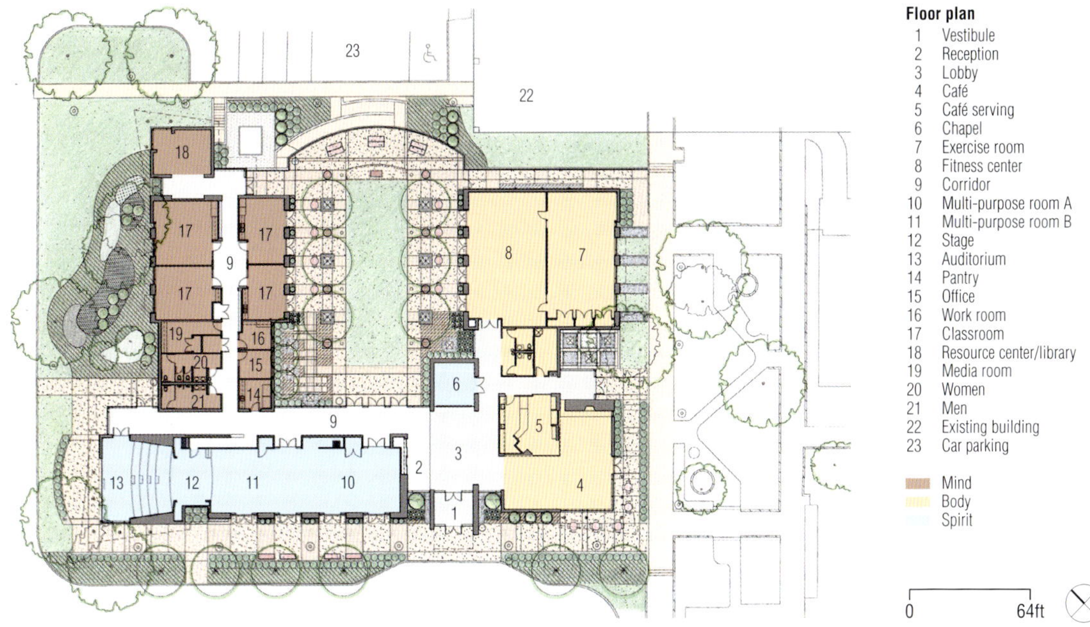

Overall project goals

As C.C. Young's leadership went through a 2015 master planning process, resident feedback indicated that they were seeking a defined heart and soul for the campus; it was clear that the existing town center was functional but uninspiring. A reinvention offered an opportunity to help residents reconnect and equip the CCRC to better meet one of its most important goals: to provide daily opportunities for personal growth and creativity. The leadership also felt strongly that these opportunities would be more vibrant, meaningful, and energizing when shared across generations, a belief that would inform the vision for The Point. The leadership and design team agreed that a new building would need a bold identity to inspire curiosity. The solution was a fresh take on a senior community center: a public, intergenerational gathering place with an eye-catching design, a strong emphasis on the arts, and programs that connect residents with each other and the local community. Design inspiration came from C.C. Young's wellness philosophy: 'Where the Spirit is Ageless.' Spaces within the new 20,000-foot center correspond to one of three specific wellness elements – mind, body, and spirit – and play host to highly interactive, creativity-focused programs that welcome people of all ages.

Provider's Statement

Provider goals for marketing and sales

The goal of The Point was to provide a venue where the residents of C.C. Young and residents of the greater surrounding community could come together and learn a variety of ideas, socialize, and improve fitness and wellness. It was designed to be a place where community collaborators could join with C.C. Young in a complementary manner to magnify individual efforts towards intensifying and broadening collective programs so that aged individuals can flourish in body, mind, and spirit.

How did the provider plan to improve the residents' quality of life?

The Point has helped define a new client beyond the traditional 'resident.' Any person who participates in a class, program, or activity for mental and physical wellness becomes a client. The Point offers an array of fitness opportunities through specifically dedicated space and equipment. The education programs are on par with those of a community college, but in many instances are equal to graduate-level courses.

How did the provider want to improve workplace quality for employees?

Many staff functions are incorporated into the building's spaces and resources. Staff training is enhanced by the various tools of the media center; the auditorium provides an excellent occasional alternative place for program, parties, or in-services improving the employees' image of their workplace and its concomitant value to the community.

Did the provider have specific goals for the project's staffing quantities, training, or distribution?

Aside from a cumulative staff of approximately five full-time equivalents (FTEs), staffing is achieved through collaboration with other organizations.

Did the provider give specific direction about the style, materials, features, or other design aspects of the project? If so, what were those directives?

The provider wanted the building to be a beacon, a lighthouse to the community that aesthetically brands it as a place of enlightenment and education. Its architecture should reflect the surrounding community and functionally meet the owner's goals of efficient and effective use of resources and space.

How did the provider's financial goals influence the project's organization, configuration, layout, or sizing of components?

As the building houses many collaborators whose vision is to create a community where every life and age is valued and enriched, The Point building and operation collaborates with all other buildings and services on the campus to raise C.C. Young up as a premier and innovative provider of services to the elderly. It functions not only in its own right, but also as a common space for other buildings on campus providing space, activities, and services that significantly improve the program opportunities for each campus facility.

Architect's Statement

Design goals

- To support the owner's wellness philosophy, 'Where the Spirit is Ageless,' which focuses on growing and expanding horizons at every stage of life: Spaces correspond to one of three specific wellness elements – mind, body, and spirit. To enrich the mind, the library offers

extensive resources on healthy aging; classrooms support lifelong learning; and a computer lab plays host to training on next-generation technologies. The body is nourished at a café offering healthy choices and strengthened at a fitness center that embraces preventative wellness. To engage the spirit, a performance hall presents live entertainment; art studios support the expression of creativity; and a meditation room and sculpture garden provide sanctuaries for reflection.

- To design a signature building that creates a heart and soul for the campus: a stated desire of C.C. Young's residents. To reinforce The Point's uniqueness, the design team used eye-catching sculptural forms and dramatic curved roof lines, balanced with simple geometric volumes that create a familiar and welcoming spirit. The expressive shape of the roofs is further tempered with generous windows on each corner that break down the building definition and create an inside–outside connection. This reinforces the inviting character of the center and symbolizes the absence of barriers. By positioning the center in a central campus location, the design team ensured it would be a beacon to visitors summiting the hill at the community's entrance.
- To develop a contextual, timeless, and vibrant aesthetic: Form and materials are a contemporary interpretation of the Texas Hill Country vernacular, carefully balanced with the existing campus architecture. This created a distinct identity for the building while providing residents with a sense of familiarity. Colors and furnishings create a welcoming spirit by incorporating natural colors and patterns that people of all ages can relate to. The relaxed environment reflects the ageless quality of the

Opposite : Lounge
Left: Library

center and its visitors and ensures that younger visitors in particular see it as a fun, lively destination. This is a direct contrast to the formal and often 'hands-off' environment of most retirement communities.

Challenges: What were the most difficult challenges in designing the project?

- Limited site availability posed a significant challenge to meeting the client's request that the center be inviting to all residents and the local community. It required the design of a standalone building versus an addition to a residential building, and the identification of a central campus location on a nearly full site. Blending these goals with the objectives of additional campus developments, including potential future expansion of The Point, the design team carved out a dedicated space for the center that is highly visible and easily accessible.

- Another challenge the design team conquered was creating a building layout that would be flexible enough to accommodate a wide variety of users and events, yet would still feel customized to each group's needs. Intensive planning and programming resulted in highly adaptable spaces where groups of all sizes are comfortable, ensuring that visitors never feel isolated in a too-large area or crowded into an undersized space. This is especially important for the older adult users of the building.

- The design team was further challenged to create an environment that would welcome users of all ages; support the needs of seniors without appearing to be age-restricted or institutional; and balance hospitality, senior living, and intergenerational aesthetics. The use of lively, friendly colors and materials that youthful visitors can relate to also creates a feeling of vibrancy in more mature residents. Today's older adults do not necessarily desire a traditional aesthetic. Other solutions included flexible spaces that support an informal functionality and a mind/body/spirit theme that centers around holistic wellness.

Innovations: Does the project offer its users unique opportunities or new features not typically available in previous similar projects?

- The most innovative design elements of The Point are subtle features that promote active and passive participation. Generous corner windows put activities on display to passers-by, encouraging outgoing residents to join the action and helping more apprehensive seniors feel connected to people and events. Inside, the flexible layout and ability to customize seating arrangements serve the same purpose, so that both individuals and groups are comfortable in a variety of spaces. The overall planning and design of the center reinforce its inviting spirit and symbolize the absence of barriers.

- The design team took advantage of the central location they selected to turn The Point into a new focal point for the campus. The center is the first thing visitors see when they enter the community, and its sculptural forms catch the eye from every location on campus. The Point has had such an influence on the community's identity that the owner renamed their quarterly newsletter 'The Lantern,' a reference to the warm glow from the center's windows in the evening.

Form shapers: What factors had the most influence on the physical form of the project?

- A critical feature to support aging guests is ease of use. The Point's central campus location and multiple entrances make it easily accessible from every building, and frailer residents in skilled care and assisted living only have to travel a few yards to reach The Point. Once inside, the design supports use by all guests, regardless of ability, through the use of senior-friendly furniture and fitness equipment, glare-resistant lighting, and floor coverings that allow the aging eye to detect surface changes.

- Older people often have anxiety related to social interactions, and The Point's design affords aging adults the opportunity to control their experience. They can choose between scheduled programming and spontaneous encounters, and decide whether to interact with close friends in the more intimate spaces or make new acquaintances in the livelier common areas.

Top trends

- Partnering with senior-friendly non-providers: C.C. Young's partnerships with nearly 30 non-senior providers are a driving factor in its success. By providing a beautiful, exciting space for use by outside entities, they have been able to attract partners ranging from health and wellness providers and institutes of higher education to arts and cultural organizations, non-profit senior agencies, and religious groups. What is particularly special about these partnerships is that they bring an intergenerational audience beyond invited family members of residents: students and professionals teach classes and give lectures; medical practitioners host clinics and seminars; and entertainers range from primary and secondary school orchestras to community church choirs.

- Integrating with the surrounding community: A desire to integrate with the surrounding community was a major influence on the design of The Point. It shaped the center's location, program and layout, and aesthetic in a variety of ways. The central campus positioning makes it approachable to residents and guests; spaces are flexible and customizable to support a wide variety of programs and events; and the interesting, ageless design welcomes the public.

C.C. Young's CEO and President, Ken Durand, noted that, 'Now more than ever, our residents and people from the Dallas community come together to explore new ideas and have fun. We are so pleased with the emphasis The Point has brought to our residents and Dallas as we pursue our vision of affording greater value to older people.'

- Addressing a holistic sense of wellness: The community's previous community/fitness center was a typical, non-branded building with a few multipurpose rooms and fitness equipment – wellness was not part of its appeal. The concept for The Point presented an opportunity to articulate C.C. Young's wellness philosophy, 'Where the Spirit is Ageless,' in both form and function. Growing and expanding horizons at every stage of life is a core principle of the philosophy, and The Point's ageless aesthetic and rich programming are the perfect complement.

Community: How does the project advance the sense of community for residents, staff, families, and neighbors?

- Building a sense of community was the driving reason to create The Point. The center embodies this idea in both design and functionality. Its positioning in the center of campus, at the summit of the community's entrance drive, announces it presence to the public. Architectural features such as the large corner windows draw attention to the activities happening inside and exciting curved roofs reinforce the center's lively spirit. As a result, The Point has become a magnet that draws groups together to explore new ideas and have fun. Mature residents flock to the dynamic programs and amenities, and the local community is welcomed as participants, educators, health and wellness providers, and entertainers.
- The Point's welcoming environment offers an ideal setting to build personal relationships: families spend one-on-one time with staff in the fireplace lounge; staff members assist residents in the fitness room; and residents take easels onto the courtyard patio with friends. The sense

Above left: Café exterior
Above right: Café interior

of community is further enhanced by the rich selection of communal programs that create numerous opportunities for intergenerational connections. Affording aging adults access to varied activities and the opportunity to interact with people of all ages is crucial to their well-being. The project's design supports that need in its programming, layout, and furnishings.

- The Point is now host to the owner's annual Art is Ageless event, a celebration of creativity that showcases the talents of artists, writers, and musicians from within the CCRC and the local community. This year's 10th-annual event featured a juried art exhibition, performances by a six-year-old pianist and seven-year-old violinist, and presentation of a lifetime achievement award to Ebby Haliday, a 98-year-old ukulele player from Dallas.

Target market: What specific features/services/amenities were incorporated into the overall project to attract your target market?

- To attract an intergenerational market, the design balances hospitality and senior living design elements to create an ageless aesthetic. In addition to colors and materials that appeal to people of all ages, there are a variety of discreet features that support aging adults without making younger visitors feel that they are in an 'old folks home.' For example, recessed carpet prevents tripping and identifies seating areas, while porcelain pavers articulate circulation around the café. All furniture is easy to grasp and move, making it simple for all visitors to configure seating arrangements according to their needs.

- The Point also appeals to an intergenerational audience by offering guests the ability to customize their experience. The building layout has the flexibility to accommodate a wide variety of users and events, yet feel customized to each group's needs. Intensive planning and programming resulted in highly adaptable spaces where groups of all sizes are comfortable, ensuring that visitors never feel isolated in a too-large area or crowded into an undersized space. The wide variety of environments – such as the comfortable fireplace sitting area, casual al fresco dining along the esplanade, and lounge with flat-screen televisions off the café – make every visit unique.

Jury Comments

This project established a singular bold statement that created a 'defined heart and soul for the campus.' Indeed, the architects and C.C. Young's leadership created not only a 'heart and soul' for their campus, but truly an inspiring environment. The project pulls the campus together, and ensures that the setting will motivate, inspire, and energize its residents. The aggressive and inspiring design uses a Texas Hill Country vernacular of stone, wood, brick, stucco, and iron to create a highly attractive, modern design. Notable features include use of corner windows and natural light throughout the building, and a very warm, organic, interior design, including local art, furniture and textiles. The project succeeds in establishing a community center that will attract and inspire people of all ages to participate in holistic wellness and intergenerational activities.

Opposite: Living room
Left: Auditorium
Photography: © Chris Cooper

Perkins Eastman

Westminster Village Town Center

Scottsdale, Arizona // Westminster Village

Facility type: Assisted Living, Wellness/Fitness Center, Senior Community Center

Target market: Middle/upper middle

Site location: Suburban

Capacity: 23 Assisted Living Rooms

Date of completion: January 2008

Below: Front at dusk

Overall Project Goals

The concept for this project was to create a more vibrant and marketable community. Westminster Village enjoyed years of success after opening in 1988, offering Independent Living and Skilled Care to an affluent consumer base. But the community's average resident age was rising. The leadership recognized that a dramatic repositioning was necessary to attract younger consumers in a highly competitive market. The result was a complete reinvention of the existing town center and the addition of an Assisted Living product. This project involved the renovation of a small portion of the existing single-story town center and demolition of the majority of the facility to make way for a two-story, 63,000-square-foot building offering trendsetting amenities on the first floor and 23 units of Assisted Living on the second floor.

Provider's Statement

Provider goals for marketing and sales

A primary marketing goal was to complete the campus' continuum with the addition of Assisted Living. The project achieved that and the units were immediately filled with existing ILU residents; outside marketing was not necessary. The other primary marketing goal was to remain competitive in the marketplace by enhancing the center's image as a hospitality-model community. The project also achieved that. Overall vacancy rates did increase following the completion of the project in January 2008, but that has been attributed to housing and financial market conditions, as vacancy rates increased at a lower rate than that experienced by competitors.

How did the provider plan to improve the residents' quality of life?

The multiple dining venues in particular did a lot to improve residents' quality of life. They can dress up to meet in the lounge for appetizers and drinks before going to the formal dining restaurant, or they can go to the casual venue in shorts for pizza and beer. The options have really opened up social opportunities that weren't there before and have improved networking among residents.

How did the provider want to improve workplace quality for employees?

The improved aesthetics have really made employees proud. Responses from visiting family members are telling; with comments like, 'You work in a resort! I thought you worked in an old folk's home.'

Did the provider have specific goals for the project's staffing quantities, training, or distribution?

All staffing goals have been met.

Did the provider give specific direction about the style, materials, features, or other design aspects of the project? If so, what were those directives?

The two primary directives were to celebrate the Southwest aesthetic that the market was familiar with, and infuse resort styling. It was an excellent collaborative effort between the provider and the design team. The most successful design feature was the blending of the architecture and the interior design, bringing the inside out and vice versa, and tying them together with colors, fabrics, and design.

How did the provider's financial goals influence the project's organization, configuration, layout, or sizing of components?

The provider was facing stiff competition in the local market, and identified a need to update. The renovation allowed the provider to improve financial prospects with the addition of Assisted Living, which is a product that the market demanded and everyone else but Westminster Village offered. It has allowed the center to remain viable.

Architect's Statement

Design goals

- To provide a rejuvenating resort atmosphere: The design team achieved this by blurring the lines between interior and exterior spaces. Glass walls and retractable glass doors surround a courtyard oasis on the town center's first floor, creating a seamless transition between inside and out. Residents gather around the courtyard's inviting pavilion fireplace for intimate chats or group activities. It has become the focal point of the oasis, offering a versatile gathering place for both special events and daily activities. Adding to the resort feeling are floor-to-ceiling windows that capture views of the landscape and neighboring mountain range. Nearly every space in the building looks onto vegetation and water elements.

- To create a vibrant dining experience: To entice consumers seeking to preserve their existing lifestyle, the design team created six unique venues with distinct brands that are on par with restaurants the target market currently frequents. Residents can grab-and-go from the marketplace-style Garden Café; relax with poolside refreshments; dine alfresco in the Courtyard Café on a floating patio; have a casual meal at Ocotillo; sit down to a formal dinner at Donnelly's; and unwind with a drink in the Jayhawk Lounge.

- To celebrate the town center: The existing town center's undefined entrance did little to draw residents in or attract the attention of prospects entering the community. The design team created a striking entry tower to define the center as the heart of the campus and reinforce its importance in the community's re-branding efforts. The purposefully over-scaled tower is visible from the moment you enter the campus. At dusk, the glow from interior ceiling lights combine with exterior uplighting at the

base to produce a lantern-like effect. The tower features a 24-foot glass wall fronted with an aluminum sunscreen, taking advantage of the brilliant Arizona sun while offering protection from heat gain and glare.

Challenges: What were the most difficult challenges in designing the project?

- A major project constraint was fear of change. Several members of the resident council had participated in the original campus planning and had difficulty being objective about the community's weaknesses. The design team worked with the resident council to discuss the big picture before developing design concepts. They took the group to visit other communities and educated them on trends and the new consumer. As a result, the resident council recognized that the repositioning was essential for the community's continued success.
- The project's complex phasing process was a significant challenge. The project involved the renovation of 6,000 square feet of the existing town center and the demolition of the remaining building to make way for a new, two-story, 63,000-square-foot building in its place. Constructability, design goals, and operational needs were carefully balanced during the planning stage to ensure optimum resident service during the two phases of teardown and rebuild. The location of many of the program elements were driven by the need to keep core services operational during the entire project – which they were. In spite of the interruption, residents became very curious about the project and enjoyed watching the demolition and rebuild.
- Respecting the vernacular of existing campus structures while creating a hospitality-driven aesthetic required a delicate balance. It was also important to the target market that the community's Southwest heritage be celebrated. In response, the design team used stucco to blend with existing campus structures and brought in local stone and textured wood as a new material. To create a resort-like inside–outside connection, exterior materials were replicated inside as much as possible. The façade stone was used on interior columns and fireplaces, and flooring materials subtly move from colored concrete to stone pavers for a seamless transition. Colors, patterns, furnishings, and accessories offer a fresh take on the Southwest aesthetic.

Opposite: Entrance at dusk
Above: Courtyard patios

Innovations: Does the project offer its users unique opportunities or new features not typically available in previous similar projects?

- The next generation of consumers is especially sensitive to compromising their existing lifestyle, and the design team ensured that the dining experiences at Westminster Village echo those of the local cafés and restaurants the target market currently enjoys. The design of vibrant brands for each environment took that solution a step further, creating names for each venue such as Donnelly's – instead of Donnelly Dining Room as originally planned – and Ocotillo, adding a dose of personality to each space.
- By demolishing the existing town center and adding new programming, the design team had the opportunity to create a more interesting layout. Inspired by Scandinavian planning principles, they used the central courtyard oasis as an anchor around which all interior spaces are located. It is an effective tool to reinforce the constant connection to the outdoors. It also reduced signage needs, as navigation is intuitive. The demolition also allowed repositioning of the pool and led the design team to utilize open spaces between existing resident buildings to create these more vibrant outdoor recreation areas.
- The opportunity to redefine and modernize the Southwest aesthetic was an exciting innovation. Updated patterns, textiles, wall coverings, and carpets reflect the Scottsdale heritage with familiar colors: the green of cacti; the orange, rust, and sand of the desert; and the brown of stone and wood. Hair-on-hide furniture that recalls cattle and horses, accessories that appear to be local finds, and pieces from local Native American artists also help balance the familiar and the new while pushing the design vocabulary forward.

Opposite: Courtyard
Above: Courtyard dining

Form shapers: What factors had the most influence on the physical form of the project?

- By completing its continuum with assisted living, Westminster Village offers a comfortable, stylish destination to age in place as resident needs change, supported by superior care, programming, and technologies. The layout of the Assisted Living neighborhood is particularly supportive of aging in place. The 23 residences are grouped into two intimate households and share a central living/dining space, activity kitchen, and terrace overlooking the courtyard oasis. The design team ensured that these common spaces were equal in quality to those in the first-floor town center, encouraging residents who cannot easily leave the neighborhood to engage in social activities.

- Universal design principles were employed to ensure that all guests, regardless of age or ability, have equitable use. All physical spaces, furniture, and supportive fixtures are accessible, both inside and out. The numerous entrances offer flexibility in use by responding to visitor needs and preferences. The local community primarily uses the main entrance, while residents and family members can choose the entrance closest to their residential building. The design ensures that users can enjoy the facility's numerous connections to nature with low physical effort. To reduce glare from the numerous windows that bring in an extraordinary amount of natural light and access to views, the team used sun shades and low-E glass.

- The constant connection to the outdoors is also important for aging in place. Extensive daylight and views allow passive integration with nature and encourage residents to engage in more daily activities and help regulate circadian rhythms.

Top trends

- Responding to the site and local conditions: The rich texture of the Southwest had a profound influence on the project's design. It was clear that the target market, primarily from Scottsdale and Phoenix, desired a familiar local aesthetic. But to make this project extraordinary, it was important to use that inspiration in a way that would be fresh, engaging, and timeless. The new town center has taken that vernacular in a bold new direction, blending the recognizable elements of a desert motif with updated forms, profiles, patterns and colors to create an exciting new image for Southwest-style architecture.

- Addressing a holistic sense of wellness: To achieve holistic wellness, the environment must address more than physical health. The new town center at Westminster Village pushes the boundaries of wellness architecture with strategies like the wrapping of amenity spaces around a central courtyard. This created a 'see-through' effect between multiple inside and outside spaces and provides a constant connection to nature. Elements like the pavilion fireplace, which is kept on at all times, draws residents together at all hours and creates new opportunities for social wellness. And the ability for residents to seek nourishment in the environment of their choosing at a variety of times is transformational. This project sets the tone for designing holistic wellness.

- Offering a hospitality experience: If you were to move out of your family home, and you had a choice between a retirement home and an all-inclusive, luxury resort, which would you choose? The answer is obvious. Westminster Village is on the leading edge of the trend to infuse hospitality styling into the residential environment. The design offers not only the visual elements of this aesthetic, but also creates opportunities for resort-style experiences. The courtyard oasis is a strong example of this trend. Features like the floating patios, intimate pavilion fireplace, and cozy seating areas allow residents to travel from their apartment to a rejuvenating vacation in a matter of minutes.

Sustainability: Does the project conserve energy, water, and other natural resources? Does it reuse existing material or buildings, or include recycled building materials? How will the project improve indoor air quality in operation?

- Sunshades reduce heat gain/glare. Vertical sunshades on the entry tower and assisted living lounge windows are positioned 10 feet above the base to afford views to the landscape. All south-facing windows feature horizontal sunshades and low-E glass.

- To reduce the heat island effect, the team used a flat white reflective roof with a Solar Reflective Index (SRI) of 78. Evaporation from the reflective ponds in the courtyard oasis also helps keep the temperature down.

- Features like retractable glass walls on the first floor and operable windows in the second-floor Assisted Living residences optimize indoor air quality by providing natural ventilation. Residents also have individual thermal control in their units.

Community: How does the project advance the sense of community for residents, staff, families, and neighbors?

- Building social interactions around food is an intuitive human practice. To ensure that this tradition would be part of the lifestyle at Westminster Village, the design team created six distinct dining environments. By using the courtyard oasis as a hub around which the venues are organized, every space on the first floor is just steps away from an opportunity to socialize over a meal or refreshments. The Garden Café takes this concept even further, offering grab-and-go options that residents can choose to enjoy in any of the town center's inviting lounge spaces.

- The hospitality design aesthetic is a major contributor to the sense of community. It creates the experience of being at a luxury resort, not a retirement home. The success of this concept can be attributed to the fact that it is embodied not only in a visual manner – from forms and colors to materials and furnishings – but also programmatically. It is both the lively exterior and interior design and exciting amenities of the new town center that are drawing residents from their apartments and bringing them together with neighbors in ways that the community hasn't seen before.
- A prospect's first glimpse of a campus shapes their perception of its identity, and what often defines that identity are the community spaces – not the residential spaces. The previous town center blended in so completely with the residential buildings that arriving visitors were not immediately drawn to it. The new town center desperately needed a 'wow' factor to distinguish it as the place to be on campus. The design team created a striking entry tower to define the center as the heart of the community. The purposefully over-scaled tower is visible from the moment you enter the campus. At dusk, the glow from interior ceiling lights combine with exterior uplighting at the base to produce a lantern-like effect.

Right: Second floor exterior

DONNELLY'S

Target market: What specific features/services/amenities were incorporated into the overall project to attract your target market?

- Westminster Village's target market indicated a desire for an upscale resort feeling. In response, the design team blurred the lines between interior and exterior spaces. Glass walls and retractable glass doors surround the courtyard oasis, creating a seamless transition between inside and out. Residents gather around the courtyard's inviting pavilion fireplace for intimate chats or group activities. It has become the focal point of the oasis, offering a versatile gathering place for both special events and daily activities. Adding to the resort feeling are floor-to-ceiling windows that capture views of the landscape and neighboring McDowell Mountain Range. Nearly every space in the building looks onto vegetation and water elements.
- Creating multiple dining venues was an important stimulant for Westminster Village's marketability. The next generation of consumers simply won't accept a single dining room with rigid service schedules anymore. They want choice and control over when and where they enjoy their meals, and they expect the physical spaces to look and feel like the restaurants they frequent with their friends and family.
- An important service opportunity arose from the new consumer's demand for a Residential Care option in addition to Independent Living and skilled care. The new Assisted Living units have been a great success – all 23 units are occupied and have a waiting list for future availability.

Left: Bar/lounge

Photography: © Chris Cooper

Jury Comments

Westminster succeeded in creating a vibrant hub to their CCRC campus. The building exudes a sophisticated interior and exterior design, reflecting an upscale hospitality approach. Creating an important anchor to the aging campus, this single building revitalizes the campus. The addition of Assisted Living to the campus was an important goal for the organization. The Town Center gives the feel of resort-style living, and the amenities clearly provide excellent choice to the consumers – six dining venues! Dining areas are elegant and inviting. The design is highly successful by using local materials to reflect local heritage and the existing environment. This project addresses energy conservation with sun shades to reduce heat gain/glare, retractable glass walls on the first floor, and operable windows. The design maximizes the visual imagery of the surrounding outdoors, capitalizing on views of the mountains. The indoor–outdoor terrace creates an oasis accessible to the Assisted Living residents as well as the entire community.

DiMella Shaffer

The Legacy at Willow Bend

Plano, Texas // Legacy Senior Communities, Inc.

Facility type: Independent Living, Assisted Living, Skilled Nursing, Dementia/Memory Support Unit, Wellness/Fitness Center

Target market: Mixed income

Site location: Suburban

Capacity: 233 units: 115 Independent Living apartments, 40 Assisted Living apartments, 60 Skilled Nursing rooms, 18 Dementia/Memory Support rooms

Date of completion: July 2008

Below: Exterior courtyard

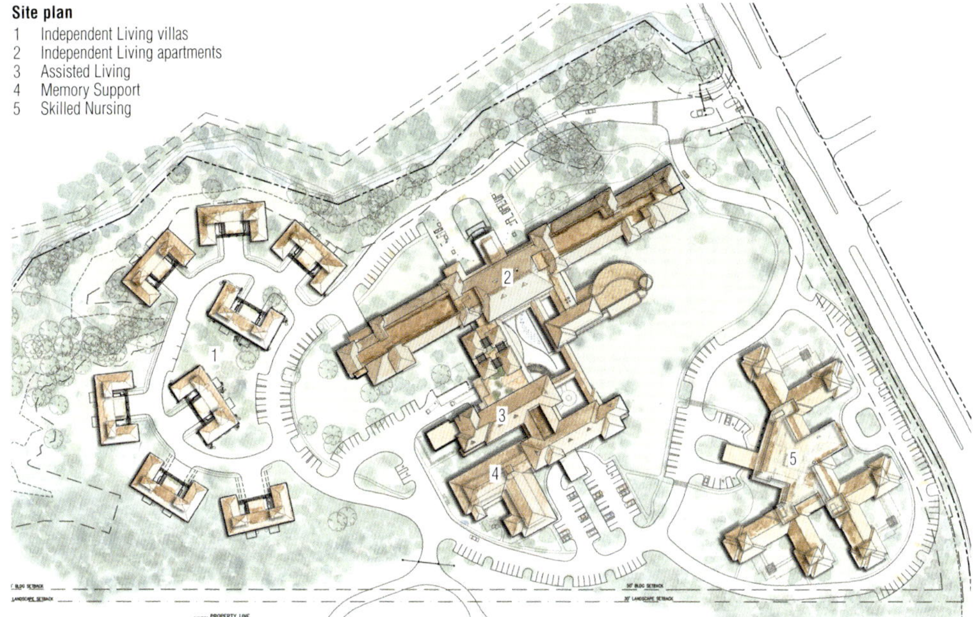

Overall Project Goals

The Legacy at Willow Bend is a Continuing Care Retirement Community (CCRC) conceived, developed, and ultimately built to serve the Dallas Jewish community. Located slightly to the north of the City of Plano, this CCRC of approximately 400,000 square feet provides housing options for seniors that enhance residents' vibrant years while also providing the best supportive living environments should they be needed. The design creates a residential community for seniors that is conceived as a 'village' of buildings ranging in height from one to four stories. Those individuals living independently have the option of living in a semi-detached one-story villa, or in a four-story apartment building with one- to three-bedroom optional living arrangements and also contiguous to a central 'community commons.' The commons provides an extensive array of social and fitness/wellness program spaces. Interconnected to this commons is a three-story Assisted Living building, providing housing for 40 residents as well as spaces for corporate administrative offices. Adjacent to the Assisted Living building is a secure building housing an 18-bed Memory Support unit. Close by on-site, a one-story 60-bed Skilled Nursing facility has been designed as a separate building with its own community commons.

Provider's Statement

Provider goals for marketing and sales

Sales have remained consistent with the feasibility study even through the economic downturn. Occupancy is slightly below plan in Independent Living. However, Assisted Living, Memory Support and Nursing/Rehab have done better than planned and have achieved over 85 percent occupancy. Budgeted numbers have been met and exceeded in these three areas and are on plan for Independent Living.

How did the provider plan to improve the residents' quality of life?

The wellness spa with salon, fitness center, resistance pool, hot tub, and personal trainer are popular with residents. The bar is beautiful. Also important are the sanctuary, screened-in porch, home theater and lovely dining room with fine dining. The center courtyard with fountain adds to the beauty of the community, as does the entry fountain with oversized porte cochère. In the nursing building, the intimate dining rooms, courtyards, and wide hallways interspersed with common game areas help give a family atmosphere to this building. The outside courtyard on the second floor of the Assisted Living building is unique to this area and enjoyed by residents and families. Memory Care has a spa and intimate dining room, which are appreciated by residents.

How did the provider want to improve workplace quality for employees?

The building is aesthetically pleasing and affords a lovely place in which to work. Large-screen TVs in employee break rooms, which are also well appointed, have a positive effect on employee morale. Staff members enjoy Stanley's Café for lunch and break times. The fitness center is available to senior staff members. Work areas are clean, well lit, and appealing.

Did the provider have specific goals for the project's staffing quantities, training, or distribution?

Over 250 staff members have been added since opening and staffing has remained stable. Ongoing training is important, starting with employee orientation. Because of the kitchen and dining room configuration, full-time equivalents (FTEs) in dining are above original projections. Nursing FTEs are also above the original plan due to the layout of three hallways. However, census has supported the higher staffing levels.

Did the provider give specific direction about the style, materials, features, or other design aspects of the project? If so, what were those directives?

The provider has been very involved since inception with an active building committee chaired by a well-known architect. The president of the organization was intimately involved with all aspects of the building project as were senior staff members. Studio Six5, the project interior design team, was also very involved and a senior staff member worked closely with the designer.

How did the provider's financial goals influence the project's organization, configuration, layout, or sizing of components?

The Legacy at Willow Bend was designed to meet not only the care needs of its residents, but also to allow the project to meet its financial and operations objectives. All levels of care were designed to be operationally efficient and thus financially sustainable. The provider's experience in skilled nursing is reflected in the design of the Health Center with its focus on short-term rehabilitation. These services will contribute significantly to the financial performance of the project and enhance the project's services to both its Life Care and direct admission residents. Assisted Living and Memory Support are 'boutique' in nature with premier amenities and services, thus allowing the project to attract its target clientele at its desired price point. Independent Living boasts a variety of unit types, which will help accelerate the occupancy process thereby enabling the project to benefit financially and meet its financial goals.

All 'back-of-house' operations were designed and built to accommodate additional units in subsequent phases. This will reduce future construction timelines and costs and add significant financial benefits to the organization as additional residences are added to the project in future years. All of these factors will enable the project to meet both its financial and operational objectives.

Architect's Statement

Design goals

- Maximize daylight and control glare: People feel better and respond positively to their living and working environments if an ample supply of daylight is provided throughout the day. To make one's experiences more pleasurable as eyesight deteriorates with age, it is critical to provide ample natural and artificial light without glare. As a result of the careful analysis taken to locate and size the window openings throughout the project, the residents were encouraged to comfortably take full advantage of their physical environment.
- Encourage socialization: To encourage residents who are in Independent Living apartments or villas to meet informally, the common program areas have been strategically located along natural circulation paths, close to elevator lobbies and most often grouped around the three exterior courtyards. This creates an opportunity for multiple chance meetings as the residents informally bump into each other.
- Consistent quality: A consistent quality of experience is provided within each different living alternative. Although the four different living environments (Independent, Assisted, Memory Support, and Skilled Nursing) each have their specific design requirements, the quality of the exterior and interior architecture, lighting, and furniture has been carefully integrated so that the community appearance is seamless. Where additional supportive assists are required, they are provided. However, the casual observer will most probably not be aware that they have been included. This particular goal makes a resident's transition from a more independent environment to one that is more supportive seem natural and therefore more likely to be openly embraced.

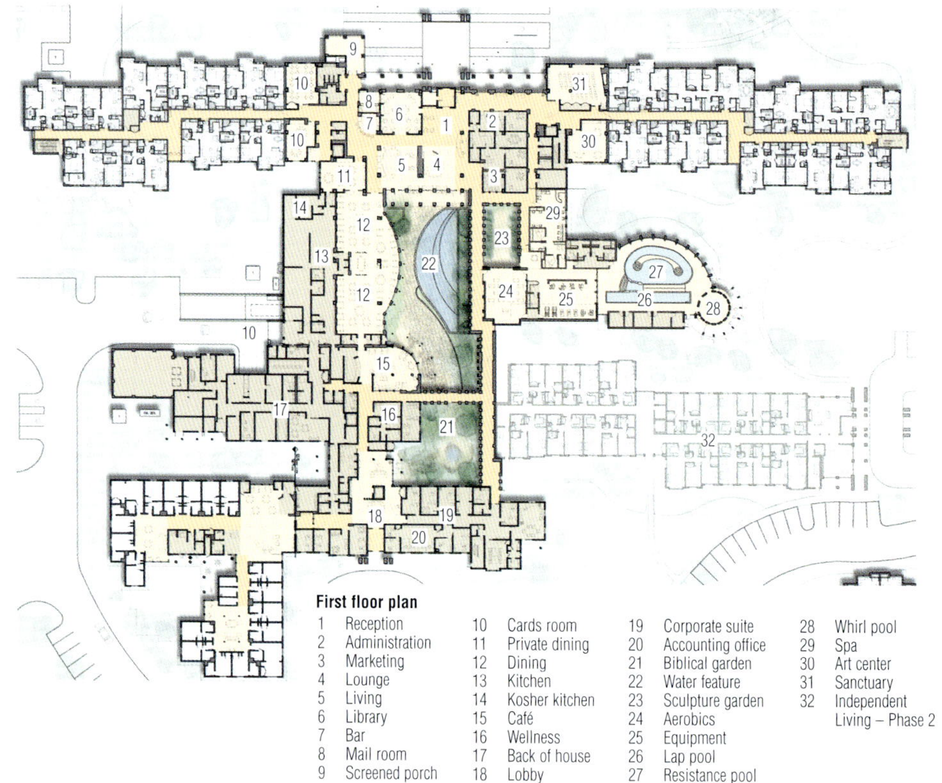

First floor plan

Challenges: What were the most difficult challenges in designing the project?

- Owner's desires versus owner's budget: The most difficult challenge was to balance the client's high expectations with modest resources in order to create an extremely high-quality CCRC product. This included an extensive programming phase incorporating the best and latest thinking regarding what seniors of today as well as seniors of the baby boomer generation would expect to have available to them if they decided to move into The Legacy. Eventually the size of the initial development was scaled back and allocated to a second phase. Extensive review and value engineering enabled the final product to retain the appearance and character of the original design at a much reduced construction cost.
- Dealing with approval agencies: A concerted effort was undertaken at the beginning of the programming phase to develop an innovative design focused on the health-regulated living environments of Assisted Living, Memory Support and Skilled Nursing to embody the current philosophy of providing resident supportive care. The project was successful in providing smaller living communities appropriate to each resident's limitations. However, the local authorities remained inflexible when considering alternative approaches to the positioning of the skilled nurse stations and the food delivery and preparation area in the Memory Support community. Greater flexibility on the agency's part could have resulted in an even more successful living environment.
- Dealing with the financial marketplace: As is often the case with the financing of CCRCs, the particular financial marketplace greatly affects the speed with which the project can be pre-sold and therefore financed and eventually built. In the case of The Legacy, because of the tight financial marketplace, fewer people than originally anticipated were willing to commit to selling their homes for their needed equity. This resulted in a necessary reduction in the size of the overall project where it was necessary to remove a few program elements (multipurpose room/sanctuary) and design modifications were required.

Innovations: Does the project offer its users unique opportunities or new features not typically available in previous similar projects?

- Creative site solutions: The site is surrounded on three sides by major roads and on the north by a creek with mature live oak trees and native vegetation. One enters along this natural feature driving west along the creek under the oak canopy providing a transition from the neighboring residential community. The east–west layout of the Independent Living building provides northerly views of the vegetated creek and southerly views of the new courtyards, water features and fitness pavilion. Independent villas nestle close to the creek along the property's west edge. Distinctive porte cochères and convenient parking provide the Independent, Assisted, Skilled Nursing and Memory Support buildings a distinct 'front door' identity.

Top left: Assisted Living: apartment
Top right: Assisted Living: living room

- Unique materials: The Legacy's exterior design palette utilizes indigenous materials that reflect the local area north of Dallas and has proven to endure, taking full advantage of how a strong southern sun can contribute to the richness of a building's geometry. For instance, the building's exterior stucco has subtle color differences selectively combined with deep, saturated stucco colors and contrasting white accents. These all contribute to create a variety and richness to the overall residential community's character. Deep roof overhangs, undulating façades, trellises, and balconies afford welcoming cool shadows from the sun and create pleasant contrasting elements to the generously sized windows and (synthetic) limestone accents.
- Creative architectural design elements: Perhaps the most important design element was the decision to organize the majority of the community program elements around three exterior courtyards bringing controlled natural light into the interior and providing views throughout the day to the courtyard's beautiful landscape, water-features, and sculpture garden. Circulating between activities is made more pleasant as one walks along the stone and glass enclosed 'cloistered' pathways, which, by design, define the courtyards. The views to the courtyards provide an organizing element that contributes to orientation and increases emotional well-being.

Form shapers: What factors had the most influence on the physical form of the project?

- The owner's philosophy has always been to make available the full spectrum of supportive care that is most appropriate to the senior resident, relative to their degree of independence. The design of all elements throughout the community intentionally maintains a quality level that makes no distinction between whether the resident is living in an independent apartment or villa, or whether they are residing in a more supportive environment that may be provided in Assisted Living, Memory Support or Skilled Nursing care. All spaces are designed consistent with the principles of universal design.

Above right: Assisted Living: dining room

- The entire campus takes advantage of wireless access in helping to provide instant and needed communication between residents and the operational staff. For independent residents, this generally takes the form of telephone, internet access, security oversight, and operational maintenance of equipment throughout the community. For those residents living in Assisted Living, Memory Support, or Skilled Nursing care access to assistance from staff is made easy through a variety of wireless options. All mechanical and electrical systems are monitored by the facilities staff, who oversee, monitor, and maintain the efficiency of the building's operational systems.
- This CCRC's program for the 8,000-square-foot aquatic/fitness center is a definitive statement attesting to the importance placed on staying fit and healthy well into the later years of life. The unique shape of the fitness pavilion captures the southern light with clerestory windows and the splayed interior shapes deflect the direct sunlight while maximizing daylight in both the aquatics center and the exercise and aerobics areas. The full-height windows enclosing the resistance pool face north, bringing in light while diminishing glare. The aquatic center's sloping roof is a byproduct of these light control features and provides an interesting geometric form, especially to the residents when viewed from their overlooking apartments.

Top trends

- Integrating with the surrounding community: The Legacy at Willow Bend is designed as a resource for the entire Plano community and particularly the North Texas Jewish community. A variety of spaces within the project are available for community meetings, religious services, and other events and the main kitchen can provide catering for hosted events. To support the integration of the elder residents within the broader community, The Legacy sponsors and supports educational, cultural, and social events and encourages the residents to invite their guests to partake. Conversely, the residents frequently venture out into the immediate neighboring community as they did when living in their own homes.
- Addressing a holistic sense of wellness: The program for the interior of the community is focused on both the needs of today's residents as well as the desires of the large baby-boomer population that will begin to back-fill the community in approximately 10 years. For instance, an extensive 8,000-square-foot fitness/aquatics center is a major feature for the target market of tomorrow along with an array of common areas that are appointed with furniture and artwork comparable to what one would find in a fine hotel.
- Offering choice through a diversity of housing options: The Life-Care Senior Community of the future will need to appeal to the large baby-boomer population that is beginning to retire. This large population demographic will demand multi-family housing options that consider not only the last vibrant years of one's life but also consider and provide the best supportive environments (should they be required) thereby allowing seniors to remain independent and enjoy the fullness of their lives for as long as possible. The Legacy at Willow Bend proudly states that their marketing motto for their targeted senior population is 'discover the art of living.' This new community provides everything to make that possible and easy to achieve.

Sustainability: Does the project conserve energy, water, and other natural resources? Does it reuse existing material or buildings, or include recycled building materials? How will the project improve indoor air quality in operation?

- Storm water and erosion are controlled utilizing natural vegetation and limited underground irrigation. Open spaces were maximized and deciduous/evergreen trees were planted providing shading of parking areas reducing the heat island effect.
- Daylighting and task lighting increases illumination levels and Low-E glass provides glare control. Views are maximized for the resident units, commons and activity areas, and the administrative spaces looking out onto natural landscape areas.
- Energy Star appliances, low water-consumption fixtures and energy-efficient lighting fixtures were provided throughout the commons areas and residential units. Bamboo flooring and millwork provided by local companies were used in the commons areas.

Community: How does the project advance the sense of community for residents, staff, families, and neighbors?

- A major advantage of living together in a senior community is the ability to interact with neighbors on a regular and informal basis. The design of the community helps to encourage these chance meetings by organizing the majority of the most commonly utilized spaces close to and as central to living arrangements as possible. In this way, a person choosing to spend time in the library may casually meet someone listening to music or painting in the art studio or someone going to the coffee shop. Other common spaces include a sanctuary, movie theater, dining room, card rooms, and a fitness/aquatics center.
- The wonderful aspect of a CCRC is that as the members of the community 'age in place' and may need to be relocated, they can move

into an adjacent, albeit separate, physical community but will find a very similar quality of interior environment. As the Independent Living community has its own commons areas suitable to residents' needs and physical and cognitive abilities, in a similar manner the Assisted Living community, the Memory Support community, and the Skilled Nursing community each have their own commons areas that encourage socialization at a somewhat smaller scale, similarly appropriate to residents' abilities and limitations.

- The Legacy at Willow Bend is designed as a resource for the entire Plano community and particularly the North Texas Jewish community. A variety of spaces within the project are available for community meetings, religious services, and other events and the main kitchen can provide catering for hosted events. Already, numerous events and conferences have been hosted by The Legacy. To support the integration of the elder residents within the broader community, The Legacy sponsors and supports educational, cultural and social events and encourages the residents to invite their guests to partake. Conversely, the residents frequently venture out into the immediate neighboring community just as they did when living in their own homes.

Target market: What specific features/services/amenities were incorporated into the overall Project to attract your target market?

- Enhanced exterior/interior appeal: An upscale senior life-care marketplace provides comparable quality of living opportunities regardless of whether the resident occupies Independent Living or the most health-supportive living arrangement. Healthy and independent prospective residents may not comprehend that someday they may need to relocate to a more supportive environment, suggesting a potential frailty that may inhibit a decision to move into a senior community. The Legacy at Willow Bend's success is that the quality of the exterior and interior materials is purposely similar throughout and the 'village' of living options comfortably fit together providing the individuality of discreet front doors.
- An active healthy resident population: Today's typical senior community resident is more discerning than in previous years when communities were designed specifically for the elderly. Potential residents often have had the opportunity during their active working life to partake in significantly more physical and educational activities and therefore expect to remain very active and healthy in their retirement years. The design of The Legacy provides for this continuing active lifestyle. The 8,000-square-foot aquatics/fitness center features a lap swimming pool, resistance walking pool and a therapeutic jacuzzi pool connected to a large equipment exercise room and an aerobics center accessible to an outdoor sculpture garden for tai chi classes.
- A unified community with discrete destinations: The Legacy at Willow Bend is the first Life-Care Senior Community in Plano, Texas that guarantees the lifetime use of one's residence along with many fine services and amenities. The spacious and well-equipped fitness and aquatics center, dining room and café, and the educational and recreational meeting rooms are available and easily accessible to all community members. The sponsor also guarantees priority access to on-site Assisted Living, comprehensive Skilled Nursing care and Memory Support care, should they ever be required. The physical community is organized in a series of buildings, many of which are linked together to create the impression of a 'village' within a landscaped setting.

Jury Comments

This wellness center, particularly the aquatics portion, is a beautiful, elegant facility. Its sculptural, curvilinear form is unique to the architecture of the campus. It forms an inviting beacon from the exterior, and creates an embracing volume on the interior. The understated elegance of the exterior is also evident on the interior, where the natural light is controlled and the colors are restrained. The support spaces for the pool area maintain the same attention to detail, color, and image.

The overall layout is efficient and spacious. Vistas between different spaces encourage social interaction and entice residents to expand their wellness activities.

Left: Aquatics center exterior
Bottom left: Aquatics center pool
Bottom right: Aquatics center therapeutic jacuzzi pool

Photography: Charles Davis Smith

Rivera Architects Inc

Three Links Care Center Lodging Facility

Northfield, Minnesota // Pat Vincent

Facility type: Dementia/Memory Support Unit, Hospice

Target market: Mixed income

Site location: Urban (city or town)

Capacity: 20 bedrooms

Total project cost: $3.25 million

Date of completion: September 2008

Below: East elevation

Overall Project Goals

This facility for memory and end-of-life care was built as an addition to the continuum of care offered at the Three Links Care Center campus in Northfield, Minnesota. The $3.25-million, 23,200-square-foot facility consists of a 12-bed Memory Care wing and an 8-bed End-of-life care wing linked by a 1,400-square-foot glass conservatory. Prior to construction of the new facility the campus population consisted of senior Independent Living, Assisted Living, and Supervised Living and Skilled Nursing care. The addition broadens the type and quality of care offered on campus.

Provider's Statement

Provider goals for marketing and sales

Cottage on Forest filled within its first 30 days and has experienced 95 to 100 percent occupancy ever since. The beauty of the building and grounds sells itself to families that tour the facility. A campus-wide DVD tour is available for marketing to people who cannot come for a tour. Reflections, for end-of-life care, has been a little slower to fill up and, naturally, resident turnover is greater due to the nature of care provided there. As families have had end-of-life experiences with their loved ones their word of mouth has provided excellent marketing. Families are so impressed with the focus of comfort not only for the resident, but also for the entire family. The beautiful, peaceful surroundings sell themselves for all who visit. The attached glass conservatory has been a powerful marketing tool as families are enveloped in the peaceful, comfortable surroundings. No matter the season, one can find peaceful solace in the conservatory with the tropical plants and the trickling sounds from the wall of water.

How did the provider plan to improve the residents' quality of life?

Cottage on Forest: Each resident has a private room that provides an alcove for sleeping and an alcove for a sitting area. The rooms are large enough that many residents have set up the sitting area with furniture from home including a sofa or loveseat and a small dining table along with favorite chairs, pictures, and accessories. Each resident's room has a large private bathroom and shower. There is a spa that includes a whirlpool bath and special furnishings that create a warm, comfortable environment. Many cozy sitting areas have been created throughout the open floor plan. This allows many family and resident groups to enjoy the common spaces at the same time. The four-season porch is reminiscent of a Minnesota Lake Cabin with a two-sided fireplace and cabin-type furniture.

Reflections: each room is designed to have a resident space and a family space within the room. All rooms have a private bathroom. Oxygen is piped in to each room but the oxygen equipment and the sphygmomanometer are hidden behind a framed picture that is easily moved away if access is needed. The spa features a whirlpool tub, shower, and beauty shop.

How did the provider want to improve workplace quality for employees?

There is a wonderful, large serving kitchen that is the heart of the home. The computer is located in a roll-top desk. There is nothing that resembles a nursing station or any signs of a medical model. Staff members are encouraged to sit with residents at mealtime but they do have a beautiful staff room for times to break away from residents for their meals or a cup of coffee. Cabinets are provided to staff to store personal belongings. Because the Cottage model promotes staff empowerment and autonomy, satisfaction and retention are fairly high. Staff appreciate working in the beautiful environment and are encouraged to put on a concert for the residents or join in the activities and outings.

Did the provider have specific goals for the project's staffing quantities, training, or distribution?

There are two other Cottage models on this campus. In those models the universal worker model is used. In our new project we use a modified, blended worker model and supplement care-giving staff with an activity director, a housekeeper, and dietary staff. We are able to tap into the staff development department on the campus to assist with new employee and anniversary training. Education specific to the Cottages and Reflections is provided by the manager of each building.

Did the provider give specific direction about the style, materials, features, or other design aspects of the project? If so, what were those directives?

In the initial planning meetings each building was discussed separately. For the Cottage on Forest a warm, cheerful, welcoming feeling was desired. The carpet was selected early in the process and that set the tone for the warm, cheerful atmosphere that was to be the basis for all further design features. Accessories were incorporated into the building that would help remind residents of their past. For Reflections the desire was to have softer, more subdued colors that would radiate peace and comfort without being dreary. The initial carpet selection again set the tone for the design features. By its very nature the conservatory brings the outside in. Furnishings create cozy spaces for visiting and give the impression of the outdoors without distracting from the beauty of nature.

How did the provider's financial goals influence the project's organization, configuration, layout, or sizing of components?

Minnesota is a state with equalization of rates in the care center. This means the state sets the Medicaid rates and providers cannot charge

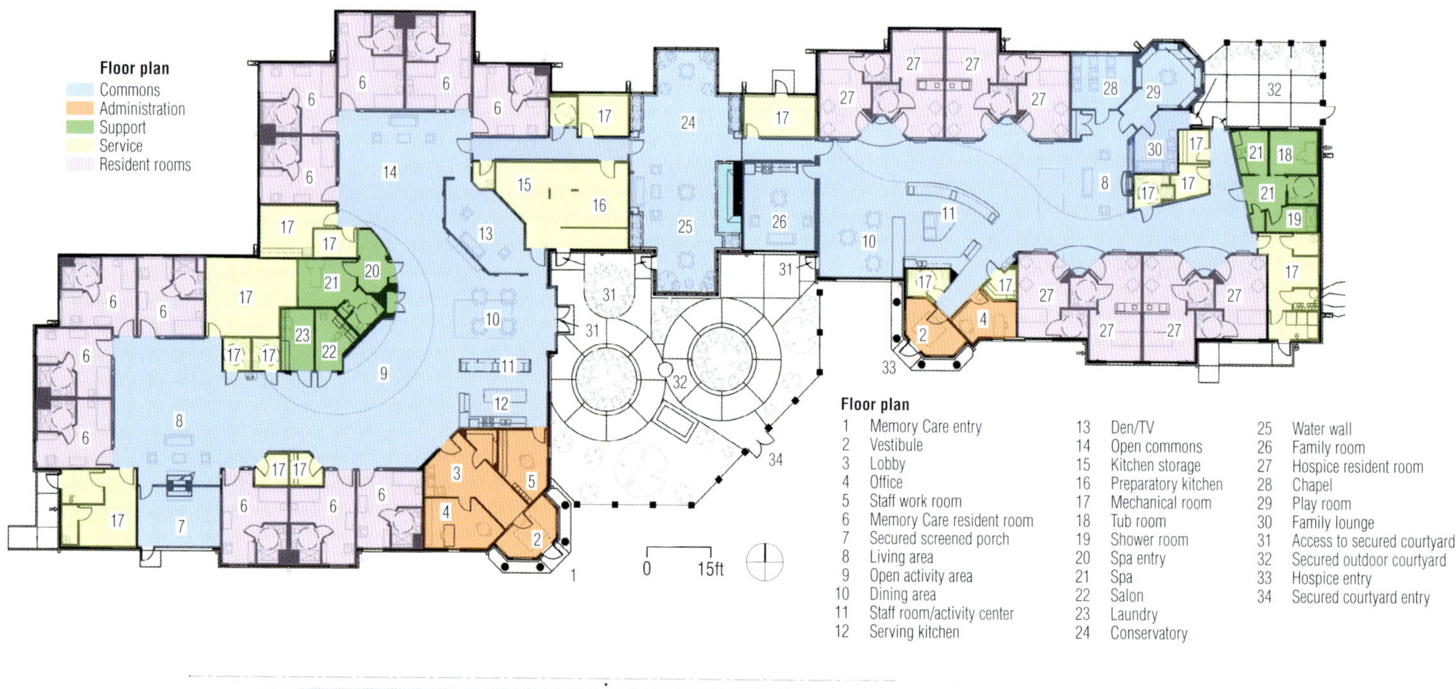

private paying residents higher rates. By building this project the provider is able to set rates that the market will bear. Therefore, this project, once fully occupied, will demonstrate a positive operating margin.

Architect's Statement

Design goals

- In designing the Cottage on Forest for Memory Care the goal was to create a homelike cottage where clients could come to live through all stages of dementia. Existing cottages were not designed to care for those with need for wheelchairs or patient lifts. We wanted to create a secured environment to address the wandering aspect of the early stages of memory care while also allowing a resident to be cared for in the later stages of memory loss where physical dependencies require more supportive care.

- The goal for Reflections was to create an end-of-life facility that supported the family as well as the resident. Many amenities support the resident through the end-of-life process such as private rooms, private bathrooms, space for the family to stay in the resident's room, flat-screen TVs, telephones, and piped-in oxygen. To help support the family through the end-of-life experience the design included a family room to encourage family gatherings, a family restroom with a shower, pull-out beds in the resident rooms and tea kitchens in 50 percent of the resident rooms. To make sure children were included in the process a children's playroom and outdoor playground were added.

- An overall goal was to provide holistic support to families dealing with dementia as well as the end of life. A glass conservatory joins the two separate care areas. Since Minnesota winters are long and cold the design team wanted to find a way to connect residents with nature year-round. A beautiful wall of water provides a peaceful solace for those who visit.

Challenges: What were the most difficult challenges in designing the project?

- The project was located at the only available area on the campus large enough to accept the new facility. This area was previously open, and represented the entrance and first impression of the campus. The new facility takes advantage of this location to present an image that is familiar and open to the public. Colors and materials are consistent with the existing structures on campus. The building's style, shape, and scale are all consistent with the residential neighborhood. The glass conservatory is open and inviting, and reveals to the community the quality of care offered to campus residents.

- A design was sought that met the primary needs of the target occupancy group and, if necessary, an alternate use if demand for the primary use changes in the future. This adaptive design was achieved by identifying to the owner occupancy groups with similar program, physical plant, and budget requirements.

Innovations: Does the project offer its users unique opportunities or new features not typically available in previous similar projects?

- The two resident care buildings were conjoined by a beautiful two-story glass conservatory. The conservatory is available for residents, families, and staff to use. It provides peaceful solace for those who seek comfort when dealing with various stages of memory loss or a terminal illness. The wall of water adds tranquility to the setting. Tropical plants blooming throughout the year bring feelings of hope and joy.

- The building is slab-on-grade construction. In-floor heating was added to the project for reasons of comfort as residents with memory loss often wander barefoot. Residents receiving end-of-life care often do not take time to put on slippers when transferring from bed to chair. In a Minnesota winter, this feature is appreciated by residents and families alike.

- In order to integrate the family into the end-of-life experience, many speacial features were incorporated in the design of Reflections. To include children in the end-of-life journey a children's playroom was designed to beckon children into the warm, cheerful space. Jungle murals, cheetah carpeting, jungle-themed table and chairs, toys, books, and a Wii appeal to children of all ages. Parents can relax in the attached family lounge and observe their children at play. Children can go outside to the fenced-in playground complete with table and chairs, hard-surface play area, grassy play area and whimsical animal figures to ride.

Form shapers: What factors had the most influence on the physical form of the project?

- The most unique feature of the project is the one-and-a-half-story glass conservatory connecting the Memory Care and End-of-life buildings. This space can be the most stimulating environment in the building because it offers an alternative to each household living space and during the colder months of the year the outdoor environment can be brought indoors for residents to enjoy.

- The Memory Care den has a projection television mounted from the ceiling. Equipment controls are housed in the staff area hidden from the residents. This feature avoids damage to televisions or equipment by agitated residents. The projection television can display daily programming, movies, or images. For example, viewing photos or events shown on-screen can stimulate resident memories.

- Memory Care public areas and circulation are defined by ceiling treatment, soffits, or furniture groupings. No partitions are needed to define these spaces, which allows for greater visibility. Interior accessories used for ambiance are either secured to walls or placed on shelves out of reach.

Above: End-of-life commons

Top trends

- Integrating with the surrounding community: The glass conservatory is more than just a common area for the Memory Care and End-of-life residents, it is also a meeting place for all residents and staff on the campus and the community. The Independent, Assisted Living, and Board and Care facilities on campus only provide basic common areas, so a space such as the conservatory offers another point of choice in close proximity to residents.
- Offering choice through a diversity of housing options: Prior to construction of the new facility the campus population consisted of Independent, Assisted Living, Board and Care and Skilled Nursing care. The addition of the Memory Care and End-of-life facilities broadens the type and quality of care offered on the campus.
- Adaptive building design: If demand for the intended use changes, an alternative use is available without substantial modifications to the facility. The building was designed with program and physical plant requirements expanded to accommodate more than one occupancy type. The current occupancy type could be changed to memory care, board and care, adult care, or other types of care without substantial physical modifications to the facility. This design flexibility gives the owner multiple financial options.

Community: How does the project advance the sense of community for residents, staff, families, and neighbors?

- The conservatory has become a focal point of the campus. 'High tea' has been held in the conservatory this summer for residents across the organization. The peaceful, tranquil surroundings highlighted by tropical plants and the wall of water add to the special feelings residents express when they receive an invitation to tea in the conservatory.
- Cottage on Forest serves those with all stages of memory loss. The heart of the cottage is a wide, open community space. Each area of a community space has a focal point, which appeals to a variety of interests. For example, there is a baby grand piano and seats for the audience, a craft table, Dad's Garage (the TV room decorated with pictures and items reminiscent of the golden age of automobiles) as well as places to relax, read a book, or visit with friends.
- For End-of-life care Reflections brings community to the residents. Within Reflections there is a small chapel, a children's playroom, a resource library for children and adults who are grieving, a place for families to connect with the CaringBridge and a beautiful family room. The private rooms are surrounded by appealing commons areas that draw people in for visits. Each resident room has a window to the commons area so that even though confined to bed, the resident can see activity in the commons areas if they wish.

Target market: What specific features/services/amenities were incorporated into the overall project to attract your target market?

- The target market for Cottage on Forest is people with varying stages of memory loss. The building and the wandering garden are secured so residents do not wander away. Accent pieces throughout the building are designed to trigger memories.

Left: Conservatory interior
Opposite: Conservatory water wall

Photography: Stuart Lorenz, Photographic Design Studio (© Ken Rivera)

- The Memory Care and End-of-life households have no corridors. This feature provides better visibility throughout the commons area and can also reduce discomfort for Memory Care residents who may become agitated in small spaces. Wandering can be a problem for Memory Care patients, but with no corridors a resident can wander throughout the open commons area instead of down a dead-end corridor. Memory boxes next to unit entry doors, resident entry doors and open common areas can be viewed front-on instead of at a 90-degree angle from a narrow corridor.
- To address the need of families to be present during the end-of-life experience there are many special areas for families to use as they attend to their loved one's needs. A Family Lounge complete with kitchenette, a dining room space for the family to gather, and sofas with a large-screen TV provide families with a home-like environment during the end-of-life journey. The Family Restroom contains a shower and vanity furnished with toiletries and luxurious towels so family members can freshen up during their vigil at the bedside. A desk area with computer access allows families to update others on the CaringBridge website.

Jury Comments

This unique, four-season conservatory/winter garden with waterfall concept brings the outdoor environment inside throughout the year. Family spaces such as the children's room with games and media entertainment will promote family visits to support the mission of hospice, which sensitively goes the extra step relative to amenities in a hospice environment. The facility provides a serene and peaceful space at the end of a life.

Fusco, Shaffer & Pappas, Inc.

Bloomfield Township Senior Center

Bloomfield Township, Michigan // Charter Township of Bloomfield & Bloomfield Township Senior Services

Facility type: Wellness/Fitness Center
Target market: Mixed income
Site location: Suburban

Capacity: 400 persons
Total project cost: $6.3 million
Date of completion: July 2009

Below: The exterior terrace maintains access to the fitness area overlooking wetlands to south
Opposite: Punch openings through the masonry columns create a dramatic façade in the main entrance canopy

Overall Project Goals

In July 2007 a campaign was directed toward residents of Bloomfield Township who were eligible to use the local Senior Center. The campaign resulted in an extensive wish list of desired events and activities. Additional in-house facilities were required, such as an adult daycare center and a staging area for Meals on Wheels delivery and pickup. Adhering to a budget of $6.3 million, Fusco, Shaffer & Pappas, Inc. provided a flexible design, which was the key element to supporting both small and large-scale activities. Utilizing the natural topography of the site, the 24,260-square-foot building was designed into a four-cell structure. The main level provides direct access to parking, with drop-off and service access. The separation of adult daycare, the computer room, and administrative offices into the outer wings of the main level provides adequate distance from potential noise associated with large group activities. Operable partitions connect the café, craft, and activity rooms, facilitating a wide range of activities. The continued health of the individual is the focus of the lower level, providing a warm-water therapeutic pool, an exercise area encircled by a walking track, as well as a billiards room. Additional fitness rooms with operable partitions allow for fitness classes of variable sizes. Exterior terraces ground the building to the sloped site while providing flexible exterior space for activities or fitness.

Provider's Statement

Provider goals for marketing and sales

The provider's goals for marketing and sales include a seasonal community outreach newsletter that outlines classes, trips, programs and special interests that generate revenue.

How did the provider plan to improve the residents' quality of life?

The following specific features add to the residents' quality of life:

- increasing social interactions
- creating community
- promoting wellness through offered programs
- promoting continued education through offered programs
- providing therapeutic opportunities
- building relationships
- improving independence and wellness.

How did the provider want to improve workplace quality for employees?

The following project features provide employee quality of workplace:

- unified office space
- separate restrooms
- private space
- lunch area
- air conditioning
- interaction with residents to build relationships.

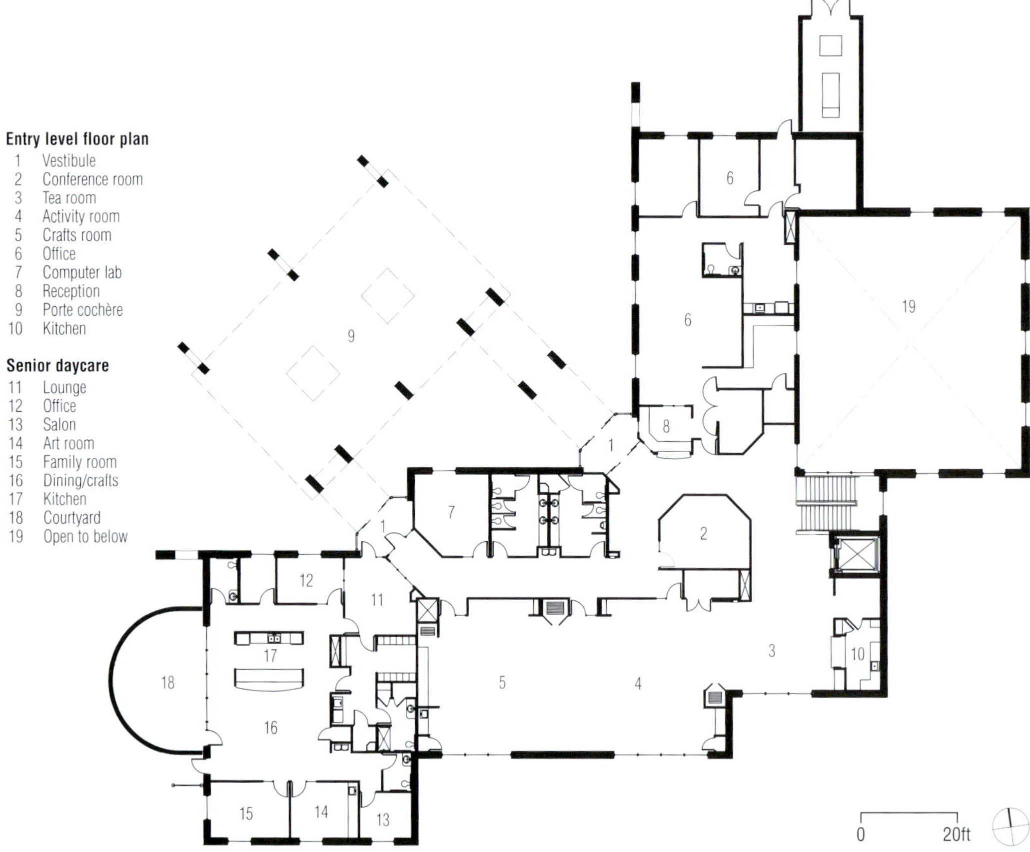

Below: The lobby and reception area lead into activity, computer, craft, and tea rooms

Did the provider have specific goals for the project's staffing quantities, training, or distribution?

The existing staff has been successfully relocated and additional employees have been integrated into the team. The training and staff distribution have been efficient in providing supervision and security for all members.

Did the provider give specific direction about the style, materials, features, or other design aspects of the project? If so, what were those directives?

The Senior Center was to be integrated within the Bloomfield Township Civic Center Campus, while blending into the existing topography and preserving the existing landscape. Security and accessibility features were a must throughout the

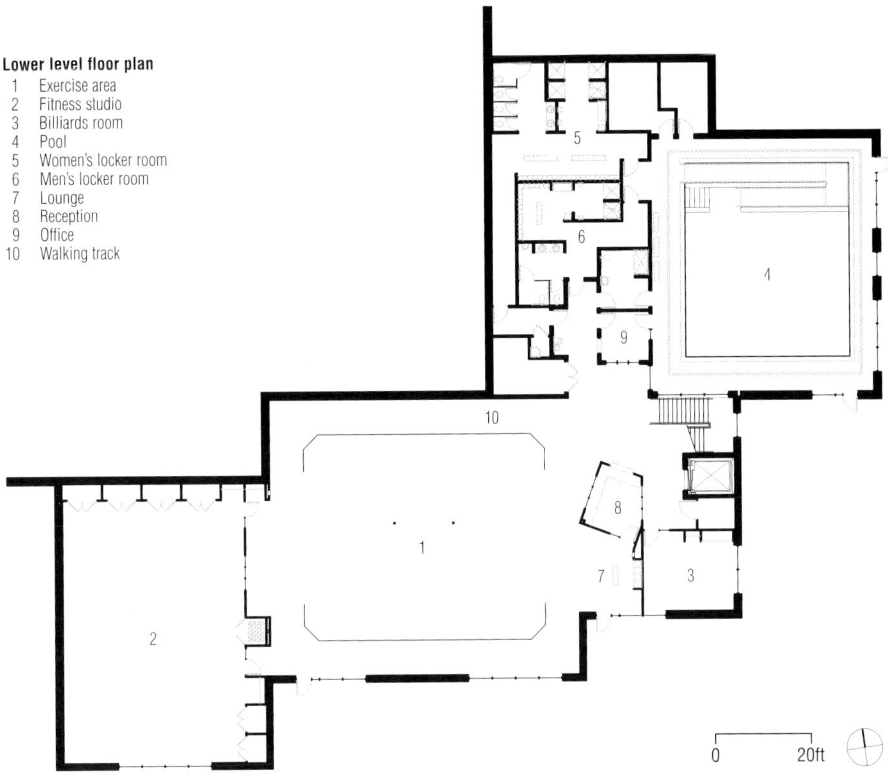

building. The interior was to be contemporary through the use of color and light.

How did the provider's financial goals influence the project's organization, configuration, layout, or sizing of components?

Revenue is generated through unique classes and programs that the building is designed to support.

Architect's Statement

Design goals

- The center was required to accommodate the needs of seniors visiting the new building, and those reliant upon home-based services provided by Bloomfield Township. The design was therefore required to integrate fitness activities, adult day care, and distribution for Meals on Wheels.
- Converting an old elementary school into a Senior Center posed limitations on the size and quality of many programs. The segmentation of the various classrooms provided no flexibility for large group functions and class sizes were limited to the existing room layouts. The new facility needed to conform to the spatial needs of the core activities as well as size requirements associated with varying group functions.
- Building placement within the allocated 4-acre parcel was limited by the amount of required parking, therefore the design of the building focused on a compact building layout. The building would also need to address the rough topography of the 35-foot bluff, while blending into the adjacent Civic Center Complex.

Challenges: What were the most difficult challenges in designing the project?

- While numerous precautions can be administered to ensure the safety of the users within the building, staff members are still required to assist with equipment, teach classes, and facilitate day-to-day operations. The floor plan is designed to maximize visibility within the exercise and activity rooms, providing open space that allows for secure oversight of activities on both levels.
- Prior to the design of the building, an extensive survey was conducted to establish the activities most desired by seniors in addition to established programs. The overall form of the building was therefore based on an efficient allocation of internal building activities. The floor

plan was divided into a mixture of specialized yet flexible spaces for group activities as well as those focusing on individual needs.

- The allotted site presented an array of design challenges for the architects, including limited site access, steep topography, restricted site size, substantial parking requirements, and integration within the existing Civic Center Campus.

Innovations: Does the project offer its users unique opportunities or new features not typically available in previous similar projects?

- Located on a steep 35-foot bluff, the south side of the 4-acre parcel provides a panoramic view of the adjacent lake and property below and beyond. Locating the building footprint within the bluff, the facility blends nicely with the existing topography, creating a façade that nestles into the contours of the steep incline.

Form shapers: What factors had the most influence on the physical form of the project?

- All public areas are universally accessible, accommodating the varying needs of the senior population.

Top trends

- Responding to the site and local conditions: The building responds to the natural topography of the site, nestling into the rugged hillside while exploiting the panoramic views of the adjacent lake.

- Integrating with the surrounding community: The Senior Center provides in-house adult daycare for elderly persons who are unable to care for themselves. This enables a spouse or family caregiver to use the facility freely, attend to tasks, or go to work.

- Addressing a holistic sense of wellness: The entire building promotes community by creating and encouraging a new and exciting environment for local seniors to join together for a wide array of activities and events.

Sustainability: Does the project conserve energy, water, and other natural resources? Does it reuse existing material or buildings, or include recycled building materials? How will the project improve indoor air quality in operation?

- To reduce heat gain associated with asphalt paving, parking is shared with the adjacent courthouse. A retractable fence allows for additional parking after business hours and on weekends.

Opposite: The adult daycare is equipped with a full-size accessible kitchen for activities for seniors and staff members
Above: A centrally located café is placed for seniors to gather, socialize, and build relationships

- The Senior Center provides energy efficiency through high-efficiency lighting and mechanical equipment. Materials with high recycled content are also used throughout the structure.
- Floor-to-ceiling glazing is incorporated into the south-facing walls to maximize solar heat gain, while minimal glazing is located on the east- and west-facing walls.

Community: How does the project advance the sense of community for residents, staff, families, and neighbors?

- The entire building promotes community by creating and encouraging a new and exciting environment for local seniors to join together for a wide array of activities and events.
- Internally, the lounge area on the main level acts as a catalyst for socializing among seniors as it is centrally located within the building, providing a place to rest between activities, waiting for friends.

Target market: What specific features/services/amenities were incorporated into the overall project to attract your target market?

- The universal accessibility of all public areas within the building promotes ease of use for the senior population.
- The facility provides a fully staffed adult daycare, providing time for a spouse or family caregiver to attend to other tasks.
- The previous Senior Center layout was rigidly defined by its former use as an elementary school. The new Senior Center utilizes movable partitions allowing for a greater degree of flexibility within the internal spaces of the building for large groups or functions.

Opposite: Large storefront windows provide natural light to the walking track and fitness area to allow patrons to view scenic wetlands
Top: Aerobic, dance, and yoga classes are held in the spacious fitness studio that opens to accommodate larger classes and a game of pickle ball
Bottom: The therapeutic pool provides universal accessibility and is utilized for rehabilitation and promoting wellness

Photography: Michael Raffin, Mia Photography

InSite Architects

Boutwells Landing Care Center

Oak Park Heights, Minnesota // Presbyterian Homes

Facility type: Skilled Nursing; regional education center for the sponsor; child daycare center; campus auditorium

Target market: Mixed income

Site location: Suburban

Capacity: 81 Skilled Nursing Rooms, 27 Dementia/Memory Support Rooms

Date of completion: February 2009

Below: Care Center entry
Opposite: Front façade of the Care Center

Overall Project Goals

This new care center is the final component of an 80-acre, Continuing Care Retirement Community that first opened six years earlier. The original campus included a town center, townhomes, smaller 'Brownstone' apartments, Independent Living, Assisted Living, and Memory Care apartments built in two previous phases. The development of the new care center was strongly encouraged and supported by existing residents and consists of 105 units, of which 102 are single-bed units and 3 are 2-bed units, in 'neighborhoods' of 12 to 14 residents. Also included are a large, campus-use auditorium and a daycare center for children. The new building completes the enclosure of a new landscaped courtyard that connects the care center to the existing town center. The new building is accessible from the existing town center at two levels, and is connected to a tunnel that provides safe and easy access for the entire campus to shopping facilities and additional parking on the north side of a busy street.

Provider's Statement

How did the provider plan to improve the residents' quality of life?

Wide hallways, attractive features, sufficient space, and smaller households are a few characteristics of the building that increase residents' quality of life. Boutwells Landing Care Center is also attached to the campus' Assisted Living and Independent Apartments. Therefore, if a resident has friends or a spouse that live in one of these areas, this aids in supporting relationships throughout the continuum. Each resident room in the care center is very spacious, carpeted, equipped with a television, private shower, and bath, as well as a tea kitchen with microwave and fridge. All of these amenities increase independence for residents and add to their quality of life.

How did the provider want to improve workplace quality for employees?

Staff at Boutwells Landing Care Center take pride in the beautiful building, and recognize that standards and expectations are very high. Their productivity has increased, with teammates pushing each other to perform at higher levels. When staff members are provided with sufficient tools to complete their job, their morale increases.

Did the provider have specific goals for the project's staffing quantities, training, or distribution?

The training for employees in this start-up facility had to mimic the opening of the center; therefore, the waves of household openings within the building had to correspond with training and hiring waves of new employees. Boutwells Landing Care Center began training their first wave of new employees in February 2009. From that point onward, the facility has held training sessions for new employees every two weeks. Each employee is given the same training, which encompasses three days in a classroom prior to training in the household with a partner. The classroom training educates the

employee on the philosophy of the center and its standard of care prior to them entering the household and performing direct care duties.

Did the provider give specific direction about the style, materials, features, or other design aspects of the project? If so, what were those directives?

This project, a skilled care center, is an addition to the existing Independent and Assisted Living center. Therefore it was important that the exterior of the building match the existing structure in materials, color, and style. Where the existing building interior is very traditional, the provider wanted the new addition to be more contemporary and light. They asked that the wood finishes be lighter in color and that corridor materials be very durable. It was the provider's goal that the resident rooms be clustered into neighborhood groupings with a very homelike atmosphere.

How did the provider's financial goals influence the project's organization, configuration, layout, or sizing of components?

Due to the continued restricted reimbursement limitations for Skilled Medicaid residents the project needed to address the issue of high efficiency. The neighborhood design with private suites supports the small-house quality of life concept. To make it efficient, the neighborhoods are self contained in most functional areas and it was determined that approximately 12–16 residents created an optimum grouping for two-hour staffing without compromising the small-house feeling. In addition, the demographic profile of Medicare residents was considered and they were specifically located on the first floor with direct access to a well-designed and equipped physical and occupational therapy program. This final small-house model was adapted to successfully include multiple floors and specialized

Left: The courtyard is shared by Care Center, Assisted, and Independent residents

care needs. The design makes day-to-day living a homelike experience and still maximizes the greater scale of staffing efficiency and proximity. The project has multiple kitchens. The small neighborhood kitchens have the versatility to serve as both preparation and serving areas and staff with universal worker training can use them comfortably and efficiently. Additional preparation kitchens and dining rooms on each floor provide an opportunity for residents to choose more formal dining venues depending on their individual interests. The link to the existing Boutwells provides the opportunity for some bulk food delivery of those menu items that are conducive to larger production.

In addition, the project was also slated as a corporate training resource center and fulfilled the need for greater community conference facilities. The design created the necessary parking through the use of a tunnel across the street and direct access to these spaces without entering the resident areas. The dining capacity in the main kitchen makes catered food services efficient and profitable.

Architect's Statement

Design goals

- To provide skilled care in a new 'neighborhood' model offering flexibility for types of care – a hospitality model, not a medical model.
- To provide single-bed rooms that are units, not just bedrooms, including full bathrooms and kitchenettes.
- To tie into, and enhance, the existing buildings with a seamless look so that levels of care are not identifiable by the differing appearances of buildings.

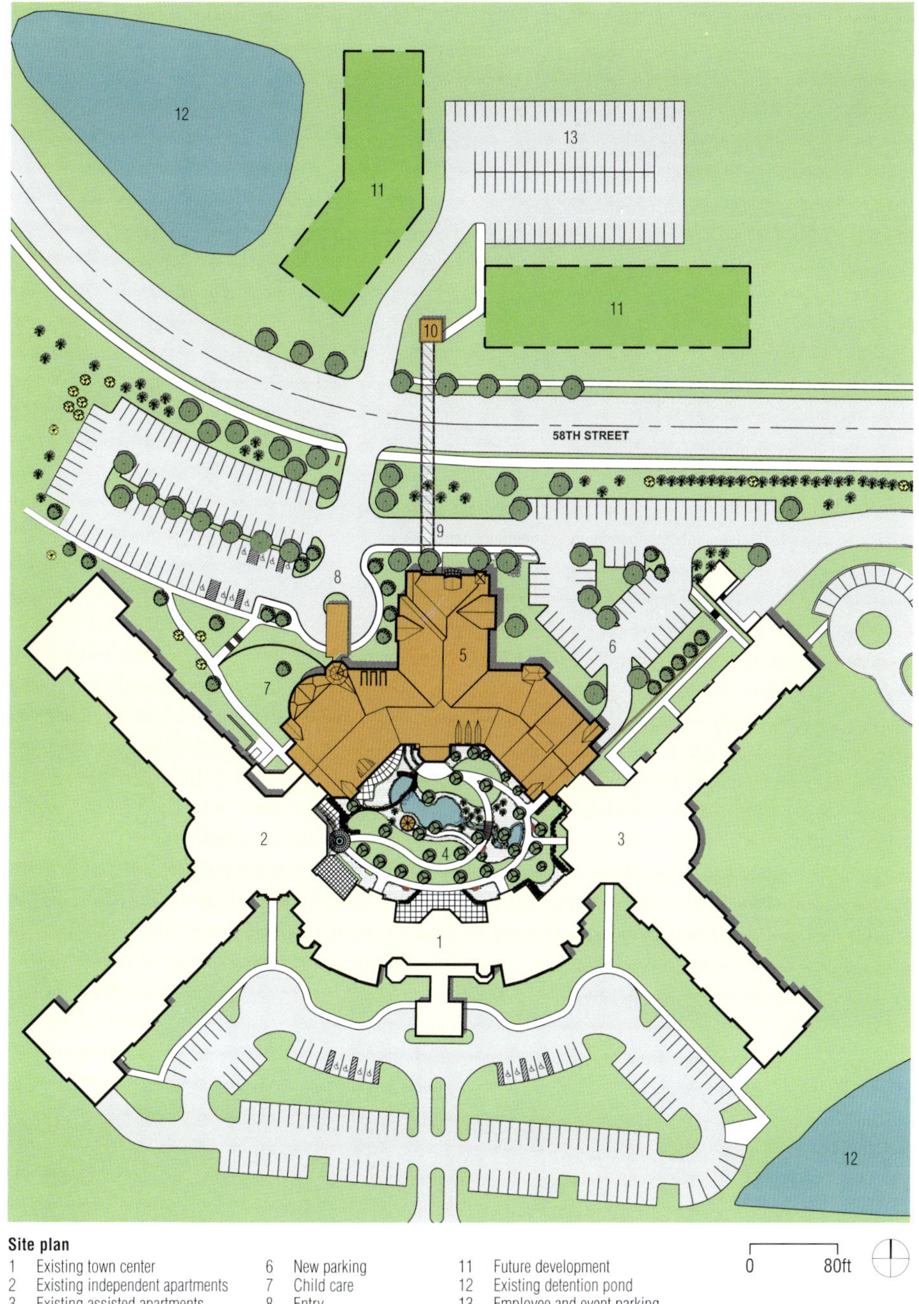

Site plan

1 Existing town center
2 Existing independent apartments
3 Existing assisted apartments
4 Courtyard
5 New care center
6 New parking
7 Child care
8 Entry
9 Underground tunnel
10 Elevator/stair to tunnel
11 Future development
12 Existing detention pond
13 Employee and event parking

0 80ft

Challenges: What were the most difficult challenges in designing the project?

- One challenge was creating the northern 'Greenhouse' skilled-care neighborhoods to offer a sense of individual 'homes,' but to also offer the operational efficiencies made necessary by the far-north climate. The building was designed with three distinct neighborhoods on each of the three floors. Each neighborhood contains all services required for an independent skilled care unit – soiled and clean utility, personal laundry, medications, storage, kitchen, dining, family room – so that the staff never has to leave the neighborhood to provide full service and care for residents.

- Providing flexibility for future needs was another challenge. Because neighborhoods can act independently the types and levels of care can be modified as a unit based on the current and future needs – Memory Care, Transitional Care, Long-term Care, and so on.

- Blending and connecting with the existing campus building was another challenging requirement. The exterior features and finishes of the existing building were continued throughout the new building, as well as using the courtyard landscaping to tie the buildings together. The interior connections, as originally planned, needed modification as the program requirements for the Skilled Care building changed considerably from seven years earlier.

Innovations: Does the project offer its users unique opportunities or new features not typically available in previous similar projects?

- The new care center takes advantage of the close connection to the existing Independent and Assisted Living residents. The campus residents as a whole were very positive about and influential in building the new care center, and the benifit of their input is seen daily as residents freely move about volunteering in 'their' new addition.

EXIT

- The courtyard was enhanced with walks around a new water feature that includes quiet pools, rock rapids, and a waterfall that connects the upper-level courtyard to the lower-level terrace in a half-acre, secure, landscaped space.

Form shapers: What factors had the most influence on the physical form of the project?

- Creating neighborhoods of a 'Greenhouse' fashion that can be part of a larger community, and yet maintain the sense of an independent home for a smaller number of residents.

Top trends

- Integrating with the surrounding community: The existing campus already had great outside community involvement within its buildings, including adult education classes from the local school district, Lions and Rotary Clubs meetings, and use of the fitness center by the local hospital. The new building builds on that with the new child daycare center and a meeting space for larger groups that could not be accommodated previously.

- Addressing a holistic sense of wellness: The neighborhood model of care strengthens the relationship of residents and staff to further residents' sense of physical and mental health.

- Offering choice through a diversity of housing options: The new care center added a part of the existing campus that was previously missing and a cause for concern for many of the existing campus residents. They wanted to stay on this campus as many had moved from townhomes to Independent and then Assisted Living apartments and could not see themselves having to leave their home – which was not necessarily a particular building, but the overall senior community they lived in.

Sustainability: Does the project conserve energy, water, and other natural resources? Does it reuse existing material or buildings, or include recycled building materials? How will the project improve indoor air quality in operation?

- The new care center HVAC system was designed to replace the existing building's system, and the single-campus system is much more energy efficient.

- The building underwent design review and completion verification by the regional utility company to include more energy efficient HVAC equipment and lighting systems.

- The building underwent utility company material comparison reviews to determine the most energy-efficient windows and wall insulation systems.

Community: How does the project advance the sense of community for residents, staff, families, and neighbors?

- While the neighborhoods provide a sense of home, a sense of community is brought to each floor by a common dining area that residents may use if they desire not to dine in their neighborhood dining area.

- The auditorium brings residents from throughout the care center as well as the entire campus together. As part of the auditorium a large lobby with an open stairway and fountain are adjacent for pre- and post-event gatherings and conversation. There is also an outdoor terrace with a waterfall pool to bring the outside in and the inside out.

- The child daycare center is very connected to the residents in the care center. On the exterior the playground is in view from both the walking area and the second-floor roof garden. On the interior large windows allow residents to look into classrooms and infant rooms, and the kids to look out at the lobby and fountain.

Target market: What specific features/services/amenities were incorporated into the overall project to attract your target market?

- Ninety-seven percent single-occupant rooms including full bathrooms with showers and kitchenettes.

- Easy access for residents from the overall campus to visit and volunteer in the new care center, and to share the new auditorium.

Opposite: Entry lobby
Top: Neighborhood great room
Above: Typical unit

Photography: Saari Forrai

K. Norman Berry Associates Architects PLLC

Episcopal Church Home St. Luke's Chapel

Louisville, Kentucky // The Episcopal Church Home

Facility type: New Chapel
Target market: Middle/upper middle
Site location: Urban (city or town)
Date of completion: October 2009

Below: View looking southwest at the entry and passenger drop off
Opposite: View looking north at the southern entry

Overall Project Goals

The Episcopal Church Home St. Luke's Chapel is a 10,000-square-foot chapel that is physically connected to the original senior care facility. The chapel has a Greek-cross plan, with concrete masonry unit and brick walls, Douglas fir timber trusses and decking, a standing seam metal roof, and aluminum windows. The intent of the new chapel was to house the ever-growing congregation that had outgrown the original 500-square-foot chapel. Given the opportunity to enhance the mass experience it was foremost that the chapel integrate parishioners at all levels of aging. Therefore, an open flexible plan for the sanctuary was accepted allowing integrated wheelchair seating alongside chairs. One integrated sitting scheme allows 75 wheelchairs and 75 chairs in the sanctuary, totaling 150 congregants. A separate room, known as the Inclusion Room, was integrated at the rear of the sanctuary space separated by large glass windows and allows 35 wheelchairs. This room is dedicated for residents with the inability to control bodily functions, and allows them to feel part of the congregation. The entire facility, including the chancel, is designed around the notion of Universal Design, allowing wheelchair access to all areas.

Provider's Statement

Provider goals for marketing and sales

Sales and marketing goals were not directly considered for this project. Rather, the Board of Trustees and Episcopal Diocese of Kentucky believe that the emphasis on the spiritual needs of residents must be as strong as the emphasis on their health and wellness. 'Church' is the middle name of the Episcopal Church Home and the previous chapel accommodated only 40 individuals, leaving not nearly enough space for the 150-plus people who choose to worship on this campus. While two services were offered, most wheelchair-bound people were often segregated, having to sit in a wide hallway and watch the service on a movie screen due to the inflexible layout of pews and limited open space.

Approximately 70 percent of residents have some form of dementia, thus various architectural accommodations have been made to comfort and support this population. The prominence of St. Luke's Chapel is an outward expression of the home's inward and special focus on the spiritual needs of the individuals it serves.

How did the provider plan to improve the residents' quality of life?

The 'Beauty of Holiness' and iconography that reminds one of worship space are emphasized features of St. Luke's Chapel and because approximately 70 percent of residents have some form of dementia (the nationwide average is 50 percent in nursing homes) various architectural accommodations have been made to comfort and support this population:

a. High beamed ceilings (large, lofty, cavernous spaces) can be frightening for cognitively impaired persons; therefore 'clouds' were inserted throughout the Chapel to make the space feel more intimate and less intimidating. Additionally, the lattice this creates affords acoustical benefits.

b. Where the chancel begins the clouds are removed to guide the eye up unhindered to the open-sky ocular window over the cross and altar. The vaulted space then reaches and lifts the eye heavenward.

c. Downward spotlights create shadows and insufficient lighting for older and sometimes-confused eyes. Instead, a series of elongated high-wattage 'task lights' – long rectangular bars of light that are shadow-free – are threaded throughout the wired ceiling.

d. Ornamental lighting (larger than normal for the space and greater in number than one might expect) is included for its valuable Church cues. It adds extra light, but also adds a 'churchy' ambiance to help those who need to be reminded where they are.

e. Abundant natural light is brought into the sanctuary, chancel and narthex spaces because studies have shown that the elderly experience less depression when exposed to natural light.

The altar rail is designed wider to allow one to lean on it and use it for support.

Green has been utilized for its calming qualities, its resonance with the color of the longest liturgical season of the church year, but also because it resonates with the 'green on green' cloister garden, fresh and vital year-round.

The altar rail is designed to facilitate four ways of receiving communion with standing room, a place cut out for wheelchairs, regular-height kneeling pads (although they are wider and deeper than most), and then a demi-kneeler designed by a physical therapist and the architect to accommodate those who want to kneel but no longer can in the regular way. The altar rail itself is considerably wider than most, and slanted so that it does not just support one's hands but the entire forearm.

How did the provider want to improve workplace quality for employees?

The chaplains have adequate space, sound equipment, storage and worship space to allow them to see all individuals in the congregation. The HVAC system is more than adequate for the space. Caregivers assisting residents in the Chapel have adequate space to allow them to worship with the residents and observe their participation. Restroom space is within the Chapel and easily accommodates two to three people.

Opposite: Interior view looking at the chancel

Did the provider have specific goals for the project's staffing quantities, training, or distribution?

The Episcopal Church Home did not increase the staffing as a result of the new St. Luke's Chapel. The current Pastoral Care, Environmental Services, and Maintenance Departments have adequate staff to perform all services required for the operation of the Chapel.

Did the provider give specific direction about the style, materials, features, or other design aspects of the project? If so, what were those directives?

The architect worked closely with a Chapel Design Committee of the Episcopal Church Home on all aspects of the style, materials, features, and design of the St. Luke's Chapel. The Design Committee included the Chapel Committee Chair, campus residents, a retired interior designer and Episcopalian, a non-trustee Episcopalian committee member who owns a hardware store, a chaplain, CEO, and a director of facilities who acted as the owner's representative, a member of St. Luke's Chapel who moved onto the campus during the design development and is a nationally known interior designer, now retired. Sample drawings were shared, sample products shared, and field trips taken to view any product or element under consideration.

How did the provider's financial goals influence the project's organization, configuration, layout, or sizing of components?

Many residents and potential residents view the opportunity for Church attendance and the receipt of pastoral care services as one of the reasons they choose the Episcopal Church Home. A minimum of three worship opportunities are held each week in the Chapel. The one service on Sundays allows for greater opportunity to visit with friends and loved ones; no one is marginalized by being separated into another area. Additionally the Chapel is frequently used by families for their loved one's funeral upon their passing.

Architect's Statement

Design goals

- The trellis 'clouds' serve three purposes: one is to diffuse light, the second is to make a voluminous space feel more intimate, and the third is to add interest to the ceiling. People with Alzheimer's are often uncomfortable in open voluminous spaces. The application of hanging wood trellises in the sanctuary space pulls the ceiling closer to the floor, making the space feel more intimate while allowing views of the heavy timber. The trellises arch up at the center of the sanctuary heightening awareness of the center of the Greek-cross plan. Many visual cues are integrated into the facility to hark back to memories of other churches.
- Prior to construction of the new chapel the area was a covered passenger drop off and entry into the facility. This entry also permitted seating and views across the street to a popular shopping mall. Many residents enjoyed sitting outside to watch the action. Keeping this in mind the design of the narthex and a covered outdoor sitting area incorporated concepts of viewing.
- Glare affects the vision of Alzheimer's patients and careful consideration was given to the natural lighting of the sanctuary. Indirect lighting is used substantially throughout. At the rear of the chancel a hidden skylight and windows allow natural light to wash the rear chancel wall. A skylight over the center of the sanctuary and circular windows at the gable ends allow natural light to enter the space, while being diffused through trellises.

Challenges: What were the most difficult challenges in designing the project?

- Seating: Because 70 percent of the residents have some form of dementia and may be confined to a wheelchair an open flexible plan for the sanctuary was accepted that would allow

Above: Interior view of the narthex towards the main entry

Photography: Chris Fieldhouse Photography

integrated wheelchair seating alongside individual chairs. One integrated sitting scheme allows 75 wheelchairs and 75 chairs in the sanctuary. This allows any number of visitors to sit with their family member who may be in a wheelchair.

- Light control: Early on it was agreed that natural light needed to be introduced to the interior of the sanctuary. Glare affects the vision of Alzheimer's patients and careful consideration was given to the natural lighting of the sanctuary. Indirect lighting is used substantially throughout. At the rear of the chancel a hidden skylight and windows allow natural light to wash the rear chancel wall. A skylight over the center of the sanctuary and circular windows at the gable ends allow natural light to enter the space, while being diffused through trellises.
- Contrast: The weakening of vision is common in aging as well as people with Alzheimer's. Again, visual cues were maximized innovatively while maintaining a sacred space. Contrasting colors were used at the chancel to better define the furniture as well as to enhance the visual effects of the chancel area. The light stained wood paneled rear wall is washed with natural light during the day and artificial light at night. The wall is curved to minimize glare. The handrails throughout the narthex and halls have a dark wood stain that contrasts with the light wall finishes. The flooring consists of anti-microbial carpet tile with a dark contrasting border to help define the areas of movement or 'lanes.'

Innovations: Does the project offer its users unique opportunities or new features not typically available in previous similar projects?

- The new chapel was located on the site where residents enjoyed a connection with the outside world. Keeping this in mind the design of the narthex and a covered exterior sitting area incorporated concepts of viewing the adjacent neighborhood. The narthex's walls are

85 percent glazing to maximize views out within a conditioned space, which also maximizes daylighting from the north. A covered seating area to the north of the site directly off of the narthex triples as an outdoor seating area, a reflective cloister space (due to its rectangular shape and regulated column spacing), and a garden. It is also the cover for passenger drop off.

Form shapers: What factors had the most influence on the physical form of the project?

- The chapel fully and respectfully integrates the elderly residents of the facility by following Universal Design concepts, applying design techniques that will enhance the experience for Alzheimer's patients, maximizing visual memory cues, integrating techniques to enhance the audio and visual experience, and integrates prior uses of the existing building.
- The sanctuary space ductwork is oversized and encapsulated within an insulated wall to minimize air movement and vibration. Acoustical panels are integrated above the trellised clouds and along walls as well as angling the Inclusion Room glazing 6 degrees. The trellised design was irregular to minimize sound issues such as 'zipping.' Lastly, an amplified sound system was installed and carefully tuned to the acoustics of both the Inclusion Room and the sanctuary.

Top trends

- Integrating with the surrounding community: The design of the new chapel will accommodate various denominations of religious faith as not all residents are Episcopalians. This attribute was an essential design goal. In addition to flexibility for different denominations, the new chapel is equipped to be used for various religious events from funerals to weddings, baptisms, and choirs.

Sustainability: Does the project conserve energy, water, and other natural resources? Does it reuse existing material or buildings, or include recycled building materials? How will the project improve indoor air quality in operation?

- Sustainable design concepts were embodied architecturally in several ways. On the exterior the use of standing seam metal roof, copper roof, limestone, clay brick, and aluminum are all durable materials. Reusable carpet tile with antimicrobial backing, level E0 VOC emission, and a recycled content of 50 percent was installed. Ceramic tile is used in the restrooms and the plumbing fixtures have low-flow infrared sensors with inline water heaters.
- Insulated windows and highly efficient dimmable fluorescent lighting is used throughout. All finishes are low/no-VOC and HVAC demand controlled ventilation using carbon dioxide detection has been utilized. Fans have variable frequency drive control and an outside air economizer.

Community: How does the project advance the sense of community for residents, staff, families, and neighbors?

- The new chapel now allows the congregants to worship as one community since they had outgrown the original 500-square-foot chapel. The additional residents that could not be accommodated in the small chapel had to assemble in the hallway outside the chapel and watch a video of the service. Given the opportunity to enhance the mass experience it was foremost that the new chapel would accommodate the larger population so that people at all levels of aging and health condition could celebrate together. Therefore, an open flexible plan for the sanctuary was accepted that allows integrated wheelchair seating alongside chairs. This allows residents and their family members and guests to worship together.
- The new chapel is connected to the existing nursing home so it is on axis with the facility's 'social corridor.' This social corridor provides linkages to the dining room, library, and reception areas. This allowed the new chapel to remain on this social corridor that the residents had already indentified and could relate to. The wings of the residential units surround this corridor proving a common community link with the chapel and the residents' rooms.

Target market: What specific features/ services/amenities were incorporated into the overall project to attract your target market?

- The Episcopal Church Home was founded on Christian values and thus always had a chapel within its complex for the residents and staff to use for both personal worship and mass. This attribute has always been core to the existence of the Episcopal Church Home and in turn a marketing tool. The design and construction of a new chapel that is based on Universal Design, all-inclusive strategies, and with special attention paid to the disabilities of aging residents is a marketable addition to the services and amenities awarded to residents. While directly benefiting the current residents, the new chapel will attract future residents as a unique feature of this senior care facility.
- The design of the new chapel will accommodate various denominations of religious faith.
- Flexibility, all-inclusiveness, and symbolism are what the new chapel represents to the outside world. This image will attract future residents, grow the community, and educate people through integration of generations, allowing the Episcopal Church Home to continue growing in its ability to care for the aging population.

DiMella Shaffer

Fox Hill

Bethesda, Maryland

Facility type: Independent Living, Assisted Living, Wellness/Fitness Center

Target market: Upper

Site location: Suburban

Capacity (units): 240 Independent Living apartments, 29 Assisted Living apartments, 54 Dementia/ Memory Support rooms

Date of completion: December 2008

Below: Main entry porte cochère
Opposite left: Residence bay windows
Opposite right: Commons at dusk

Photography: Maxwell Mackenzie

Overall Project Goals

This $189-million, 700,000-square-foot, 323-unit community was developed by Sunrise Development, one of the nation's premier senior living developers. Prior to choosing a senior living community, seniors have enjoyed lives of significant purpose and achievement. It is important that they continue to pursue activities and opportunities that promote a sense of community and individual freedom. With this in mind, Fox Hill was marketed as luxury condominiums with amenities that are unmatched in the Washington, Virginia, and Maryland marketplaces.

The project was built on a 21-acre sloping greenfield site surrounded by protected forest and adjacent to the Capital Region beltway, interchange and a major access route to the District of Columbia. In addition to Independent Living residences, the facility also includes separate Assisted Living apartments and special care wings for residents with memory impairment within the main common area.

A grand two-story great room provides views to the central activity spaces, which include an art studio, library, bank, bistro, tavern, café, lounge, recording studio, game and card room, formal dining and grille dining room, winter garden, and resort-quality fitness and swimming areas.

Provider's Statement

Provider goals for marketing and sales

Although there has been a slowdown due to the economy and housing market, sales of condominiums and Assisted Living and Memory Care units continue to exceed census goals. The condominiums are a fee-simple real estate sale so contingencies have been required due to home sales involving longer timeframes. The design, amenities, and location offer a senior option on the cutting edge of the industry. Fox Hill continues to market its unique qualities and the advantages of the self-directed lifestyle versus the traditional Continuing Care Retirement Community inside the Capital Beltway.

How did the provider plan to improve the residents' quality of life?

Senior design throughout includes wide doorways and accessibility. Discreet handrails appear to be woodwork in hallways with seating areas halfway down the halls for those who desire a place to sit down. Condominiums are designed with call-buttons located 12 inches off the floor in the bathrooms and voice-to-voice emergency system. Digital phone design allows residents to carry hand-held phones throughout the property and to send and receive calls from their home phone. Grab bars are available in bathrooms. Shower stalls are accessible. Open floor plans allow for aging in place with space for walkers and scooters. All amenities are accessible from the condominiums and garages without the need to go outside in the elements. Residents enjoy the artist studio, recording studio, performing arts center, and wine cellar.

How did the provider want to improve workplace quality for employees?

A suite of staff break rooms, training rooms, and kiosks complete the Sunrise curriculum. Additionally, there is a staff lunch program in which employees can purchase lunch for $3. The general manager and the department coordinators host a staff appreciation day in which awards are given to outstanding team members. Recognition of staff members' birthdays occur each month and highlight all the birthdays that month. Coordinators are encouraged to reward team member excellence. Length of service awards are included in monthly team meetings. Employee feedback is encouraged using an open-door policy from management. To ensure the staff feels empowered, regional and corporate HR and operations team hold skip-level meetings in addition to annual questionnaires. Annual reviews are held within a two-week period of the employee's anniversary date for hourly team members and annually in March for department heads. Time clocks are used to track labor and ensure team members are paid for hours worked. Department heads review respective team members' punch details on a daily basis to ensure paychecks are accurate.

Did the provider have specific goals for the project's staffing quantities, training, or distribution?

Staffing and training are managed by experienced top performers in the senior housing industry who are carefully selected to work at this flagship community. The Fox Hill staffing model ensures excellence in service and care delivery through the opening phases and stabilization of the community. The training curriculum and execution follow a tested and successful schedule and is outlined by Sunrise with additional training unique to Fox Hill hospitality. Completion of required training is monitored by the HR department at Fox Hill and by respective department coordinators.

Site plan

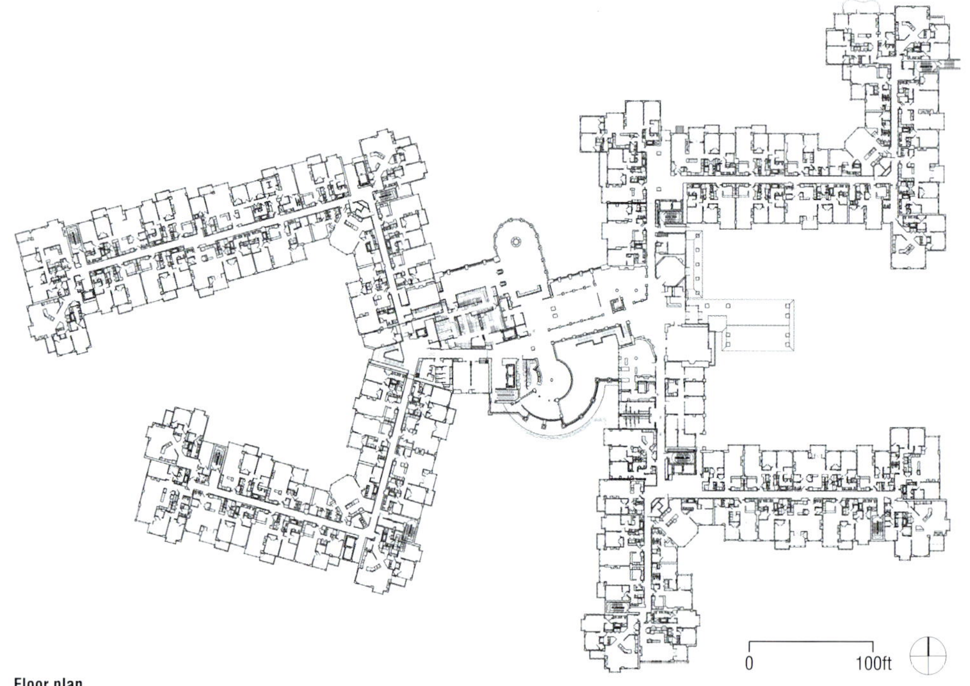

Floor plan

Did the provider give specific direction about the style, materials, features, or other design aspects of the project? If so, what were those directives?

The décor at Fox Hill is Craftsman-style country club modern.

How did the provider's financial goals influence the project's organization, configuration, layout, or sizing of components?

The project is structured to allow for strong performance in its amenities/service of the community, which has offset the slow housing market and ramped up census.

Architect's Statement

Design goals

- An important goal for the project was to provide the finest senior living environment in the greater Washington area with services not found elsewhere.
- The second goal for the project was to have a high-quality Assisted Living environment that provides views to the existing woods and allows for ample natural light.

Challenges: What were the most difficult challenges in designing the project?

- Zoning: Existing zoning allowed for the creation of less than 20 house sites as per the residential zoning requirements. A special-exception zoning route allowed for a change of use for a Senior Living Facility with careful oversight regarding conservation and stormwater design. The

Above: Winter garden

Photography: Chris Eden

process also entailed an intensive public review process with neighborhood groups, abutters, legal consul, and the county zoning board. The challenge was achieving a careful balance between program and zoning, which resulted in a continuous effort of review and revision to maintain the project within the requirements for a greater part of the project development.

- Interstate Interchange Site: The challenge centered on providing a design that accommodated a large program calling for a central activity node located on a 65-foot sloping triangular site tight against an interstate interchange. The solution utilizes a 'hill town' approach consisting of five building wings that relate to the relative ground elevation independent of each other. Each residential wing or house has its own separate garage and pedestrian entry. A pedestrian may enter the various houses at different levels or one may enter at any of these entrances and access all areas from within the building.

- Scale and Massing: The site is flanked by two residential neighborhoods located to the north and south. The design approach sought to respond to the scale of these areas by reducing potentially long, tall, multi-floor façades. Though the building consists of seven floors in the middle wing, these taller elements were moved to the middle of the site, away from the edges. Large sloped roofs, which relate to the roofs of the neighborhoods, were used to reduce the apparent height and mass of the center building while utilizing shed dormers for the higher fenestration. Residential scale windows, together with large glazed bays, aid in punctuating the façade, while building corners help to further break up the structure.

Above left: Bar lounge
Above right: Grille dining
Photography: Chris Eden

Innovations: Does the project offer its users unique opportunities or new features not typically available in previous similar projects?

- The obvious feature was the sloping site; though a challenge for horizontal travel from one end of the site to the other, it afforded a great opportunity by enabling a double-story common area to serve as a viable connector for resident passage through the building. The inclusion of the two-story Winter Garden as the central node of the building became more viable when viewed as an event along the circulation paths, which travel from the fourth floor down to the third floor.

- The beautiful adjacent Burning Tree Golf Course to the north provided a vantage point for orientation within many of the residences as well as the Independent common areas and the Assisted Living common areas. Assisted Living outdoor terraces have full views over the adjacent fairways.
- Adjacent forest conservation easements ring the site and provide a dense natural buffer, which must be maintained in perpetuity. The building language responded to this aspect of the site's character. It is more natural in material expression and color.

Form shapers: What factors had the most influence on the physical form of the project?

- Inconspicuous lean rails were integrated into the detail design throughout the building.
- Custom-designed wall sconces were used for the resident corridors, providing large quantities of light without glare.
- State-of-the-art staff-communication devices and central alerts were installed, keeping all staff in constant touch with resident needs.

Top trends

- Responding to the site and local conditions: The project offers choice through a diversity of housing options.
- Offering choice and variety daily: There is a choice of living options with many unit types to pick from, which applies to Independent Living as well as Assisted Living. The program and built environment address a need for choice and variety that benefits the community wellness approach.

Sustainability: Does the project conserve energy, water, and other natural resources? Does it reuse existing material or buildings, or include recycled building materials? How will the project improve indoor air quality in operation?

- Commitment to environmental and landscape sensitivity: A tightened building footprint facilitated the preservation and integration of trees and forests, along with pioneering sediment control solutions and integrated storm-water management.
- Energy-recovery ventilation recovers up to 80 percent of energy used. Water-conserving plumbing fixtures were used and an innovative hydronic heating and cooling system dramatically reduced maintenance costs with a saving of 30 percent in life-cycle costs.

Community: How does the project advance the sense of community for residents, staff, families, and neighbors?

- Staff members comment on how pleasant Fox Hill is. In particular, they comment positively on the Winter Garden, which is the central space – Fox Hill's grand room. Here, 25-foot-tall ficus trees grow in the sunlight surrounded by café tables and chairs where residents and staff mingle and pass through throughout the day. This space also accommodates events, cocktail parties, presentations, celebrations, and other resident gatherings. It is on display every day for all to experience. This grand hall sets the tone for community and interaction for everyone at Fox Hill. Bathed in light from the sun or the array of cove and ceiling fixtures, it radiates a positive feeling to all and physically expresses the sense of community.
- Located above the Winter Garden on an elevated platform is the Rock Creek Grille, where breakfast and lunch are served every day. All routes pass by or below this restaurant located in the epicenter of the building; it is center stage, a meeting place that radiates activity. Complementing this space is the Winter Garden Café. A beverage or snack can be ordered throughout the day and can be enjoyed in the café seating area in front of a six-paneled digital television or under the ficus trees flanking the garden. In addition, adjacent to this café is the resident mailroom, a space frequented by everyone on a daily basis. As a result the café and Winter Garden provide a convenient place for residents to pause with others after visiting their post box.
- Through resident meetings held in clubrooms, musical entertainment held in the performing arts room, or casual meetings at the lounge, bistro, and on the promenade, social mingling is promoted by design. Seven sitting areas with fireplaces are located on the main floor of the commons. The appeal of fireplace flame in different scale settings appeals to the resident's desire for variety and choice. From the small setting to the larger scene in the grand living room or dining room lounge, fireplaces work their magic. One night, Robert Lee, a resident of Fox Hill, commented 'I am in a point in my life where there is no left turn, there is no right turn, we are here to stay and we thank you for making our lives so enjoyable in such a beautiful place.'

Target market: What specific features/services/amenities were incorporated into the overall project to attract your target market?

- The upscale condominium amenities include a wine cellar, pet spa, art room, demonstration kitchen, golf and game room, heated garage, formal and informal dining, social library, fully functional bar, and piano bistro.
- There are over 80 Independent Living condominium unit options to choose from.
- Fox Hill is sited within the National Capital Beltway.

RLPS Architects

Mennonite Home Skilled Care Reinvention

Lancaster, Pennsylvania

Facility type: Skilled Nursing

Target market: Middle/upper middle

Site location: Suburban

Capacity (units): 133 Skilled Nursing beds, 28 Dementia/Memory Support beds

Date of completion: September 2009

Below: The new façade treatment includes bay windows, peaked roofs and curved elements
Opposite: The discreet nurse station allows resident living areas to be the centerpiece of the household

Overall Project Goals

To support the transition to a resident-centered care model, Mennonite Home is renovating and adding modest additions to each of its nursing floors making small, separate households of 18 to 22 residents. The conversion of a 40-unit Assisted Living floor along with the nursing floors will redistribute the 195 nursing residents, providing a smaller number of residents on each floor, an increase in privacy through the use of 'toe-to-toe' bedroom arrangements and expanded living areas. A new visitor hallway at the first floor and elevator addition reorganizes the circulation from the recently renovated main entrance to each household, eliminating the intrusion of going through one household to get to another. The new public elevator allows the existing elevator located between two households on each floor to become a dedicated service elevator, bringing service unobtrusively from the basement level. Each reconfigured household has its own entrance leading into the living areas providing a comfortable, homelike environment with more privacy as well as social spaces for family visits and interaction among residents. Each household includes its own spa bathing room and communal living and dining rooms. A residential-style kitchen with an open cooking area serves as a focal point of activity much like a traditional home. The required nurse station, medications, and other service areas are tucked away to allow the resident areas to become the new centerpiece of the household.

Provider's Statement

Provider goals for marketing and sales

This project was a reinvention of a medical model nursing home into households. The last phase was completed in October 2009. Staff, resident, family, and peer reactions have been extremely positive.

How did the provider plan to improve the residents' quality of life?

The nurses' station has been eliminated. Each household contains a living room with a fireplace and LCD TV, parlor, dining room, and kitchen. Tray service has been eliminated. Residents' meals are served on Fiesta® ware. The parlor has become a great location for families to visit or have small family parties.

How did the provider want to improve workplace quality for employees?

The facility has had zero turnover as a result of the project. More staff members have interaction with residents and express increased job satisfaction as a result. The staff has expressed appreciation for the households of 16–22 residents as opposed to the original large floors of almost 50 residents.

Did the provider have specific goals for the project's staffing quantities, training, or distribution?

Staffing ratios did not change as a result of the project.

Did the provider give specific direction about the style, materials, features, or other design aspects of the project? If so, what were those directives?

Facility representatives and the architect spent 7–8 months in an extensive design phase addressing every aspect of the reinvention to ensure the households were homelike.

How did the provider's financial goals influence the project's organization, configuration, layout, or sizing of components?

The project was foundational in allowing the facility to initiate person-centered care. The facility leadership believes it also positions them extremely well from a marketability perspective, which will ultimately yield strong financial performance.

Architect's Statement

Design goals

- To support the operational shift to resident-centered care the environment needed to facilitate that change by reorganizing the existing institutional nursing units into smaller residential styled households that are reinforced by separate household living and dining areas. Household identities were established through a variety of interior finish material and color selections. Two long-term care households are arranged back-to-back to allow staff work areas to be shared efficiently.
- To offer more privacy and dignity to residents by improving visitor circulation to each household and separating the service circulation to complement the residential experience. Resident privacy is also improved by decreasing the quantity of side-by-side bedrooms by converting pairs of side-by-side semi privates into 'toe-to-toe' arrangements providing accessible bathrooms with showers and staff support areas off of the hallways. The existing main entrance continues to function in accessing all households on all levels, including a short-term rehab on the first floor, without the need to go through one household to get to another.
- To maintain continuing operations of the nursing home by a phased construction approach over two years and in five phases. The conversion of the Assisted Living and three small additions to nursing provided the initial 'swing space' for maintaining census throughout the project.

Top: In the rehabilitation unit, a wall with a window between the two beds provides a higher level of privacy
Bottom: The spa features warm and inviting finishes for a calming effect

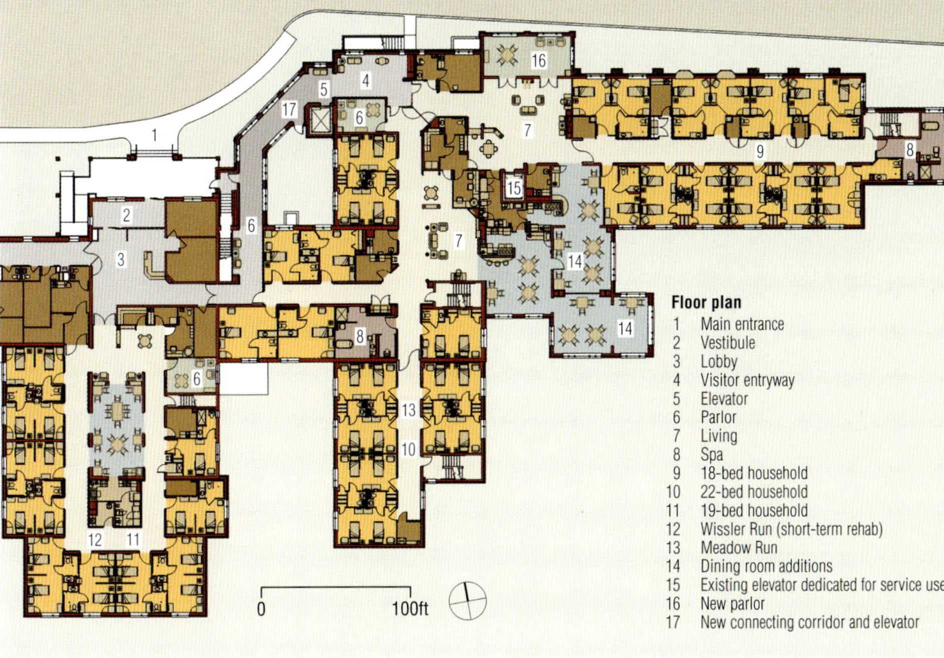

Challenges: What were the most difficult challenges in designing the project?

- The greatest challenge for the project was meeting the impervious coverage limitations of the site. Existing unused sidewalks, an ambulance entrance, and a patio were removed to allow the coverage for the three small additions.

- Balancing the goals of the project with the constraints of the budget and existing building posed another challenge. Careful prioritization and analysis of the tradeoffs between various options helped lead the design team in complex choices.

- With limited expansion opportunities and the owner's need to maintain the total bed capacity, there needed to be a carefully orchestrated phasing plan that would allow for full census to be maintained throughout the entire renovation project. Similar to solving a Rubik's Cube puzzle, the design team partnered with an experienced Construction Manager and mapped out steps that have lead to bringing the project to completion ahead of schedule.

Innovations: Does the project offer its users unique opportunities or new features not typically available in previous similar projects?

- The relatively short distance from the main entrance to the central hub of the L-shaped wings provided an easy opportunity for connection with the construction of the new visitor hallway. Visitors coming from the main entrance pass through this short hallway, bypassing a resident room corridor and connecting between the two legs of the building, which define two separate households.

- The existing elevator located between the two households was conveniently dedicated to a service function with the construction of the new first-floor visitors' hallway and elevator. Now this service elevator can handle vertical circulation from the basement level to the service core between both households.

- Conversion of the existing one-story Memory Care unit to a separate short-term rehab allowed this more ambulatory and cognitively intact population to be immediately adjacent and to utilize the first floor main entrance and main street amenities. The opportunity to connect with natural light in this one-story household was enabled through the use of skylights.

Form shapers: What factors had the most influence on the physical form of the project?

- The limited expansion opportunities meant that it was not possible to provide exclusively private rooms in the Short-Term Rehab Unit. Believing that privacy is defined to include acoustic privacy and that a cubicle curtain is insufficient, the design team experimented with the use of a wall with a window between the two beds in side-by-side bed rooms to provide a higher level of privacy. Recognizing that short-term rehab residents are the most independent and most likely to return to their homes suggested that their bathrooms include a fully accessible 'European' style shower to provide this subpopulation the option of showering in their own bathrooms without the need to use a common spa bathing room.

- The project incorporated the new [m]Power brain fitness system as part of its mental wellness program. The fully automated system supplies a constantly changing menu of challenging activities that are scientifically designed to maintain brain health as well as combat the onset and effects of dementia and Alzheimer's disease.

- Creating private rooms with private bathrooms in long-term care can be beyond the financial means of many providers as well as the size limitations of an older building footprint. A number of 'toe-to-toe' bedrooms are provided that share an

Above: Eliminating tray service helps residents adjust mentally and physically to the dining experience

Photography: Larry Lefever Photography

accessible bathroom. Here the design team explores the definition of privacy by including a wall between the bed areas, with the intention of giving residents a sense of ownership of their own space or territory without the disruption of unwanted circulation through it.

Top trends

- Responding to the site and local conditions: The cosmetic re-skinning of the façade with residential details complementary to the residential quality of the Independent Living across the street and the surrounding community has transformed this institutional icon into the fabric of the surrounding residential community.
- Taking advantage of existing infrastructure: By using the existing infrastructure, the owner was able to maintain an affordable solution and work within a timeframe beneficial to their budget.
- Effecting culture change: The most influential driver to the project was the owner's vision and conviction to create both a resident-centered care operation and a supportive physical environment that embraces flexibility and resident self-determination, counter to the culture of dependence that is prevalent in institutional long-term care. Architectural decisions to reinvent the environment were made based on establishing a functional program of creating a home. Design decisions were based primarily on the ability to reinforce this functional objective and where they would have the most impact.

Sustainability: Does the project conserve energy, water, and other natural resources? Does it reuse existing material or buildings, or include recycled building materials? How will the project improve indoor air quality in operation?

- This project reinvented existing building stock with minimal additions rather than building new.
- Particularly since the building remained occupied during this phased renovation project, low-VOC materials were utilized.

Community: How does the project advance the sense of community for residents, staff, families, and neighbors?

- Similar to the kitchens in our homes, the residential-style kitchen serves as the center of activities for the household. Here residents have the opportunity to get a snack between meals, see and smell cookies baking, or find other residents and staff to chat with.
- The new resident hallway and elevator now connects the main entrance to a lower level with daylight access that includes rehabilitation therapy, a coffee shop, chapel and other main street amenities. This connection now allows outpatient rehab services to conveniently utilize these services.

Target market: What specific features/services/amenities were incorporated into the overall project to attract your target market?

- The use of residential-style kitchens is incorporated into each household as a central focus and means to establish a sense of home.
- Each household contains multiple dining rooms and living rooms that break up the household into even smaller groups of residents, resembling more closely the intimate scale of a home.
- The design team experimented in the short-term rehab unit in an attempt to provide a higher sense of privacy in side-by-side bedrooms with the use of a wall with a window between the beds intending to give the resident a sense of ownership of their own space or territory.

C.C. Hodgson Architectural Group

Montgomery Place

Chicago, Illinois // Montgomery Place Retirement Community

Facility type: Independent Living, Assisted Living, Skilled Nursing, Dementia/Memory Support Unit, Wellness/Fitness Center, Senior Community Center

Target market: Middle/upper middle

Site location: Urban (city or town)

Capacity: 232 rooms

Total project cost: $12.3 million

Date of completion: October 2008

Below: Front façade

Overall Project Goals

Located in the Hyde Park neighborhood on the southside of Chicago, Montgomery Place was repositioning the community from a rental to entry-fee based financial model. This strategy centered on improving marketability by adding new lifestyle components and completing the continuum of care by adding Assisted Living. A 7,365-square-foot, two-story addition created an opportunity to present a new active lifestyle image at the front door. New amenities on the first floor of the addition include a fitness center, pool, massage therapy, and informal café. The second floor of the addition allowed for development of a clustered rehab household that was able to break free from its existing double-loaded corridor model. The roof of this addition includes a rooftop garden accessible from the third floor Memory Support and Assisted Living. Other additions included a working greenhouse, a private dining room, and a conservatory that serves as a gathering area, helping to alleviate congestion at the dining room while creating additional connection with the existing gardens. Extensive renovation of the second floor included development of two households, one for short-term rehab and one for long-term care, each with its own great room. A third floor renovation provided conversion from Skilled Care to an additional two households, one for Assisted Living and one for Memory Support.

Provider's Statement

Provider goals for marketing and sales

The project met pre-sales goals to reach a $40.5 million tax-exempt bond issuance in 2006 and has since exceeded bond covenant requirements for Independent Living occupancy with regard to the new 90-percent-refundable plan offered to new residents.

How did the provider plan to improve the residents' quality of life?

The creation of the neighborhood clusters was designed to ensure a more personable home-like environment, which adds to residents' quality of life. New therapeutic rooftop gardens, one on the Nursing Pavilion and the other on the Assisted Living Pavilion, provide additional health benefits. The facility's position on the shoreline of Lake Michigan allows residents to not only enjoy the view but also actively grow vegetable and flower gardens. The Independent Living residents also enjoy a newly constructed year-round Greenhouse that supplements an outdoor courtyard. Lastly, the project created a Lifelong Learning Center where educational and guest presentations are provided.

How did the provider want to improve workplace quality for employees?

The neighborhood cluster design for Skilled Nursing and Assisted Living has had a positive effect on employee morale and productivity. A new employee lounge space and amenities for stress relief have also been provided. The project also addresses the inappropriate use of revenue-producing apartments as office spaces by creating a new workspace-friendly environment in the underground parking garage. Approximately 25 percent of parking spaces were eliminated to create administrative offices and Independent Living resident storage space. Administrative employee responses have been positive. One of the directions given to the architect was to create a formal administrative entry space for meet-and-greet interactions with potential clients and several fun spaces for employees such as a putting green, pool table, and dining spaces, helping them to de-stress.

Did the provider have specific goals for the project's staffing quantities, training, or distribution?

Staffing levels were reduced due to downsizing the nursing facility, however creating neighborhood cluster designs contributed to lower staff turnover and improved quality of care.

Did the provider give specific direction about the style, materials, features, or other design aspects of the project? If so, what were those directives?

Both the provider and the architect set out to improve the visitors' first sight of the building and first impressions upon entering the building. The new addition housing the pool and Wellness Center was designed to be in the forefront and the creation of a café/library and conservatory on entry to the building added to our objective to change the long-standing negative image and perception of being solely a nursing and/or Assisted Living facility. The new design and finishes created a positive, warm and welcoming health-driven impression.

How did the provider's financial goals influence the project's organization, configuration, layout, or sizing of components?

The project's completion was unique financially as the provider was able to eliminate $6.5 million in variable-rate bond debt by August 2009. It continues to exceed covenant ratio requirements. Operational performance was maintained at excellent levels during and after the project's construction phases. There are 22 licensed Assisted Living apartments (in the Catered Living Pavilion) with one neighborhood cluster of 8 apartments for early-stage Assisted Living/Memory Support and 14 apartments for more traditional Assisted Living. Skilled Nursing was downsized from 93 beds to 40 beds with one 14-bed neighborhood cluster for sub-acute rehabilitation and a second neighborhood cluster of 26 beds for moderate to late-stage Memory Support. Neighborhood cluster designs were incorporated in both the Skilled Nursing and the Assisted Living pavilion – one of the key factors in improving quality of care and quality of life.

Third floor plan
Memory Support household
Assisted Living household

Second floor plan
Short-term rehabilitation household
Long-term household

First floor plan
New addition
Renovation
1 Pool
2 Fitness room
3 Massage therapy
4 Café/library
5 Entry lobby
6 Pre-function
7 Private dining
8 Conservatory
9 Greenhouse

Architect's Statement

Design goals

- One of the goals was to update the image and services of the community by completing the continuum of care and transforming the community into a more residential environment. This was done through the creation of a dedicated Assisted Living floor and transformation of Skilled Care from an institutional model to a more residential, household model of care. On the second floor, the new model includes both short-term rehab and long-term care households. Each household was designed with a living room, dining room, and associated staff areas. The third floor now has both an Assisted Living and a Memory Support household. Both floors have direct access to roof gardens.
- A second goal was to provide new resident services that strengthen the lifestyle experiences of current and future residents. Life in the Hyde Park neighborhood has been described as 'a rare mix of styles: sophisticated and down-to-earth, engaging and peaceful, culturally diverse and authentic.' Montgomery Place wanted to embrace these concepts in the development of its new image. This was accomplished by the development of a new wellness center, a bistro/café and an informal library directly adjacent to the existing main entry. These new spaces provided an updated casual image that complemented the existing, more formal side of the house.
- A third goal was to strengthen the connections between indoor and outdoor spaces and provide increased opportunities for all residents to enjoy the outdoors. Because of the limited amount of land on the urban site, the residents' garden is an important amenity. Understanding the value of these gardens, the architect added two rooftop gardens to provide dedicated outdoor space for each level of care. In addition, a conservatory and greenhouse were developed, creating additional connections with the garden areas of the site.

Each of these amenities was located to strengthen and enhance the visual connections with the surrounding neighborhood and views to Lake Michigan beyond.

Challenges: What were the most difficult challenges in designing the project?

- Achieving the maximum impact from judicious renovations and additions on a tight urban site: Because this 14-story vertical high-rise Continuing Care Retirement Community (CCRC) is bordered by sidewalks on one edge and a parking garage on the other, it was quite a challenge to make a real difference on such a tight urban site. The architect also wanted to make it obvious to the community that 'something was happening' at this community – so they added a 7,365-square-foot, two-story-plus basement addition. This allowed for the total transformation of the image of the building at street level as well as providing enough space to completely transform the interior feeling of the residential floors and provide spaces for the new Wellness Center.
- Providing sufficient amenity space at the first floor main entry by relocating administrative offices to the parking garage: Montgomery Place includes a parking garage whose spaces are consistently leased to neighboring buildings. The decision to relocate the administrative offices to the garage not only required careful design consideration, but also a carefully orchestrated political campaign involving multiple community meetings with surrounding neighbors as well as support from the local alderman. The design of the office suite itself included careful installation of skylights that access daylight from the garden above, in order to increase the quality of the windowless space below.
- Addressing code/regulation requirements: Illinois Department of Health (IDPH) regulations can make it very difficult to achieve the type of household design plans that Montgomery Place wanted to implement. Regulations mandate a direct line of visual supervision from all nurse stations to resident room doors, making any type of clustering plan very difficult. Strategically locating staff desk areas helped satisfy this requirement. Chicago fire code requirements forbid the opening of public spaces to the corridors without the use of fire doors. The design provided concealed fire doors in each of the great rooms to facilitate a more residential room-to-room flow and appearance from the corridors.

Innovations: Does the project offer its users unique opportunities or new features not typically available in previous similar projects?

- The City of Chicago encourages LEED compliance and requires that 75 percent of flat roofs on new construction be 'green.' Realizing the opportunity, our designers developed two accessible green roofs, one over the existing dining room as a therapy garden and one on the new Wellness Center addition as a dementia garden. Although Montgomery Place did not apply for LEED certification, LEED design criteria were followed for the green roofs. For example, the 50/50 relationship of plantings to hardscape was met, and hardier, more drought-resistant plantings were specified. Other goals included reducing the heat-island effect and tempering the storm water burden by absorbing rainwater and releasing it slowly.

Above left: Concierge desk
Above right: Informal library/café

- In order to provide sufficient amenity space on the first floor, Montgomery Place made the decision to relocate the administrative suite to the lower level parking garage. Concern centered around the emotional wellness of staff members who would be working in a windowless space. Care was taken to locate skylights that would provide access to natural light and finishes were upgraded to provide a more visually appealing environment. Additional amenities, such as a billiards area, provide opportunities for staff to socialize and relax.
- The goal of providing unobstructed views of Lake Michigan and a wonderful view of the Museum of Science and Industry directly across the street, while maintaining safety and security, informed the design of a glass-enclosed pergola for the third floor Memory Support roof garden. The enclosure helps to shelter the space from strong winds while the pergola was designed with a fine-grained perforated metal grid on top so that the shadows cast do not create the disorienting ladder effect of a typical trellis design. The planting materials were carefully selected not only for aesthetics, but also for safety so they are not harmful if swallowed. The garden also provides raised gardening beds for therapeutic gardening by the residents.

Form shapers: What factors had the most influence on the physical form of the project?

- The residents of Montgomery Place describe themselves as true Hyde Parkers. To them aging-in-place meant being empowered to directly influence the design direction of the repositioning of Montgomery Place. Their independent-minded attitudes and engaged lifestyles made for very lively design planning sessions. Although the tight constrains of this urban site limited the expansion possibilities, the residents wanted a pool, and insisted upon a pool. They saw this feature as supporting their ability to age in place with the convenience of having a pool only an elevator ride away. The design solution was to incorporate into the first floor Wellness Center a small resistance jet pool to allow for swimming in place and resistance walking.
- Montgomery Place embarked on a renovation program to upgrade the current Independent Living apartments. Improvements included upgraded finishes, accessible bathrooms, and larger kitchens, with the introduction of raised dishwashers, wall ovens, and cooktops. In addition, consolidation of one-bedroom units were provided for those residents seeking larger units.
- Montgomery Place recognized the need for Assisted Living to extend its care services for residents who were aging in place. In order to provide this service, they reduced the number of skilled care beds and renovated the third floor to accommodate 14 residential-style Assisted Living units centered around a great room, as well as an additional eight units of Memory Support with access to a secure roof garden.

Top trends

- Responding to the site and local conditions: Montgomery Place is located in the Hyde Park neighborhood, on the south side of Chicago, in a prime location with direct views and access to Lake Michigan. The design approach of the building additions was to relate in scale and setback to the existing urban fabric of the neighborhood, as well as to maximize views to the garden and Lake Michigan. The interior design was a response to the interests of existing residents who have a strong academic orientation and relate to familiar Hyde Park institutions in the neighborhood such as the Seminary Co-op Bookstore of the University of Chicago. As a result, the existing library was expanded with the addition of a new informal library and café, which helped to enliven the main entrance.
- Taking advantage of existing infrastructure: Due to the constraints of the urban site, Montgomery Place was limited in the amount of new square footage that could be accommodated. It became imperative to analyze the existing infrastructure to determine underutilized areas that would free up existing square footage for new amenities. The most important decision that allowed for development of the new wellness center was the decision to move the administrative suite to the parking garage. Many of the existing spaces were not utilized by current residents and instead leased to other buildings. By recapturing these spaces, the suite could be accommodated and additional space provided for the café on the first floor.
- Addressing a holistic sense of wellness: Recognizing the importance of a holistic wellness program, Montgomery Place was very concerned with providing not just a fitness center with a pool, but additional services such as massage therapy. In addition, the desire was to locate the center in a place of honor where residents would naturally gather and accomplish a sense of social wellness. To satisfy the intellectual needs of its current residents, an informal library and café was also created as an integral part of this wellness center.

Sustainability: Does the project conserve energy, water, and other natural resources? Does it reuse existing material or buildings, or include recycled building materials? How will the project improve indoor air quality in operation?

- Green roofs were used on the addition and over the existing dining room. Goals included reducing the heat-island effect, reducing storm-water burden, adding insulation, and extending the roof life.

Community: How does the project advance the sense of community for residents, staff, families, and neighbors?

- The new wellness center was located on the street side of the existing building rather than the garden side, near the front door, and adjacent to the new café and informal library. This was designed to provide visibility of the fitness center and pool, and to bring people together in a casual atmosphere of social, intellectual, and physical wellness.
- The existing building included a formal dining room that experienced a bottleneck at its entry prior to all meals. A conservatory was developed adjacent to the dining room to not only alleviate some of the congestion at the dining room entry, but to also provide a space for residents to gather both before and after dining. This space was strategically located to take advantage of views and direct access to the garden and Lake Michigan beyond.
- The existing building included two Skilled Care floors that were very institutional and provided very little space for socialization or activities. The renovation included the development of a separate household for short-term rehab and long-term care on the second floor, each with its own living, dining, and kitchen spaces. Additional quiet rooms provide a space for small group gathering as well as views of Lake Michigan. The third floor was renovated to Assisted Living and Memory Support, each with its own great room.

Target market: What specific features/services/amenities were incorporated into the overall project to attract your target market?

- Today's seniors expect and demand more options, so wellness principles were prioritized by incorporating a wellness center into the community, including a pool, massage, and fitness areas. This wellness center was located at the front door to emphasize this enhanced lifestyle both to the greater community as well as prospective residents. In addition, a café and informal library were located adjacent to the space to encourage and facilitate group participation.
- Many potential residents were looking for larger units with updated features and fixtures. Montgomery Place embarked on a renovation program to upgrade the current Independent Living apartments. Improvements included upgraded finishes, accessible bathrooms, and larger kitchens, with the introduction of raised dishwashers, wall ovens, and cooktops. In addition, consolidation of one-bedroom units were provided for those residents seeking larger units.

Above: Conservatory view

Photography: Barry Rustin Photography

C.C. Hodgson Architectural Group

Porter Hills GREEN HOUSE® Homes

Grand Rapids, Michigan // Porter Hills Retirement Communities & Services

Facility type: Skilled Nursing

Target market: Middle/upper middle

Site location: Suburban

Capacity: 20 units; 10 residents in each Green House

Total project cost: $3.3 million

Date of completion: May 2009

Green certification: LEED Silver Certification for New Construction

Below: Entry view
Opposite left: Courtyard view
Opposite right: Enclosed porch

Overall Project Goals

Porter Hills GREEN HOUSE® Homes consists of two Homes designed to meet the needs of elders who require Skilled Nursing care support. This project is part of a national replication project that is being funded in part by the Robert Wood Johnson foundation and is known as the GREEN HOUSE® concept. Developed by Dr. William Thomas, the GREEN HOUSE® is a model for cultural change that eliminates large nursing facilities and creates warmer social settings that are truly homes. Each of the 7,500-square-foot Porter Hills GREEN HOUSE® Homes is designed to be a home for 10 elders. They are located adjacent to the campus of Cook Valley Estates, in Grand Rapids, Michigan. The GREEN HOUSE® Homes were sited to minimize the impact on the existing wetlands as well as to maximize views toward the wetlands and outdoor courtyards. Walking paths from the homes provide a pedestrian connection through the wetlands to the existing Cook Valley Estates. The design and massing of the homes is compatible with the Craftsman style of neighboring houses and businesses, and include vibrant outdoor courtyards. The interior was designed with a residential scale and finish. Each home is a self-contained residence that includes private resident rooms with private baths, hearth areas combining the living room, dining room, and open kitchen; a dining table that seats all elders, staff, and two guests; a library; and a staff work area designed as a typical home office.

Provider's Statement

Provider goals for marketing and sales

Elders from Porter Hills Health & Rehab Center (legacy building) will move to Porter Hills new GREEN HOUSE® Homes. Twenty beds will be transferred from the legacy building which enabled Porter Hills to build two 10-bedroom homes.

How did the provider plan to improve the residents' quality of life?

Every part of the home encourages use, comfort, and ownership. Private bedrooms can become just that, a bedroom. Elders are encouraged to display their knick-knacks, favorite books, and other personal items throughout the home.

The home is small, with short distances between amenities to encourage walking.

There is open access to the kitchen with opportunities to be involved in meal selection and preparation. Access to a secured backyard is also available, providing opportunities for gardening and views of natural wetlands and wildlife.

The use of institutional equipment and design has been eliminated: the nurses' station has been replaced with a home office; medications are kept in private bedrooms, eliminating the need for a medication cart; ceiling lifts and bathing spas are included in all bedrooms, eliminating the need for Hoyer Lifts; and there are no corridors.

How did the provider want to improve workplace quality for employees?

The provider sought a non-institutional environment for self-directed work teams.

Site plan

Did the provider have specific goals for the project's staffing quantities, training, or distribution?

The initial training for all disciplines and 'Train-the-Trainer' program was provided by the Green House® Replication Initiative. This includes an extensive amount of training resources. Peer networking is also a beneficial resource that is promoted and coordinated by the Green House® Replication Initiative. Ninety percent of the staff working at Porter Hills Green House® homes are from Porter Hills Village.

Did the provider give specific direction about the style, materials, features, or other design aspects of the project? If so, what were those directives?

A design charrette was facilitated by the architect to better determine design directives. Residents, family members and staff from varying disciplines participated. Entire home design was based on the outcome of the charrette in addition to meeting the requirements of the Green House®. This also led to the decision to construct the homes to USGBC standards and apply for LEED certification.

Architect's Statement

Design goals

- The primary goal of this project was to develop a GREEN HOUSE® model that would provide a small home setting that truly reflected all of the characteristics and attributes of a home versus being homelike. Residents, staff, and designers worked together to identify institutional elements still remaining in other household designs and find more authentic solutions. For example, a foyer was designed that created a natural barrier between living spaces and the front door, thus eliminating the need for a vestibule; a required staff work space was designed as a typical home office; a required exit corridor was designed as a mud room/staff entry; and required medical preparation areas were replaced with individual locked medicine cabinets in resident rooms.

- A second goal was to provide a healthy and environmentally conscious design by achieving LEED certification. From the beginning of construction, strict regulations were set in place to ensure a reduction in indoor air quality problems; some of the products regulated for gas emissions were adhesives, sealants, paints, stains, carpets, and wood products. The use of a geothermal system and sustainable site criteria contributed to energy and water efficiency; and goals were set to ensure that recycling programs and local resources would be utilized, minimizing the impact of the construction of the homes on the surrounding environment.
- A third goal was to take advantage of the beauty and views of the wetlands on the chosen site through the careful placement of the homes. The GREEN HOUSE® Homes were oriented to minimize disruption of the existing wetlands and to allow for maximum views of the landscape from the hearth and enclosed courtyards. In addition, all of the private resident rooms were designed with two operational windows on opposite walls that would not only provide an abundance of natural daylight, but also views to the landscape beyond.

Challenges: What were the most difficult challenges in designing the project?

- The existence of wetlands on the property provided opportunities for enhanced views, but also provided challenges for the siting of the two GREEN HOUSE® Homes. In order to minimize disruption of the wetlands, the homes were located tight to one another, but offset to provide maximum privacy and autonomy for each of the courtyards. Retaining walls, both integral to the building and freestanding, were required to minimize the necessary mitigation of those wetlands that were disturbed. Careful thought and planning went into utilizing the wetlands to increase site infiltration of storm water, eliminating sources of contamination and managing runoff.
- Porter Hills GREEN HOUSE® Homes is the first stand-alone GREEN HOUSE® not located on the campus of an existing nursing home. As such, the project had to be designed and operated to satisfy the required regulations of a stand-alone nursing home. Because staff could not be shared with an existing facility, additional office space was provided. A new position was created that would meet the administrative requirements of the stand-alone facility, while also providing nursing and activity functions as well.

Innovations: Does the project offer its users unique opportunities or new features not typically available in previous similar projects?

- The heating and cooling equipment chosen for Porter Hills GREEN HOUSE® Homes is a geothermal heat pump system, utilizing a ground loop heat exchanger (GLHE). This system is the most energy-efficient system available. Porter Hills will realize an overall energy use reduction of up to 50 percent compared with a conventional heating and cooling installation.
- Electronic ceiling lifts that are out of sight until needed were installed in all resident rooms to facilitate movement of residents from their bed to the bathroom as they age in place. This provides not only a greater level of independence for the resident, but also allows for minimal aid from a single caregiver so that more quality time can be spent with each resident.

Form shapers: What factors had the most influence on the physical form of the project?

- The open kitchen is designed to allow for full resident participation as they age in place. The counter design accommodates both standing-height surfaces as well as wheelchair-height surface areas to allow for residents to help in food preparation and other tasks. Safety doors are accommodated at two access points to allow for preparation of meals while ensuring safety and allowing for the presence of residents during tasks such as boiling water.
- All private resident rooms include a private accessible bathroom with fully accessible showers. A bathing spa provides a therapeutic tub as well as access to a hair washing and styling station.

Top trends

- Addressing a holistic sense of wellness: The design of the household, with its 10 resident rooms, is intended to embrace holistic wellness by providing a design that supports the natural rhythms of life. All resident rooms are arranged to have a direct view and connection to the hearth areas of the home. These areas, including the living room, dining room, and open kitchen, are arranged in an L-shape to not only facilitate this connection, but provide abundant natural light and a sense of intimacy within each of the individual spaces. In addition, as nature was seen as an important element of wellness, the design of the homes included enhancement of views to the wetlands and ease of access to courtyards and walking paths.
- Being green/sustainable: The Porter Hills GREEN HOUSE® Homes is the first nationally to apply for LEED certification. It was this client's strong belief that the environmental and economic health and community benefits would further enhance the lives of those living

and working in the homes. The use of a geothermal system, sustainable site criteria, wetlands mitigation, water efficiency, indoor air quality measures, and an emphasis on recycling and use of local resources are just some of the criteria utilized in achieving LEED Silver Certification.

Sustainability: Does the project conserve energy, water, and other natural resources? Does it reuse existing material or buildings, or include recycled building materials? How will the project improve indoor air quality in operation?

- Sustainable site features include limited disruption of the natural hydrology and wetlands through the use of retaining walls and increased water efficiency through specially designed irrigation and managed storm runoff.
- The heating and cooling equipment is a geothermal heat pump system, utilizing a ground loop heat exchanger. This system is the most energy-efficient system available and will realize up to a 50 percent overall reduction in energy use.
- Strict regulations were set in place to ensure a reduction in indoor air quality problems resulting from the construction process. Products regulated for the gases they emit include: adhesives, sealants, paints, stains, carpets, and wood products.

Community: How does the project advance the sense of community for residents, staff, families, and neighbors?

- This client understood the importance of a strong community in not only the operation of the GREEN HOUSE® Homes, but in their implementation as well. Prior to the design of the GREEN HOUSE® Homes, residents, staff, and family members visited several existing projects to help in not only understanding the environment of the GREEN HOUSE® Homes, but to have a basis for determining what they would like to see in the design for Porter Hills. A design charrette was then facilitated by the architect, providing the opportunity to analyze and identify solutions for the new design that responded to what was liked and disliked at the toured facilities. The result was a design concept developed by a community of involved stakeholders.
- The design of the household, with its 10 resident rooms, is intended to encourage development of strong relationships and a sense of community. All resident rooms are arranged to have a direct view and connection to the hearth areas of the home. These areas, including the living room, dining room, and open kitchen, are arranged in an L-shape to not only facilitate this connection, but to provide abundant natural light and a sense of intimacy within each of the individual spaces. In addition, a dining room table that seats all elders, staff, and two guests was custom designed to encourage the gathering and interaction of this small community at mealtimes and other special events.
- Outdoor activities provide unique and varied opportunities for people to come together. Understanding this, the GREEN HOUSE® Homes were designed around access to a private courtyard with direct views and access from all of the public spaces in the Home. The design of the courtyards include shaded seating areas, walking paths, raised gardens, and natural plantings.

Target market: What specific features/services/amenities were incorporated into the overall project to attract your target market?

- Many of the families of today's seniors are looking for a much more residential environment for the care of their loved ones. The GREEN HOUSE® Replication Project, as conceived by Dr. William Thomas, is a model for cultural change that eliminates large institutional-style nursing facilities and creates warmer social settings that are truly homes. Each of the Porter Hills GREEN HOUSE® Homes is a self-contained residence for 10 elders that includes private resident rooms with private baths; hearth areas combining the living room, dining room, and open kitchen; a dining table that seats all elders, staff, and two guests; a library; and a staff work area designed as a typical home office.
- Access to nature is becoming a required amenity not only in the marketing of a facility, but in the continued health and wellness of residents and staff alike. Understanding this, the GREEN HOUSE® Homes were designed around access to a private courtyard with direct views and access from all of the public spaces in the home. The design of the courtyards includes shaded seating areas, walking paths, raised gardens, and natural plantings. In addition, all resident rooms were designed with two operable windows on opposite walls to provide natural daylighting, views to the landscape, and fresh breezes into the rooms on nice days.
- A byproduct of the development of the Porter Hills GREEN HOUSE® Homes was enhancement of the marketability of the adjacent Cook Valley Estates. These estates are a collection of single-family homes and apartments for independent seniors. The GREEN HOUSE® Homes, with their provision for skilled care, provides an option for those seniors as they and/or their spouses require a greater level of care, without having to leave the nearby community. Walking paths were provided to allow for a pedestrian connection between the two communities as well as to allow for enjoyment of the wetlands and landscaping.

Top: All meals are prepared from scratch in the residential-style kitchen
Above: The living room is oriented towards the hearth with direct views and access to the courtyard

Photography: JRP Studio, LLC

Engberg Anderson, Inc.

Sharon S. Richardson Community Hospice

Sheboygan Falls, Wisconsin // Sharon S. Richardson, C.H.

Facility type: Hospice
Target market: Mixed income
Site location: Rural
Capacity: 20 Inpatient Hospice Beds
Date of completion: September 2007

Below: View of hospice from healing garden water feature
Opposite: View to courtyard and resident patios

Photography: Mike Rebholz

Overall Project Goals

The idea of the hospice began with Joe Richardson to ensure a legacy for his wife Sharon who died of cancer in 2004. The $7.2 million project is also a tribute to the community, which helped raise the funds for construction of the first and only inpatient hospice in the county, and continues to support the patient care endowment. The one-story, 30,000-square-foot building, with a partially exposed lower level, has 16 private rooms and two family hospice rooms. The building is composed of three resident wings; each has a den with kitchenette, numerous reading nooks, and decentralized staff/support spaces. Activity spaces providing a residential feel include a living room, chapel, dining room, library, children's play room, spa, and training center. The serene views, pastoral setting and rolling hills were critical in determining this 10-acre former cornfield as the project site. The absence of substantial vegetation at the site allowed the development of healing gardens and extended walking trails. The slope of the site allowed 'back of house' support functions to be accessed from a visually concealed lower level, preserving the upper level for all resident-centered spaces and reducing the overall scale of the building. The angled configuration of resident rooms relative to the corridor allows two orientations to the exterior and focused views to the courtyards beyond. The familiar residential design incorporates utilitarian components: 8-foot corridors, medical gases, and staff/service spaces.

Provider's Statement

Provider goals for marketing and sales

The provider was extremely pleased with the response from the community, the patients, and their families/caregivers, as well as from employees and volunteers regarding the warm and welcoming feeling they experience as they enter and dwell in the building. The virtual tour on the company's website receives hundreds of hits every month and is mentioned often by visitors.

How did the provider plan to improve the residents' quality of life?

Residents are thrilled with the spa area where they can enjoy a whirlpool bath, or any spa service they might request from the staff of the Kohler Waters Spa. Community is integrated into the operation through the spa design, the landscaping with hundreds of local master gardeners, musicians utilizing the common spaces to share their talents, and memorial services in the conference room. In addition, the ability to move the hospital beds through the patio doors and to enjoy nature at the threshold of their suites is highly valued by our residents. For those more active, the common areas serve as gathering spaces with family, friends, and staff/volunteers.

How did the provider want to improve workplace quality for employees?

The wing design and work station placement support team interaction and assignment of staff; in addition, the dining room has become a hub of activity and a favorite space for interacting with other employees, volunteers, and the families served at the Hospice Center.

Did the provider have specific goals for the project's staffing quantities, training, or distribution?

The building has several spaces to be utilized for staff positioning, and the conference room design has accommodated a wide range of training and meeting needs – with furniture and space that is designed to be moved and flexible in all of the common areas.

Did the provider give specific direction about the style, materials, features, or other design aspects of the project? If so, what were those directives?

The designer and provider were engaged in an ongoing dialogue about the provider's vision for the sense visitors would experience entering the building, including the amount of natural lighting as well as the quality and color of wood and other materials. These ongoing conversations and the designer's quick follow-up in response to the discussions gave the provider confidence in the designer's commitment to exceed their expectations.

How did the provider's financial goals influence the project's organization, configuration, layout, or sizing of components?

The building supports operational and financial performance goals in a number of ways. First, the three separate wings and nurses/CNA stations allow suites and staff positions to be filled in a cost effective manner. The design of the wings (short and wide, rather than long and narrow) also accommodates staffing patterns without taxing the staff unnecessarily, with a positive impact response time. In addition, the three wings with semi-private areas for families and visitors in each wing allow the provider to utilize one of the wings for a different type of care

Site plan

1 Drop off
2 Loading at lower level
3 Gazebo
4 Terrace overlook
5 Gardens
6 Extended walking path

0 75ft

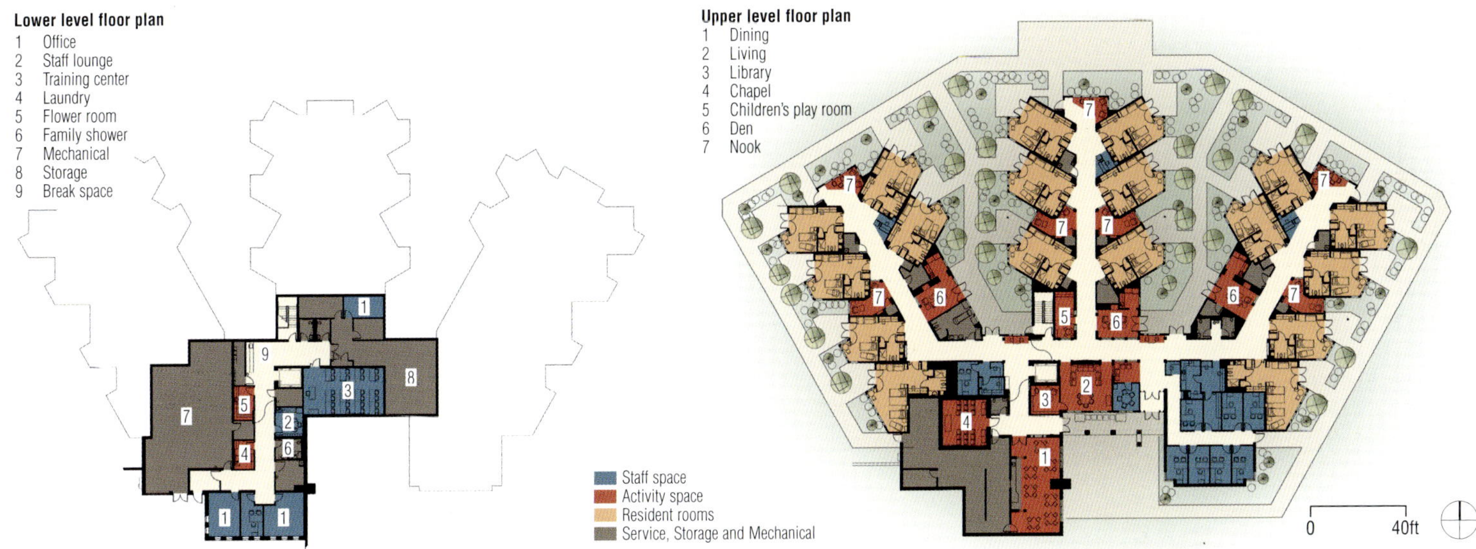

(acute assisted living is currently being considered) and the building design is conducive to this type of expansion of services. This is very important to revenue streams.

Architect's Statement

Design goals

- The weaving of the natural environment with the building, reducing the scale, and designing focused views from the resident room while protecting privacy were major goals. The building is designed with three resident wings surrounded on both sides by exterior gardens. The blending of the natural environment is further promoted with a semi-sheltered patio space at each resident room and a pair of French doors to allow easy access. The resident rooms are oriented 60 degrees relative to the corridor to promote views out of the courtyard and not into adjacent resident rooms. The partially exposed lower level was utilized to reduce the scale of the building and maintain a residential feel.
- The resident and family experience was a driving factor in the design of the building. Specifically, providing a range of locations and sizes of spaces for activities or quiet retreat. The resident rooms are large enough to allow visitors in the room, but gathering spaces are also provided directly outside the resident rooms. The extended walking trails complete the range of available spaces.
- Working in a hospice environment is taxing, physically and emotionally. The design must ease the caregiver's burden and provide interior and exterior areas for respite and relief. The decentralized service and storage areas reduce travel distances and allow staff presence in each resident wing. The resident room nurse servers reduce travel distances and response time when meeting patient care needs. The resident rooms and wings have identical layouts to help reduce wayfinding confusion and staffing errors.

Challenges: What were the most difficult challenges in designing the project?

- Incorporating construction and space requirements similar to a hospital while creating a comforting and homelike environment. Institutional components including 8-foot-wide corridors, medical gases, nursing staff spaces, and other support spaces were challenges. The building was configured into a series of smaller residential-sized wings with familiar spaces (resident rooms, reading nooks, den, and kitchenette). The corridors were enhanced with clerestory windows that allow sunshine during the day and moonlight to peek through at night. The corridors have several seating/reading nooks with hardwood half-height walls and columns to convey a sense of warmth. Staff and support spaces were reduced in size and decentralized to each wing.
- The space program had a substantial area for back-of-house functions which would have negatively impacted the scale of the building. Working with the natural topography of the site a partially exposed lower level helps hide the back-of-house functions and keeps the scale of the building at a residential level. The amount of administrative space was expanded to include an in-home hospice care center. The original space program did not account for the

extra space requirement. The lower level was utilized for office space with the addition of a large area to provide natural light and views.

Innovations: Does the project offer its users unique opportunities or new features not typically available in previous similar projects?

- The location of the building on the crest of the hill and the northern orientation overlooking the healing gardens takes advantage of a natural sloping site. The sloped site maximizes views while allowing the back-of-house functions to be tucked discreetly out of site.
- The mass of the building was pulled apart to reduce its overall scale and the resulting courtyards allow the blending of the natural environment and the built environment.

Form shapers: What factors had the most influence on the physical form of the project?

- The hospice is designed to allow the residents to do for themselves for as long as possible, but when care is needed it can be given and received with dignity. The resident rooms are the major component in providing a supportive environment. The rooms have direct access to a semi-sheltered patio space, which is large enough to accommodate a bed. The resident bathrooms have an accessible toilet and a large accessible shower with a foldable shower seat. The toilet is located to allow staff assistance from both sides and is equipped with dual drop-down grab bars.

Top trends

- Responding to the site and local conditions: The building responded to the site by taking advantage of the natural contours to hide back-of-house functions and create walking paths through a meadering healing garden. In addition the resident rooms were oriented to capture the views of the natural surroundings and wild life.
- Offering choice through a diversity of housing options: The hospice is arranged on a decentralized model of staffing, service, support, and activity spaces. The resident wings are divided into semi-autonomous smaller households of six resident rooms and associated staff and activity space.
- Person-centered model of care: Holistic architecture, interior design, and landscape are crtitical to the mission of meeting the changing abilities of the body, mind, and spirit towards the end of life. The hospice model goes beyond the care of dying individuals and considers the life-affirming interactions with family and staff as vitally important.

Sustainability: Does the project conserve energy, water, and other natural resources? Does it reuse existing material or buildings, or include recycled building materials? How will the project improve indoor air quality in operation?

- To reduce the need for artificial lighting, the building was oriented and designed to allow ample daylighting. Also, a combination of clerestory windows and seating nooks located on the exterior wall eliminate traditionally dark interior corridors.
- To reduce the need for mechanical ventilation the resident rooms each have a set of double doors with screens to allow natural ventilation and access to the gardens. The resident bed may be moved out of the room to the private, semi-sheltered patio.
- Storm water does not burden the municipal sewer system. All storm water is treated on-site by means of a retention pond that also provides an active landscaped feature and walking path destination.

Community: How does the project advance the sense of community for residents, staff, families, and neighbors?

- The dining room is a hub of activity for the hospice. The warmth of the flickering fireplace and songs from the grand piano are often used to set the mood for an evening meal with loved ones. The self-service beverage counter in the dining room is often supplemented with a plate of homemade cookies to encourage people to engage into the space. The dining room is located adjacent to the front entry patio, which is often a site for visiting with friends and family as they arrive and enter the hospice.
- The hospice has numerous socialization and gathering areas within the building and in the surrounding exterior gardens. The healing gardens extend down the northern slope of the hospice site. A winding path with occasional benches proceeds down to a prominent water feature with an overlook. A gazebo sits at the crest of the hill and invites spontaneous conversation while sitting in the shade and enjoying the surrounding countryside.
- The informal and formal sitting areas extend into the building. The gathering areas in each resident wing are varied in size and location to provide options to residents and family members. People often find peer support from conversations with family, staff, and friends in one of the retreat areas on the resident wings.

Target market: What specific features/services/amenities were incorporated into the overall project to attract your target market?

- The major element incorporated into the design to assure marketability was a person-centered residential environment. The scale and appearance of the environment is reflective of a residence and the organization of spaces and amenities will support a model of care that is person centered and non-institutional.
- The family is an integral part of the hospice experience. This is evident in the size and layout of the resident rooms, which provide family space for overnight guests. The building provides many areas for gathering with family and even a family shower for overnight guests.
- The environment is person-centered and every effort is made to provide an end-of-life experience that is individually tailored to meet the needs of the resident and family members. The environment allows operational flexibility to meet individual needs by providing decentralized staffing, support, and activity spaces.

Opposite left: Resident room showing custom cabinetry housing medical gases

Photography: Mike Rebholz

Opposite right: Resident room showing direct patio access

Photography: Dan Kabara

Bottom left: Resident wing corridor features small-scale gathering spaces and access to the gardens

Photography: Mike Rebholz

Below: Chapel with central skylight and locally crafted panoramic 'four seasons' themed backlit stained glass

Photography: Mike Rebholz

RLPS Architects

Signature Apartments

Media, Pennsylvania // Martins Run

Facility type: Independent Living

Target market: Middle/upper middle

Site location: Urban (city or town)

Capacity: 166 apartments

Total project cost: $100–$120 per square foot (varies by unit type)

Date of completion: December 2013

Below: View from balcony of reinvented living space showing open plan and kitchen improvements
Opposite: Improved view to outdoors from apartment foyer

Overall Project Goals

Like many non-profit Continuing Care Retirement Communities (CCRCs), this provider needed to update aging apartment stock to meet current market demands. The phased redesign of 80 apartments primarily entails reconfiguring units ranging from 600 to 900 square feet within the existing footprint. The project also involves combining selected units to provide larger accommodations from 950 to 1200 square feet. One of the most significant space-saving strategies was the replacement of existing wall console mechanical units with a high-efficiency vertical unit placed outside the living space. This permitted installation of four-panel patio doors, which significantly increased natural light and outdoor views. The original 5- by 7-foot bathroom was expanded and fitted with a frameless, tiled corner shower, wood console vanity with integrated bowl, wood wainscoting, hide-away hamper, linen storage, decorative wall sconces, and ceramic tile floors. Wrought-iron picket railing on the 48-inch-deep balconies was replaced with clear tempered glass panels to provide an unimpeded view. Removing the interior walls from the previously dark galley kitchen resulted in a much brighter, open living space that belies the relatively small unit sizes. The updated units feature a spacious kitchen with stainless steel appliances, energy-efficient low-E windows and patio doors, walk-in closets, washer/dryers, built-ins and bamboo flooring. Other upgrades include accent and task lighting, granite countertops, custom-style cabinetry, and space-saving pocket doors.

Provider's Statement

How have the provider's goals for marketing/sales of the project been met?

All 2009 sales were the signature-style (reinvented) apartments, proving that this design is what the current market is seeking.

What specific features of the project add to residents' quality of life?

The reinvented apartments have a more open feel, provide more living space, and add a significant amount of natural light.

What specific directions were given by the provider to the project's designer relating to the style, materials, features, or other design aspects of the project?

Expectations included adding more light, increasing the use of green features, incorporating an open floor plan, removing HVAC from inside the apartment to outside, installing a more efficient HVAC system, and incorporating the most up-to-date amenities.

How does the project uniquely address the provider's objectives for financial/operational performance?

The reinvented apartments enhance the provider's ability to sell to younger prospects.

Architect's Statement

Design goals

- The primary goal was to stop the financial hemorrhaging caused by increasing vacancies that were a result of market resistance to an aging, outdated product. Removing the interior walls of the cramped kitchen dramatically transformed the living area into an open, inviting, and significantly brighter space. The renovations turned the kitchen into an appealing amenity with upscale cabinetry, granite countertops, a breakfast bar, and task lighting.
- To maximize outdoor connections and introduce more natural light into the existing apartments, the wall console mechanical units were relocated to the exterior, which cleared the way for four-panel patio doors. Glass railing replaced the former picket railing on the balcony to extend views and further promote a sense of openness

and larger scale. Increasing window height in the bedroom similarly improved that area.

- To bring the existing apartment units up to market standards, the new design reflects considerations for a myriad of details that would make not-so-big living spaces comfortable, homelike and senior user-friendly. This encompassed a washer and dryer in every unit, ample storage, a furniture vanity and multiple layers of overhead, task, and decorative lighting.

Challenges: What were the most difficult challenges in designing the project?

- The greatest challenge for this project was providing 'outside the box' solutions 'inside the box.' Other than the combined units, the design objectives had to be achieved without the benefit of added space. This was primarily accomplished by opening up the space to create a larger sense of scale and openness while paving the way for upscale interior finishes, fixtures, and lighting to enhance the space.
- Persuading the owner that the intended spatial reconfigurations, finish upgrade, window and door replacements, and improved lighting would make the difference was a huge challenge. As a result, a critical component of the design process was educating the owner regarding consumer expectations and concept review meetings.
- Because the apartment renovations are occurring piecemeal, the disruption of services to existing occupied apartments has to be minimal for plumbing, electrical, and mechanical system upgrades.

Innovations: Does the project offer its users unique opportunities or new features not typically available in previous similar projects?

- Floor-to-ceiling, wall-to-wall patio doors erase the visual barrier between interior and exterior spaces and provide a sense of more space.
- The removal of traditional picket balcony railing and replacing it with glass further enhances transparency.
- Use of frameless shower stalls to increase the sense of space in bathrooms.

Form shapers: What factors had the most influence on the physical form of the project?

- Recognizing that most apartments are inhabited by only one person, pocket doors were utilized not only as a space-saving device but also to increase accessibility.
- Although lighting has been designed to maximize output in foot-candles, the design solution involves layers of lights to improve flexibility and offer a variety of sources: direct, indirect, ambient, task, and decorative all work in concert to provide the desired effect and outcome for comfort, safety, and well-being.
- Bamboo hardwood floors have been used in living areas and kitchens for both aesthetics and ease of mobility. Throw rugs are added by residents if desired adding to flexibility and independence.

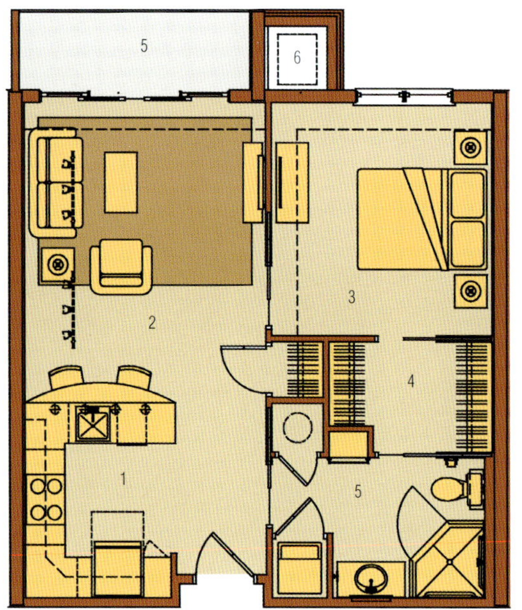

Typical floor plans
1 Kitchen
2 Living/dining
3 Bedroom
4 Walk-in closet
5 Bathroom
6 Patio
7 HVAC
8 Foyer

0 5ft

Left: Reinvented master bedroom with enlarged windows

Photography: Larry Lefever Photography

Top trends

- Integrating with the surrounding community; Addressing a holistic sense of wellness; Helping aging adults stay in their homes longer: New residents expect this move to be their last and want the physical environment to be supportive of their desire to stay 'home.' By using the existing infrastructure, the owner was able to maintain an affordable solution and work within a timeframe beneficial to their budget abilities.

Sustainability: Does the project conserve energy, water, and other natural resources? Does it reuse existing material or buildings, or include recycled building materials? How will the project improve indoor air quality in operation?

- This project reinvented existing, aging housing stock with minimal structural renovations, eliminating the need for new building.
- The apartment reinvention included replacing existing glazing with energy-efficient low-E windows and a more efficient HVAC system.
- Relocating the HVAC unit outside the apartment to add full-height glazing in the main living area, along with extending bedroom window heights significantly increased natural lighting and views to the outdoors.

Community: How does the project advance the sense of community for residents, staff, families, and neighbors?

- Increased occupancy promotes new relationships and ultimately a more vibrant community.

Target market: What specific features/services/amenities were incorporated into the overall project to attract your target market?

- To meet current market expectations, the reinvented apartments feature an open-plan, daylit living area with upgraded finishes, fixtures, and lighting, as well as ample storage including a walk-in closet and a washer and dryer in each unit.
- Master bathroom improvements include a frameless shower to make the room feel larger, a furniture-style vanity and ample storage including a clothing hamper.
- The kitchen includes a breakfast bar, upgraded fixtures, stainless steel appliances, and carefully detailed cabinetry.

Mithun

Hope House at Hope Meadows

Rantoul, Illinois // Generations of Hope

Facility type: Communal living with home and community-based services

Target market: Mixed income

Site location: Rural

Capacity: 8 Independent Living apartments

Date of completion: 2010

Green certification: Designed to LEED certification standards but not yet registered to be certified

Below: Hope Houses connect to the existing intergenerational center across from a new community hall

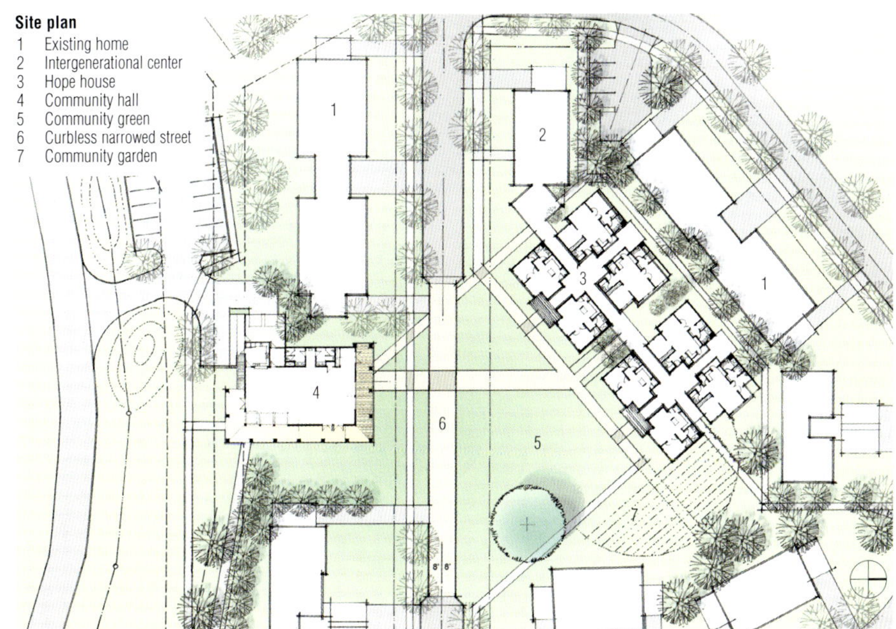

Overall Project Goals

Hope House creates a new model of housing that allows seniors to remain and age in community. Hope Meadows, the existing community, was created in 1994 to support adoptive families and children coming out of the foster care system. Located on part of a former air force base in rural Illinois, the intergenerational community contains 44 households of seniors that moved to the community with the common purpose of supporting 15 adoptive families that also live there. Many of these seniors have contributed to the community for over a decade as informal grandparents and are finding it increasingly difficult to 'age in place' in the existing housing as their health and mobility decline. The new Hope Houses connect to the existing intergenerational center and help preserve the relationships between seniors and adopted children so that the elders do not need to move away from the community as their health declines. The houses and intergenerational center front a newly developed common green at the center of the community. A new community hall located across the green serves both the intergenerational community and events offered to the broader community. It also provides a strong connection to the existing play equipment and picnic events pavilion.

Provider's Statement

Provider goals for marketing and sales

The goals and objectives for the project were more about supporting the established intergenerational community than for marketing and presales purposes. The project undoubtedly will improve interest in Hope Meadows as a place where elders can age in community, with dignity, respect, and a shared purpose until their final days.

How did the provider plan to improve the residents' quality of life?

Hope Houses are placed at the center of the community so that elders remain the center of the adoptive family's lives even at their most frail. Seniors' most valuable contributions reside not in what they do as volunteers, but in the caring relationships they develop with the children and adults. With the creation of the houses, located in the center of the community and supported by the community, important relationships are sustained even through the final stages of life. Children learn about compassion, reciprocity, and interdependence as seniors' health declines. Relationships with elders continue until the end of life. Seniors are engaged in the community on multiple levels, both through the activities of the intergenerational community as well as events hosted by the larger community at the community hall.

Did the provider give specific direction about the style, materials, features, or other design aspects of the project? If so, what were those directives?

Hope Houses and the community hall blend into the residential fabric of Hope Meadows in their size, mass, and materials. Hope elders actively sketched out what they saw as important elements to include in the design of the Hope Houses (for example, types of spaces and relationships).

How did the provider's financial goals influence the project's organization, configuration, layout, or sizing of components?

Hope Houses offers a housing option that is a step-down in size from the existing housing at Hope Meadows. Rental of the community hall by other organizations in Rantoul could potentially provide a modest source of income from this space.

Architect's Statement

Design goals

- To allow seniors increased levels of control and interaction with the larger community as they age. The houses are physically connected to the intergenerational center – the social/cultural/educational hub of the

community – allowing for short, protected travel distances from their home regardless of weather conditions. Homes are located across from the community hall, a gathering spot for large events. The front porch of each house enables residents to observe or interact with the activity of the street. Apartments within each Hope House are arranged to reinforce existing social patterns and foster a continued sense of community within each Hope House and between each Hope House and the larger community.

- To reinforce existing social patterns between seniors and adoptive families. Siting the Hope Houses and community hall as the hub of activity supports the community's commitment to care for their elders. Apartments connect to winter gardens large enough for plantings and gathering spaces. Unit entries adjoin shared atrium 'porches' and encourage neighborly interactions, similar to the role of carports in existing homes. Apartments can accommodate visits from adoptive families as well as caregivers. Bedrooms open to the living room, allowing elders to continue to be part of family gatherings if confined to a bed. Bedroom window locations allow passive participation with street life, if the elder is unable to get outside.
- To respect the scale and context of the existing community. Removing a fourplex and siting the Hope Houses in its place creates an accessible central green – the primary organizing element around which the existing intergenerational center, Hope Houses, and community hall are arranged. The architecture respects the size, scale, and materiality of the existing intergenerational center, duplexes and fourplexes. Carports in existing homes act as porches and facilitate much of the informal interaction between seniors, families, and children. These, in turn, lent cues in the sizing and proportion of the Hope House porches, the community hall porch, and the connectors between the Hope House and the existing intergenerational center.

Left: Artist's impression of daily life at Hope Houses

Challenges: What were the most difficult challenges in designing the project?

- Ideal versus existing conditions: Other foundations wish to replicate this intergenerational community around the country, so the plan had to not only respond to the 'givens' of this community (that is, the existing locations of housing, playground, picnic shelter, and intergenerational center) but also be idealized enough to maximize its potential for replication on other sites. The new site plan extracts important spatial relationships from the 'ideal' and successfully implements them with the existing fabric of the intergenerational center and the picnic pavilion/play area. The relationships are kept consistent even if the orientation and location of the elements strayed from the ideal.
- Street running through community green: An existing street that bisects the central green was a challenge to the implementation of the 'ideal' site plan and the central green. Ideally, this street would be closed at each end, and the roadway dedicated to green space. Until approval is granted, the current site plan shows the existing street being raised and narrowed as it passes through the central green, slowing traffic and permitting a curbless path from the Hope Houses to the community hall.

Innovations: Does the project offer its users unique opportunities or new features not typically available in previous similar projects?

- The project team closely studied the social patterns of the intergenerational community to understand how the existing environment fostered community and to learn what types of patterns should be reinforced in the site planning and layout of the new buildings. This study informed the design team about how unit entries should be grouped, the importance of the relationship between units and the sidewalk and, in turn, how the new buildings should be sited.

- A community green existed prior to this project but was isolated and hard to access, because it was surrounded by houses backing onto it. Removing a fourplex to clear space for the Hope Houses finally opened up the green to the community. The green became the central organizing element between the existing intergenerational center and play area with the new community hall and Hope Houses.

Form shapers: What factors had the most influence on the physical form of the project?

- Bedroom location and orientation allows a bedbound senior to have visual access to the front door as well as community life through the windows. The bedroom opens fully to the living room so that even a bedbound senior can still host events with an adoptive family within his or her home.
- Hope Houses are planned with universally designed kitchens and bathrooms with cabinets that can be lowered, raised appliances, and ample reachable storage. Walls in bathrooms and elsewhere are blocked for the installation of grab bars in multiple locations.
- The community intends to wire Hope Houses for future concierge-type programs linked to caseworker, nurse, and local community meal and transportation programs, among others.

Top trends

- Responding to the site and local conditions: The design of the buildings and their layout on the site reinforce the established social patterns of the existing community. Building forms and detailing are consistent with the region. Buildings are sited to respond to local climate.
- Helping aging adults stay in their homes longer: The new unit designs allow seniors to stay in their home through to the end of their lives. Unit sizes are generous and bedrooms open directly to living rooms in order to allow adoptive families to visit and seniors to be a part of the action even if bedbound. Units are universally designed and offer features to keep kitchens and bathrooms usable and safe. The design also allows for varying levels of involvement in the activities of the community. The units offer enough space for family or caregivers to stay at the end of an elder's life.
- Offering choice through a diversity of housing options: The community's desire was to create a living environment for seniors who need additional assistance to remain a part of the intergenerational family. This sentiment drove the *parti* for the project. Hope Houses are placed at the center of the community so that elders remain the center of the adoptive families' lives, even at their most frail.

Sustainability: Does the project conserve energy, water, and other natural resources? Does it reuse existing material or buildings, or include recycled building materials? How will the project improve indoor air quality in operation?

- Site planning: Buildings are sited and oriented around local climate data to take advantage of natural daylighting and maximize winter solar exposure. Reflective or green roofs are being considered to reduce the heat-island effect.
- Indoor environmental quality: Buildings utilize low-emitting materials (for example, carpet, coatings, adhesives/sealants, and composite wood products).

Left: Climate information informs the design

- Materials and resources: The existing intergenerational center was reused; the construction management plan diverts demolition/construction waste from disposal; materials were chosen for recycled content; and materials were extracted, processed, and manufactured regionally.

Community: How does the project advance the sense of community for residents, staff, families, and neighbors?

- Seniors requiring extra care still need welcoming places for grandchildren and families to visit, share, and continue relationships that make everyone stronger. For this reason, Hope House is intentionally placed at the geographical and experiential center of the community. The new central green weaves together the relationship between Hope Houses, the intergenerational center, the community hall, and the play area to give varied opportunities and scales of formal and informal community interaction.

- Hope Houses connect directly to the intergenerational center. This promotes the continued interaction of more frail Hope elders with Hope kids through tutoring, mentorship, and informal interactions that reinforce positive relationships.

- The community hall acts as a control between the Hope community and the broader community. The location makes it easily accessible to all intergenerational community residents for community events while serving as a gateway to the larger community. The general public is invited to take part in events there, but the hall's location toward the edge of the intergenerational community buffers the intergenerational community from the added traffic that these events bring.

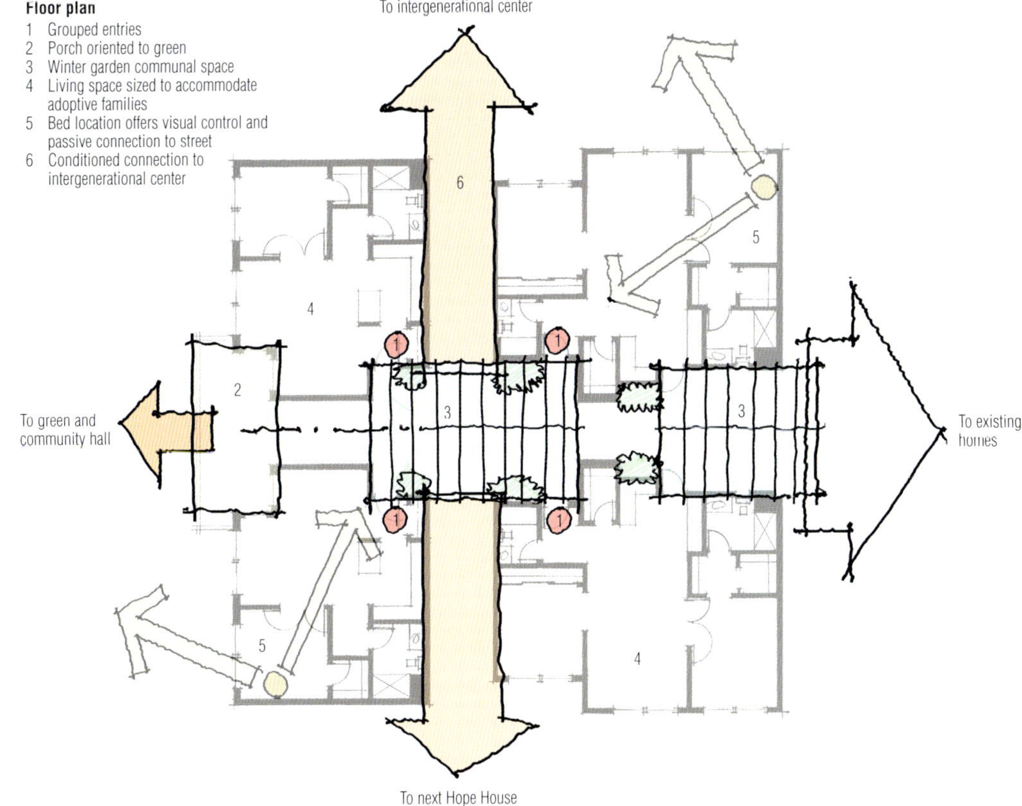

Target market: What specific features/services/amenities were incorporated into the overall project to attract your target market?

- Housing design allows seniors to age in community, keep connected with adoptive families even at their most frail, and be supported by the community and by home and community-based services.

- Upgrades to the intergenerational center make it accessible and better able to support smaller group activities (for example, tutoring, coffee, community tea, scouts, library, and so on). Direct connection between the intergenerational center and Hope Houses make it useable by seniors of all levels of mobility.

- The new community hall will host large gatherings for the intergenerational community, as well as provide a home for events hosted by the larger community. This keeps seniors engaged in the community on multiple levels.

Jury Comments

A unique, and heartwarming, senior housing concept that speaks not only of comfortable living for residents, but also the importance of self-worth for older adults continuing to contribute to their community. Definitely a win-win for seniors and vulnerable children. Sustainable features are successfully integrated.

Steinberg Architects

Taube Koret Campus for Jewish Life

Palo Alto, California // Taube Koret Campus for Jewish Life

Facility type: Independent Living, Assisted Living, Dementia/Memory Support Unit, Senior Community Center

Target market: Middle/upper middle

Site location: Urban (city or town)

Capacity: 170 Independent Living apartments; 12 Assisted Living apartments; 11 Dementia/Memory Support units

Total project cost: $107 million

Date of completion: September 2009

Green certification: LEED Silver

Below: Senior residence entrance

Overall Project Goals

The Taube Koret Campus for Jewish Life (TKCJL) is a 193-unit Continuum of Care Residential Community (CCRC) that is an integral part of a larger mixed-use, intergenerational campus filled with educational, fitness, health and wellness, cultural, and community resources. The TKCJL is a partnership between two non-profit organizations that were conceived and planned in concert with each other: the Moldaw Family Residences at 899 Charleston and the new Oshman Family Jewish Community Center. This partnership has created a multitude of opportunities for social engagement and lifelong learning. The TKCJL represents the third generation of senior housing. While the first generation sequestered its residents from the surrounding community, and the second generation emphasized lifelong learning opportunities, the TKCJL is an urban village – a residential model that provides ample opportunities for engagement with the outside environment. The community has all of the vitality of a city without the challenges that make urban living difficult for seniors, such as level changes or traffic. Residences are organized into neighborhoods that enable seniors to stay close to home or participate in activities with the residents of adjacent neighborhoods as well as the larger Palo Alto community. This project, located on a former brownfield site that was once the world headquarters of Sun Microsystems, has been designed to achieve LEED Silver certification.

Provider's Statement

Provider goals for marketing and sales

The project has been marketed as a unique, intergenerational campus where residents are offered an array of activities, from state-of-the-art fitness and wellness programs to cultural performances and educational activities. It's an enlivened village within an urban community. Sales of the units have been realized as projected, which is remarkable considering the steep downturn in the housing market.

How did the provider plan to improve the residents' quality of life?

Residents are afforded ample cultural, recreational, and wellness opportunities that increase their quality of life. The state-of-the-art recreational facility, replete with a beach-like warm-water pool that seniors can simply slide into, is often used by seniors as well as young children. Reading areas with a fireplace, the Stanford medical library, a gardening program, a cultural hall, and arts and crafts activities all give residents the quality of life they desire.

How did the provider want to improve workplace quality for employees?

Emphasis is placed on workspace design that boosts employee productivity and morale, including windows with views to the outside campus/community, as well as natural light and ergonomic furniture. The multi-generational aspect of the campus also boosts staff morale as they are engaged in more activities and with people of different ages.

Did the provider have specific goals for the project's staffing quantities, training, or distribution?

The collaboration between the Moldaw Family Residences and Oshman Jewish Community Center brings mutual benefits to the operation of the facility, among them the sharing of staff. For example, there is an overall facilities manager who manages the complex, and security guards are also shared by the partnership. The joint entity provides for a cost-effective staffing model.

Did the provider give specific direction about the style, materials, features, or other design aspects of the project? If so, what were those directives?

The design team was specifically asked to develop an architectural concept replete with symbolism. To that end, the designer came up with a medieval urban village concept that connects with the symbolism and meaning of the Jewish faith. For example, the ascent from the ground to the plaza level at a height of 14 feet mirrors the Jewish concept of *Aliyah* – ascending from the everyday life to a more spiritual existence. The color palette of the buildings resembles the colors of the seven species (*bikkurim*) brought to the Temple for the first offering: grape, wheat, pomegranate, barely, fig, olive, and honey. The textured look on the senior center exterior symbolizes experience and wisdom – or wrinkles. Use of contrasting colors is intended to assist with wayfinding. Transparent glass bridges that connect the different buildings afford seniors the option of viewing the activities on campus in comfort and security, should they elect not to participate.

How did the provider's financial goals influence the project's organization, configuration, layout, or sizing of components?

The unique partnership between two previously unrelated entities to bring about this project has aided the financial performance and operational cost of the facility. The combining of resources, for example, helped the partners to supplement each other's areas of needs, which would not have been possible if they were acting alone. Also, the sale of an unused parcel within the 12-acre site to other developers for other housing types has been helpful. Use of shared driveways, for instance, has also been cost-effective with respect to operational maintenance.

Architect's Statement

Design goals

- An intergenerational community is founded on the belief that everyone – from children to adults to seniors – benefits from the opportunity to interact with a diverse group of people of all ages on a daily basis. The TKCJL is designed to maximize opportunities for both casual and planned interactions, from

Site plan
OFJCC adult
OFJCC administration
OFJCC afterschool care
OFJCC cultural hall
OFJCC sports and recreation facility
OFJCC prechool
OFJCC café/retail
OFJCC teen center
OFJCC community organizations
MFR common areas
MFR residential units
Service
Altair townhouses
Bridge senior housing

organized activities to family events to casual strolls through the town square. Each of the eight houses is a unique community, oriented toward one of the outdoor rooms, offering seniors the option to live in a very active space with a strong focus on youth, fitness, or cultural activities. Other rooms that overlook internal program spaces have less interaction with people from outside the senior living community.

- By sharing resources, both the Jewish Home and the Jewish Community Center (JCC) have been able to offer a much broader range of resources than either could have provided on their own. While a stand-alone senior living community might have 5,000 square feet of space for fitness activities, residents of the TKCJL will have a 50,000-square-foot facility located with direct access from the senior residences. Smaller activity centers are located both horizontally and vertically within each neighborhood. The senior community also includes several large activity centers that are shared among the eight houses, as well as the much larger public facilities on the TKCJL campus that are open to all senior residents and the diverse Palo Alto community at large.
- The community is designed to offer a wide range of options for seniors to maintain their independence, and to achieve a balance between maintaining their privacy and staying connected to the larger community. They have the choice of using health and wellness facilities within their own neighborhood, or using one of the shared activity centers, which enable them to get to know residents of other neighborhoods. They also have access to the much larger public facilities of the JCC, where they can participate in fitness, educational, and community programs.

Above: Town square

Challenges: What were the most difficult challenges in designing the project?

- As the program developed, the senior housing component grew from a planned 80,000-square-foot stand-alone Assisted Living facility into a 240,000-square-foot CCRC. This challenge was embraced by seamlessly integrating facilities both horizontally and vertically in order to create a village-like scale. The vertical stacking also helps define a series of outdoor rooms that encourage socialization. These outdoor rooms include the town square, the Midrachov (walk street), a cultural courtyard, a children's courtyard, and senior housing courtyards uniquely designed to accommodate the visual and movement sensitivities of the elderly.
- Because the TKCJL was built on a brownfield site, the entire community had to be elevated on a 14-foot platform. This feature was used to the community's advantage by locating all parking at grade and creating a plaza at 14 feet. The plaza is a car-free community, with modern architecture superimposed over a plan with the characteristics of a medieval city. The result is a series of meandering, asymmetric walking streets where one can move through outdoor rooms underneath bridges or through portals to another outdoor room experience.
- When the Jewish Home and the JCC began their partnership, their first instinct was to create distinct, segregated areas of activity – community center and residential. The architects worked with both partners to

demonstrate the benefits of interconnecting horizontally and vertically through the sharing of cultural, food, service, and maintenance facilities. By teaming together, they have created shared opportunities that neither partner could have created on their own. This relationship has had broad benefits for senior housing residents, JCC members, and the Palo Alto community.

Innovations: Does the project offer its users unique opportunities or new features not typically available in previous similar projects?

- By linking the Jewish Home and the JCC, synergies were created that resulted in a sum greater than its parts. Health and wellness, education, fitness, and cultural amenities are shared by residents, JCC members, and the general public, making it economically viable to create larger, more fully featured facilities. The TKCJL will be a hub not only for residents and members of the JCC, but throughout Palo Alto and nearby cities.

- The TKCJL represents the third generation of senior housing. While the first generation sequestered its residents from the surrounding community, and the second generation emphasized lifelong learning opportunities, the TKCJL is an urban village – a residential model that provides ample opportunities for engagement with the outside environment. The community has all the vitality of a city without the challenges that make urban living difficult for seniors, such as level changes or traffic. Residences are organized into neighborhoods that enable seniors to stay close to home or participate in activities with the residents of adjacent neighborhoods as well as the larger Palo Alto community.

Form shapers: What factors had the most influence on the physical form of the project?

- The TKCJL includes a broad range of unit types, depending on the senior resident's ability to continue living independently. All units feature sliding doors that are easier for seniors to operate and triangulated mirrors in the bathroom, with special lighting adapted to seniors' visual capabilities. Other suites provide living space for live-in home healthcare workers who can provide 24-hour support while enabling senior residents to maintain their privacy.

- When seniors feel connected, they often remain active, engaged, and independent. The site plan is divided into a series of eight outdoor rooms of different scales and varying landscapes that encourage a variety of programmed and unprogrammed interactions. Residents walk from outdoor room to outdoor room beneath a transparent glass bridge. Each outdoor room has its own unique personality with varying size, scale, and atmosphere.

- The TKCJL community has a rich mix of programming that appeals to a broad intergenerational audience, including educational, fitness, retail, cultural, residential, and wellness uses, offering a plethora of opportunities for interaction, including volunteering, lifelong learning, and organized fitness activities.

Top trends

- Partnering with senior-friendly non-providers: Since this CCRC Facility is fully integrated into a mixed-use development that is anchored by the Jewish Community Center, its residents can receive a broad array of services from senior-friendly non-providers, including a store that sells Judaica and the Stanford Medical Center Health Clinic. The community also includes other retail outlets and restaurants. Multiple dining options include the main dining room, coffee shop, restaurant, and dairy and meat catering kitchens for residents who keep kosher.

- Integrating with the surrounding community: The TKCJL is not a fortress where seniors live behind concrete walls, but an integral part of the Palo Alto community. Many of the JCC's programs are open to the public, including cultural programs, lectures, and health and wellness facilities. In addition, the TKCJL has partnered with local arts and cultural organizations to create further opportunities to share resources. For example, the Palo Alto Chamber Orchestra has made an agreement to use the Cultural Hall three times a year for free. In return, they will play a free concert once a month in one of the outdoor squares. On Shabbat, when the soccer fields and basketball courts are not in use, the City of Palo Alto will use them for local amateur matches.

- Offering choice through a diversity of housing options: In addition to the 8-acre TKCJL, the original master plan includes an adjacent 4-acre site that includes market-rate family housing and very-low-income senior housing. These housing developments share driveways, access plazas and recreation, and cultural resources with the TKCJL, providing further diversity within the TKCJL community.

Opposite: Cultural hall

991

Sustainability: Does the project conserve energy, water, and other natural resources? Does it reuse existing material or buildings, or include recycled building materials? How will the project improve indoor air quality in operation?

- The brownfield site was redeveloped with the implementation of soil remediation and engineered control systems.
- Natural daylight and views are provided for all living spaces and over 90 percent of the regularly occupied non-residential spaces.
- More than 70 percent of demolition and construction debris will be recycled.

Community: How does the project advance the sense of community for residents, staff, families, and neighbors?

- Each of the eight outdoor rooms has a unique identity that encourages residents to participate in their own community. The town square offers easy access to restaurants, fitness facilities, preschool, administrative offices, and afterschool activities. The cultural courtyard hosts indoor and outdoor social and cultural events for campus and off-campus users. The children's courtyard houses preschool and afterschool activities. Several large common facilities are shared between the eight houses. This encourages residents to socialize with residents who live in nearby houses within the TKCJL.
- Since this CCRC facility is fully integrated into a mixed-use development that is anchored by the JCC, its residents can receive a broad array of services, including a store that sells Judaica and the Stanford Medical Center Health Clinic. The community also includes other retail outlets and restaurants.
- The buildings that make up the TKCJL community were designed in a similar architectural style, but each has unique architectural features that reflect its primary use. The fitness center has an exposed frame, a metaphor for 'skin and bones.' The children's c'enter has a panelized building system with bolts and connectors on its exterior, symbolizing the building blocks used by children and the notion of building for the future. The senior center has a textured look on its exterior, an evocation of experience and wisdom. The cultural hall is covered in glazed tiles – befitting a community where unique individuals have come together to form a vibrant mosaic.

Target market: What specific features/services/amenities were incorporated into the overall project to attract your target market?

- The TKCJL was designed to have broad appeal to the Bay Area Jewish community, enabling residents to live in a community with other Jewish seniors without sequestering them from society. The social, cultural, and fitness activities offered by the JCC have a Jewish cultural focus, but also appeal to the large percentage of JCC members who are not Jewish. Kosher dining is available in the CCRC. Typically, 40 percent of the membership of a JCC is non-Jewish.
- The TKCJL has partnered with community institutions to create highly effective services targeted to the senior population. For example, the adjacent Stanford Medical Center Health Clinic has established a satellite healthcare facility on campus. This world-renowned facility encourages residents to take advantage of opportunities for preventative care and also gives them access to state-of-the-art care for more serious conditions, as well as best practices and research in gerontology.
- TKCJL promises to be a catalyst for the redevelopment of an aging industrial district within the City of Palo Alto, an upscale community adjacent to Stanford University and Google's world headquarters. Sustainable design is an integral element of this urban village, which is located on a former brownfield site. Extensive studies of solar orientation to maximize natural sunlight were conducted to reduce the use of artificial lighting. Natural ventilation flows freely within interior spaces and common area terraces, minimizing energy use. The project is designed to receive LEED Silver certification.

Jury Comments

A very engaging concept and initial image that demonstrates the interrelated strengths of combining intergenerational facilities by including a CCRC in a mixed use development with cultural programs and childcare. The architecture is contemporary, but produces interesting and intimate spaces consistent with pedestrian-scale village streets. The project embraces the best attributes of urban streetscapes, namely the visibility and vitality of community activities shared by people of all ages. The project represents an important and emerging trend of avoiding isolation or creating 'islands' for seniors, while offering an environment with fewer physical barriers while still maintaining a sense of security.

Opposite top left: View of cultural hall, looking towards the mountains
Opposite top right: Staircase to JCC and senior residences
Opposite bottom: South courtyard

JSA Inc

The Ridge and Boulders of RiverWoods at Exeter

Exeter, New Hampshire // Exeter, New Hampshire

Facility type: Independent Living, Assisted Living, Skilled Nursing, Dementia/Memory Support Unit, Wellness/Fitness Center, Senior Community Center

Target market: Mixed income

Site location: Rural

Capacity: 192 Independent Living units, 51 Assisted Living apartments, 31 Skilled Nursing beds, 8 Memory Support beds

Total project cost: $48 million

Date of completion: February 2010

Below: The Boulders arrival court
Opposite: The Ridge arrival courtyard

Overall Project Goals

In 2001, RiverWoods, then a well-established Continuing Care Retirement Community (CCRC) consisting only of The Woods, began to explore the potential for expansion for aging in place, changing demographics, and the increasing needs of residents. This expansion would attract younger, more active residents desiring larger units, thus adding vitality and financial sustainability to an already successful community, securing its position as the preeminent CCRC in the area. Expansion options were limited to adjacent parcels separated by a secondary rural road. Using the natural break between the parcels, the resulting master plan outlined the opportunity for two new additional communities with distinct identities. Designing the project as three separate small-scale CCRCs was a departure from the traditional design approach for similar projects. The unit sizes, configurations, programs, and identity of Phase 2 – Ridge and Phase 3 – Boulders at RiverWoods provide the diversity of living environments necessary for an active community-centered lifestyle in which a stimulating environment encourages personal growth, an accepting and responsible community that participates in the life of the larger community around it, and a forward-looking community dedicated to remaining at the forefront of excellence in senior living.

Provider's Statement

Provider goals for marketing and sales

Marketing for The Ridge and The Boulders has been aided by the design of the buildings. Their unique qualities of being large (part of the overall RiverWoods complex) yet small (100 or less Independent Living units) add to the home-like feel. The Ridge achieved a presales figure of 84 percent when it opened in October 2004 and the community filled to 75 percent within the first four months. In less than 12 months 95 percent stabilized occupancy was achieved. The Boulders is currently 87 percent presold with an opening anticipated for March 2010. These sales and occupancy figures far exceeded the requirements of the financing documents and projections. Sales were achieved through a combination of direct mail, advertising, informational events, and word of mouth.

How did the provider plan to improve the residents' quality of life?

Many features add to residents' quality of life – the beautiful grounds, the open and light apartments, the many common rooms that encourage activity, and the dining venues that allow for more formal and casual get-togethers.

How did the provider want to improve workplace quality for employees?

Employees have the opportunity to work in an environment that offers a fully equipped fitness room, a clean and attractive workplace, and freshly cooked meals in a well-equipped employee lounge. Staff members have the opportunity to connect with their 'neighborhood' while still enjoying the advantages of working in a larger organization, providing benefits and opportunity for growth among staff.

Did the provider have specific goals for the project's staffing quantities, training, or distribution?

Staffing quantities for The Ridge have been right on the projected numbers. Staffing quantities for The Boulders are projected based on Ridge staffing. The smaller size of the communities allows for personal service from a reasonable-size staff – with most overhead and department director positions continuing to be filled by existing staff. The Ridge and The Boulders allow the provider to offer development and growth opportunities to our existing staff from the original campus. With the opening of The Ridge three of the six manager positions were filled by internal growth and the same is anticipated with The Boulders.

Single and duplex cottages provide transitional scale for neighbours
Abutting single-family subdivision
Emergency egress road, planning board requirement
50 FOOT WIDE
NO DISTURBANCE BUFFER
AT EXEMPLARY WETLANDS
Underwater storm-water gallery
Individual parking garages
WETLAND
EXEMPLARY
WETLAND
The Boulders
The Ridge
50' WIDE
PEDESTRIAN ACCESS
EASEMENT
50' WIDE EASEMENT
TO PORTLAND
NATURAL GAS CO.
CONSERVATION
EASEMENT
BOUNDARY
Underwater storm-water gallery
Public parking for scenic trail
MAINT
RED OAK DRIVE
WHITE OAK DRIVE
JOLLY RAND TRAIL
BLACKFORD DRIVE
BLACKFORD CONNECTOR
0
100ft
Site plan

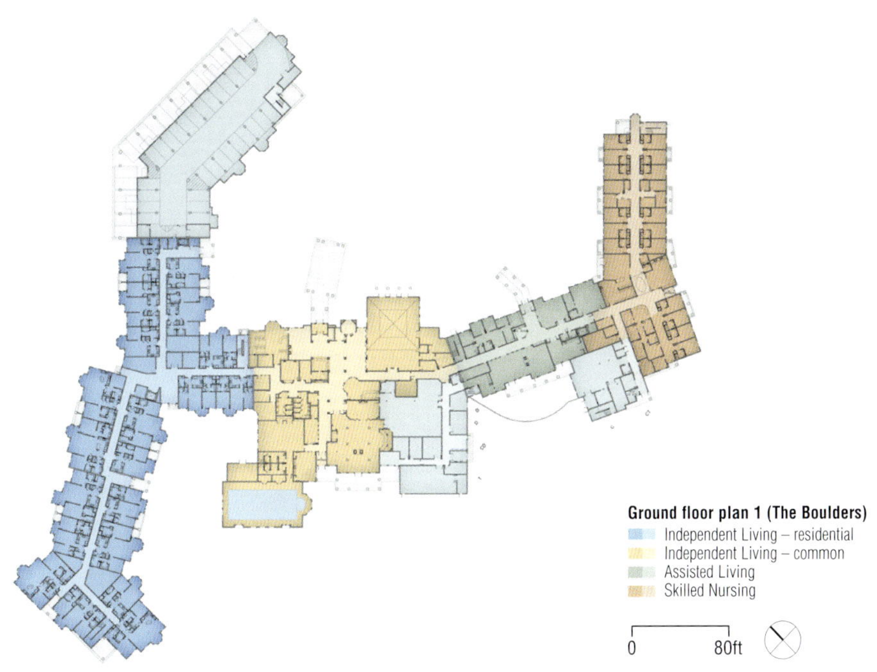

Did the provider give specific direction about the style, materials, features, or other design aspects of the project? If so, what were those directives?

General input was provided to the project designer to maintain the 'New England' sense of style, to make the project as efficient as possible from an energy standpoint, to make common space multipurpose, and to create as much 'fresh air' space as possible in The Boulders. Additionally, the designer attended multiple resident charette meetings where residents from the existing campuses weighed in with their input on the buildings (from comfort, environmental, and efficiency standpoints) and implemented those suggestions in their designs.

How did the provider's financial goals influence the project's organization, configuration, layout, or sizing of components?

The Ridge has improved, and the Boulders will improve, the financial performance of the RiverWoods Company as a whole. By adding cottages to the mix of units available, and weighting the overall apartment mix toward larger units, the project is able to improve the operating margin for the organization, improve the cash and investment balances and liquidity ratios, and lower the required monthly service fee increase for existing residents. These goals were achieved because the community was staged in such a way that there was no need to add expensive overhead positions as the facility grew, and the complement of apartments in the newer 'neighborhoods' of Ridge and Boulders are weighted toward larger and higher-margin apartments.

Architect's Statement

Design goals

- To create a supportive community environment providing amenities and services that promote wellness, independence, and security while providing appropriate healthcare to residents.

- To foster an accepting and responsible community that participates in the life of the larger community around it.
- To design a secure community where quality of service is carefully monitored and long-term financial strength is ensured.

Challenges: What were the most difficult challenges in designing the project?

- The expansion site, while located in proximity to The Woods (Phase 1), was also surrounded by very vocal opposing abutters. The opponents feared that a site egress connector mandated by the Planning Board would adversely affect their way of life. The site design accommodated this challenge by negotiating with the Town to accept a narrow, winding connection to the existing neighborhood. This narrowed connection gives the appearance of a residential driveway rather than a connecting road. This passive form of traffic control was acceptable to all parties and reinforces the rural-residential character of the neighborhood. Also, as a buffer, cottages were arranged as a partial subdivision to act as a transition to the neighbors.
- The existing topography on the 115-acre parcel for Phases 2 and 3 (The Ridge and The Boulders) contained over 50 acres of wetlands and buffers. The site and building design for both projects respect the wetland setback line in all cases, only traversing the wetlands with access roads. The meandering nature of the building design is completely consistent with the nature of the land.
- The Ridge residents were invited to take part in the planning and programming of the subsequent phase, The Boulders. This involvement presented a number of challenges regarding access, identity, and amenities. The resulting design of The Boulders responds in a way that complements the design of The Ridge. Each building includes amenities not found in the other, creating an opportunity for residents to 'visit one another' to see and experience something new.

Opposite top: The Ridge dining courtyard
Opposite bottom: The Ridge Independent Living

Innovations: Does the project offer its users unique opportunities or new features not typically available in previous similar projects?

- The wooded site has many protected wetlands. As previously mentioned, these wetlands play a pivotal role in shaping the organization of the project, but also provide a wonderful natural amenity that benefits the residents. Walking trails take residents from a paved perimeter to woodland trails and back. More adventurous residents will take an alternate detour off-site to a nearby municipal dam and waterfalls.
- The namesake of Phase 3 was literally the most prominent existing feature of the site. This site was blessed with boulders of all shapes and sizes, some as large as a single-story house. The residents themselves were instrumental in selecting the name 'The Boulders'.
- While the phasing of the The Ridge and The Boulders is largely a byproduct of a well-conceived development plan, the opportunity to create three distinct communities reflecting different generations and sensibilities; the reduction in scale; and the ability to responsibly 'shoe horn' a rather large project into a tight and environmentally sensitive site to the satisfaction of scrutinizing abutters, a discerning town, and future residents all result from the unique opportunities offered by the site.

Form shapers: What factors had the most influence on the physical form of the project?

- A Technology Coordinator was engaged to coordinate all low-voltage wiring and systems including WanderGuard, cable, computer, emergency call, and telephone. This will afford all three communities better internal and external communications. Future healthcare and diagnostic technologies as well as an ever-increasing demand for computer use and connectivity to the resident via laptop and handheld devices were given careful consideration.
- All units including kitchens and bathrooms at The Ridge and The Boulders are fully adaptable. While the fully accessible Independent Living units meet all local and national requirements, additional units have been customized or personalized by the owners to meet their specific or anticipated special needs. Convenient and out-of-the-way electric cart parking has been provided for major public spaces including the dining and multipurpose areas. A shuttle service is provided around the clock between each of the communities, to downtown Exeter, shopping, entertainment, restaurants and religious services.
- Unlike most large-scale CCRCs, in each of the individual communities there is a full spectrum of services and continuum of care. If a resident of The Ridge or The Boulders for instance requires Assisted Living or Skilled Nursing, they do not have to move to another location. Rather, they can stay within the familiar setting of their own community, close to spouses, relatives, and friends while receiving the specialized services they may require with minimal lifestyle compromise.

Top trends

- Responding to the site and local conditions: The organization, phasing, and overall development of the entire RiverWoods campus was dictated by the site, wetlands, abutters, and local market conditions.
- Offering choice through a diversity of housing

options: The RiverWoods communities offer three distinct identities responding directly to cultural and generational lifestyle preferences. Moreover, unit personalization options allow residents to tailor their homes to their specific needs and choices.

- Addressing a holistic sense of wellness: The Ridge and The Boulders represent a consistent progression towards a holistic commitment to wellness and fitness. Both communities feature pools, elaborate fitness and therapy facilities, walking trails, and a medical clinic.

Sustainability: Does the project conserve energy, water, and other natural resources? Does it reuse existing material or buildings, or include recycled building materials? How will the project improve indoor air quality in operation?

- Limiting sprawl/designing to context: Underground parking and three smaller communities allow RiverWoods to integrate well with the scale of its two- and three-story residential neighbors. Coverage (7 percent) is well below the zoning allowance.
- Storm-water management: Underground rainwater collection/filtration chambers capture, manage, and cool rainwater runoff prior to release. Cooler temperatures have a beneficial impact on wetland plants and wildlife near the two facilities.
- Energy: Solar heating for the pool; enhanced R values for walls and attics; central energy recovery units; occupancy sensors for lights; individualized control for heating/cooling; and dual-flush toilets all combine for a high level of sustainability.

Right top, middle and bottom: The Ridge and Boulders cottages
Opposite top: The Boulders independent living commons
Opposite bottom: The Boulders typical three-storey independent living

Community: How does the project advance the sense of community for residents, staff, families, and neighbors?

- Paved walking paths are provided that encompass the entire perimeter of each building, providing a variety of distances for exercise opportunities. Beyond the physical connectivity, each community is linked by RiverWoods' own fiber optic CATV station, which serves as a central information source for all residents.
- As part of their charitable mission, RiverWoods hosts an annual Gala Event for local non-profits (chosen from applications submitted from the community). This event is a highlight for the residents as it showcases their contributions to the community at large. Residents take great pride in offering their artistic creations (woodworking, pottery, and painting) in the silent auction that benefits the selected charity.
- Each of the three communities contained within the overall campus offers unique identities and programs. For instance, the bakery at The Ridge offers an attraction that The Woods does not have, offering an incentive to residents to travel between the communities and sample the unique amenities that each has to offer.

Target market: What specific features/services/amenities were incorporated into the overall project to attract your target market?

- Although The Boulders is a new phase for the RiverWoods community, the marketing effort takes full advantage of almost 20 years of success, often with current residents acting as unofficial marketers. Residents Ron and Ellie Bernasconi, when asked what they liked best

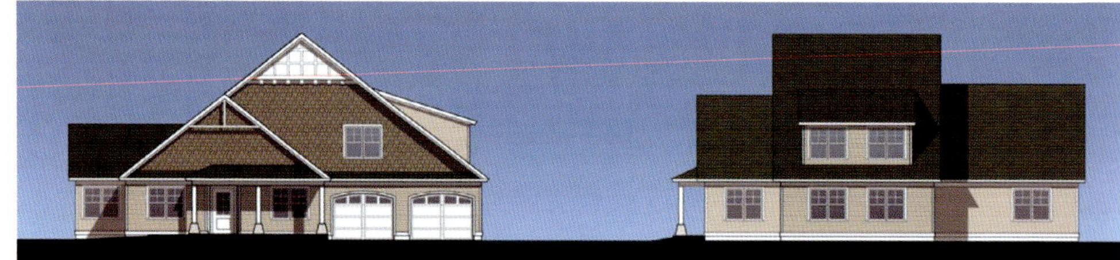

about the community, responded, 'The people. There's a widespread mix of personality and talent and everyone is so willing to share their time with others.' In addition, the RiverWoods board members have become natural recruiters with Ivy League educators and connections to universities and prep schools.

- The marketing also targets people wanting a more intimate environment with a strong connection to the local community. Resident Thomas Adams reflected on the level of community involvement and support, 'We have contributed in major ways to the New Outlook Teen Center and Seacoast Hospice by hosting fund-raising events. We do volunteer work through outreach programs. We use our skills to create fine furniture and works of art in paint and fabric and clay for auctions for non-profit organizations. We improve walking trails; and we help clear fallen trees and invasive plants from the Exeter River.'
- This community aggressively markets to affluent out-of-state retirees, focusing on the fact that retiring in New Hampshire offers distinct financial advantages over other states. New Hampshire has no general sales tax, no personal income tax, and no capital gains tax. The top-ranked New England state with the lowest tax burden, New Hampshire is also number 6 in the United States in terms of the lowest taxes.

Jury Comments

The concept of three campuses in immediate proximity to each other represents an interesting CCRC model that allows for consumer choice between three separately identified and vibrant campuses, without the feel of a mega 500-unit CCRC. The approach will still permit the provider to integrate and share services.

This is a handsome project based on carefully proportioned buildings using the regional vernacular. Even with a 35-foot height limitation, the buildings show attention to a variety of images and façade treatments. The interior design is equally appealing and interesting.

The smaller campus size is sensitive to the integration of each CCRC into the unique context of the surrounding site and community. Sustainable components include underground parking, cooling and filtering of rainwater to protect the surrounding wetlands, and a solar heated pool.

Lawrence Group

Villa at San Luis Rey

Oceanside, California // Senior Partners West LLC

Facility type: Independent Living, Assisted Living, Skilled Nursing, Dementia/Memory Support Unit, Wellness/Fitness Center, Senior Community Center

Target market: Middle/upper middle

Site location: Urban (city or town)

Capacity: 180 Assisted Living apartments, 40 Skilled Nursing apartments, 12 Dementia/Memory Support apartments

Total project cost: $48 million

Date of completion: 2011

Green certification: The project is being designed according to LEED Gold standards

Below: The CCRC (foreground) matches the architectural style of the historic Spanish Mission (upper right)

Opposite: Public spaces face the many courtyards: this plaza faces an historic lavanderia

Overall Project Goals

The project will help realize one of the Mission's priorities: to support the older demographic of the population and provide a stabilized income source to maintain the Mission. The historic nature of the setting and its relationship to the Mission provides a unique market opportunity for a senior-living community. The City and the Mission required that the site and community design be congruent and in harmony with the Mission's past and future. The Mission also requested that the building and site be as ecologically balanced as possible. A commitment was made to create one of the greenest senior-living communities in the country. A significant departure from traditional construction was investigated and the structural skeleton will be recycled steel shipping containers. There are 242 one-, two- and three-bedroom apartments with concierge services, a fitness center/therapy spa, an outdoor pool, multiple dining venues, gardens, and a salon. These units will all be licensed as Assisted Living in order to provide a full range of aging-in-place services to the residents as required, keeping them independent for as long as possible. A special five-unit suite has been designated for the friars and has Alzheimer's/Dementia Care units as part of the healthcare area with some units designed to convert in the future to a Skilled Nursing facility. Socialization of residents and integration into the Mission community are key program goals.

Provider's Statement

Provider goals for marketing and sales

Because the Villa is a rental-based model, significant marketing will not occur until closer to opening. However, because of the connection to Mission San Luis Rey and the enormous support it has in the community, an affinity market has already developed. Over 100 prospects are on a priority reservation list, far exceeding expectations because little marketing has been carried out to date.

How did the provider plan to improve the residents' quality of life?

One of the most distinguishing factors, which will contribute to the quality of life of many of the residents, is that the Villa is on the grounds of the Mission with its rich heritage and ongoing activities. This is the Villa's greatest asset as it will not only provide residents with rich opportunities, but also encourage family and friends to visit and belong. Whether Catholic or not, the Villa's residents will be enriched by the wealth of experiences available at the Mission.

Additionally, the project team has worked together around the country in four-season climates and immediately recognized the opportunity to use the outdoors year-round for quality living, social, and recreational spaces. Significant effort has been made to enhance this feature of the community to the benefit of the residents. The common and outdoor areas add to the residents' quality of life, as do the programs and events that foster

Site Plan

wellness, independence and social, religious, physical and emotional well-being.

The residents will feel secure that the structural elements of the recycled shipping container structure will protect them in the case of an earthquake. However, there will be no outward evidence of this 'steel womb' structure from inside the units, which are welded together in a remarkable way that will be extremely safe. Within this structure, resident apartments are well designed with warm and attractive finishes, fully equipped kitchens, senior-friendly bathrooms with grab bars and step-in showers, and ample closet space. Residents have the security of an emergency-response system, which provides immediate assistance in case of an emergency.

How did the provider want to improve workplace quality for employees?

The atmosphere of the Villa with its historic and tranquil Mission setting also sets the tone for the workplace environment. The high-quality equipment in all work areas including the kitchen, housekeeping, and maintenance enables staff to be productive and efficient. The POS, emergency response, telephone, and computer systems all facilitate service delivery. Employees have attractive benefits and competitive salaries. The management staff understands the importance of recognizing employees for the work they do, as well as assisting them through training and opportunities for advancement.

Did the provider have specific goals for the project's staffing quantities, training, or distribution?

The provider and management have extensive experience in establishing staffing schedules and in recruiting and hiring quality employees to its senior communities. The provider is committed to creating a positive work environment and to the on-going training of its employees.

The building and its systems facilitate excellent service delivery assisting employees to not only meet their job requirements, but to experience job satisfaction.

Did the provider give specific direction about the style, materials, features, or other design aspects of the project? If so, what were those directives?

It was specified that the design must be in harmony with the Mission's historic heritage as well as green and operationally effective for seniors and staff. The proposed architectural theme for the project will emulate a California Mission Revival style in accordance with the guidelines. The project incorporates various design elements that are in harmony with the existing Mission buildings. Common elements of the Mission-style architecture include buttresses, large patios, low-pitched tile roofs, arcaded corridors, arches, curved gables and a tower element. Vast open interior courtyards provide open space and building articulation, which breaks up the east- and west-facing façades. Other intricate articulations, such as a tower element, a pediment with a San Luis Rey profile, balconies, arcaded wing walls, and wood fascia are incorporated to provide interesting visual elements.

The Villa and its campus will be 'green,' starting with the structure of the building being completed out of recycled shipping containers and moving outward to include many LEED-recognized qualities, from insulation and lighting, to water recycling and landscape features. The entire Mission campus is set to be an eco study lab and the Villa will be part of that effort.

The program design accounts for an effective and friendly layout of units, commons areas, outdoor areas, and service areas. They will meet ease-of-use and directional-orientation standards and be effective for staff and senior utilization.

How did the provider's financial goals influence the project's organization, configuration, layout, or sizing of components?

From a market perspective, it was important to embrace four provider initiatives. The first was capturing and showing reverence for the historic nature of the Mission site, which provides a unique market setting for a senior-living community and assists both initial and long-term occupancy goals. Secondly, the project will financially support the Mission through a long-term ground lease, thus helping it to remain a vital and vibrant entity, which further supports the project. The third objective from a market perspective was to provide a diversity of spaces, indoors and out, that would provide for a more demanding senior population in the future. This translated into additional unique and multiple dining venues; activity, social, and recreational areas; gardens; and so forth. Finally, the project was to be very green, which meets the criteria of the provider and is something that is fast becoming essential in the consumer world, including the senior-living sector. All four initiatives are important to the market performance and occupancy stabilization and thus the financial performance of the project.

From an operational perspective, the facility provides staffing efficiencies in several areas including food service and production areas. Additionally, energy-efficient lighting and HVAC systems, capturing natural cooling with operational windows to capture prevailing ocean breezes, will reduce the consumption of power and thus lower operational costs.

Architect's Statement

Design goals

- The owner wants to develop a state-of-the-art Continuing Care Retirement Community (CCRC) that provides seniors with a high-quality and flexible aging-in-place lifestyle that embraces the traditions and historic style of Mission San Luis Rey. The building needs to fit into the historic district and not overpower the 1798 Mission on the hill.
- Because the building needed to touch the land with a light hand, green building technology has been developed and incorporated into the design. Using more than 500 recycled shipping containers for the structures makes a green statement and fits into the historic nature of the site, while simultaneously offering residents safe, yet comfortable living arrangements that meet their needs. Just as the Mission has become a centerpiece in the history of education in Southern California, this development, planned in concert with the Mission's development plans, will make this a national eco study lab for sustainability.
- Using new green building and innovative prefabrication technology to improve the construction schedule and reduce the cost of the overall project allows the construction period to be reduced by as much as 30 percent and significantly reduces general costs.

Challenges: What were the most difficult challenges in designing the project?

- Since the project site has a substantially lower elevation than the Mission, the structure was designed as a four-story building less than 50 feet in height so that it does not obstruct the views of the historic Mission. Recycled shipping containers will be used as the primary structure, which will keep the floor-to-floor height lower than conventional in a Type 2 construction and thus accommodate the design of a four-story building under the maximum allowable building height. The container skin is encased in a decorative and insulating material to match the Mission's architecture.

- The project required fill dirt to create a relatively level building pad for the proposed structural system and had to be specifically suited for senior living. The necessary fill required a retaining wall along the property's western boundary backed with carport structures. The carport structures will have a trellis with vine pockets installed behind the screen wall. Since the shipping containers have their own floor, yards of concrete were necessary, saving the project money. Imported fill was minimized and large crawl spaces will be provided under most of the buildings, to be utilized for mechanical, electrical and plumbing (MEP) and other uses.
- The project had to meet all of the goals and objectives of the City's General Plan and Zoning Ordinance, including the Historic District Overlay, and the City Mission Design Guidelines. The senior-living community is compatible with the surrounding land uses and is consistent with the senior and age-restricted communities in areas west of the project site. The project has been designed to complement the existing facilities of the site, and has been developed under the standards set by the approved Mission San Luis Rey de Francia Planned Development (PD) Plan. Significant environmental sensitivities have to be solved to meet the plan requirements.

Innovations: Does the project offer its users unique opportunities or new features not typically available in previous similar projects?

- The use of a sustainable structural system is a novel and unique aspect of the project. The challenge was to meet historic preservation requirements, market expectations, as well as become a successful senior-living community. The project team conducted massing and seismic studies. Room layouts were developed to meet quality residence standards and criteria. The Mission embraced the idea after it was presented that more campus structures for the Friars will be built from the new technology. A partially finished demonstration container was displayed at the Mission-sponsored Earth Day with great acceptance and excitement. This challenge is now a clear opportunity to move forward with making this truly an innovative project from the inside out.
- The history of the Mission and its relationship with the native people is accentuated by the Lavenderia. The challenge was to set a facility among the orchards and crops to complement the surroundings. This presented a unique opportunity to open up the primary courtyard to its history. Open pathways from the courtyard to the Lavenderia will encourage residents and visitors to partake of its beautiful masonry and stonework. The eastern border of the site is surrounded by historic prickly pear cactus covering an ancient adobe wall. The Villa grounds are framed and secured by this significant element. It creates a historic landscape feature preserved to the benefit of the project and the community as a whole.
- The project team recognized the opportunity to use the outdoors as quality living, social, and recreational spaces year-round. Significant effort has been made to enhance this feature of the community for the benefit of the residents. The courtyards each have a distinct ambiance particular to the courtyard location, level of activity or privacy, and views into the courtyard or looking out. Courtyard experiences may include activity elements such as bocce courts, a putting green, an outdoor fireplace, a spa, and outdoor eating. The courtyards feature sensory garden plants, outdoor pool, and a variety of fire and water elements for visual enhancement.

Form shapers: What factors had the most influence on the physical form of the project?

- Using California standards, the design layouts considered the variety of activity and care levels of the residents in Assisted Living communities. As the residents age in place individually, the facility has the ability to manage their continuing care. More intense care may require a short-term move to another room with a higher care level available in the same building. Several rooms have been designed for conversion to Skilled Care in the future as the population may require. Dementia care will help couples stay in proximity, even if one chooses to reside in Independent Living while the other is in Special Care. The combination of the design and licensing approach provides the management with significant ability to assist the residents.
- Many seniors, Catholic or not, who have already asked to be put on the priority reservation list have done so because of their connection, either direct or through family and friends, with the Mission and its work. There is comfort and trust associated with the long history of the Mission. The Villa helps translate that into a new home place for residents with its building, gardens, and services. The Mission brings special opportunities to make it a place with meaning, such as volunteering for the annual Oceanside Earth Day, helping to tend the rose garden, or being a guide to local school children. Situated on the grounds of the historic and vibrant Mission San Luis Rey, the Villa will be a special place to age in.
- The site is located within walking or very easy driving distance to restaurants, a bakery, a grocery store, salons, and many other commonly used services. Offsite improvements include a stoplight for ease of entry/exit, a bus stop and a bus shelter structure with sidewalk,

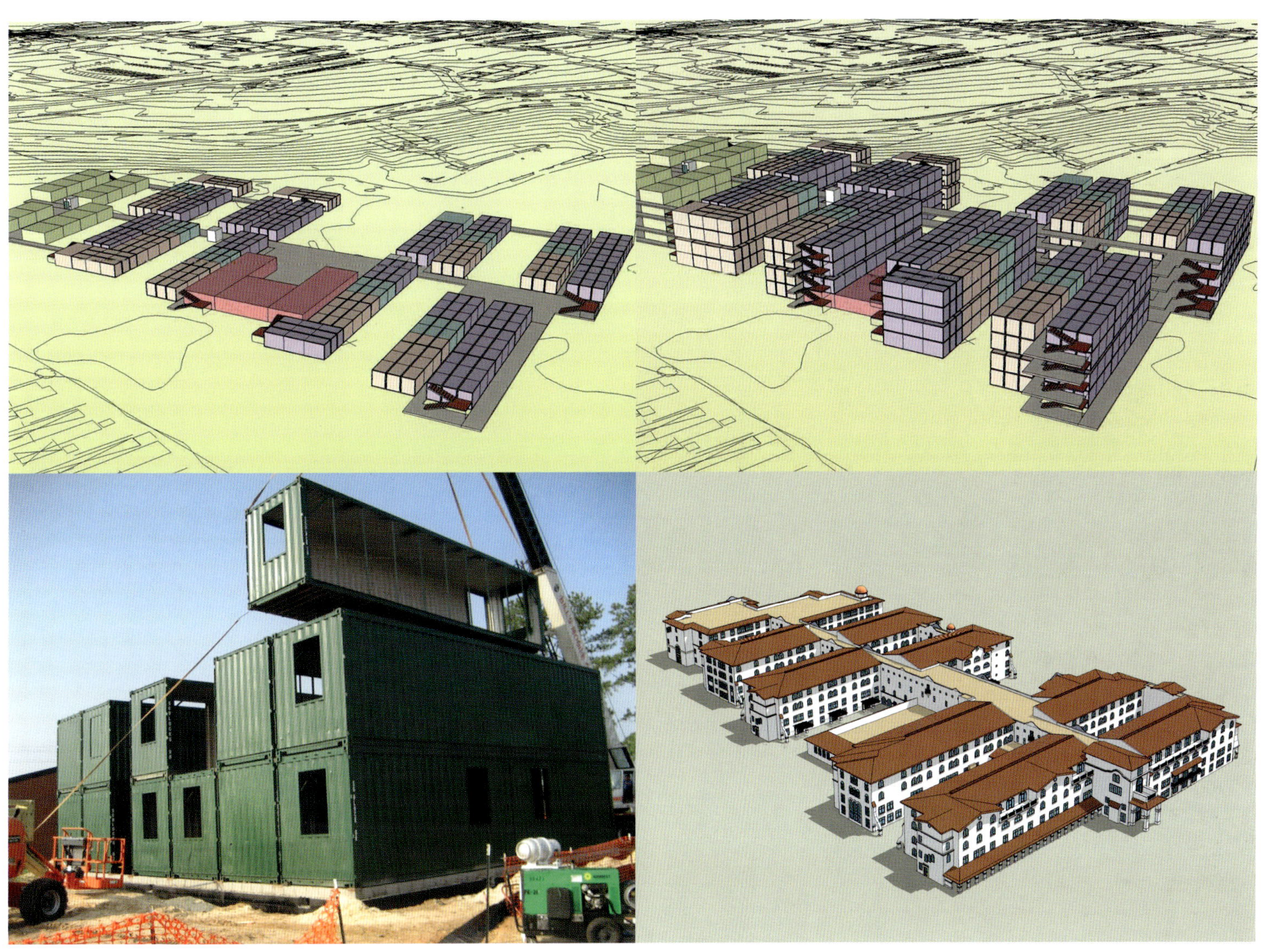

Above: Modified recycled shipping containers are the building's structural skeleton

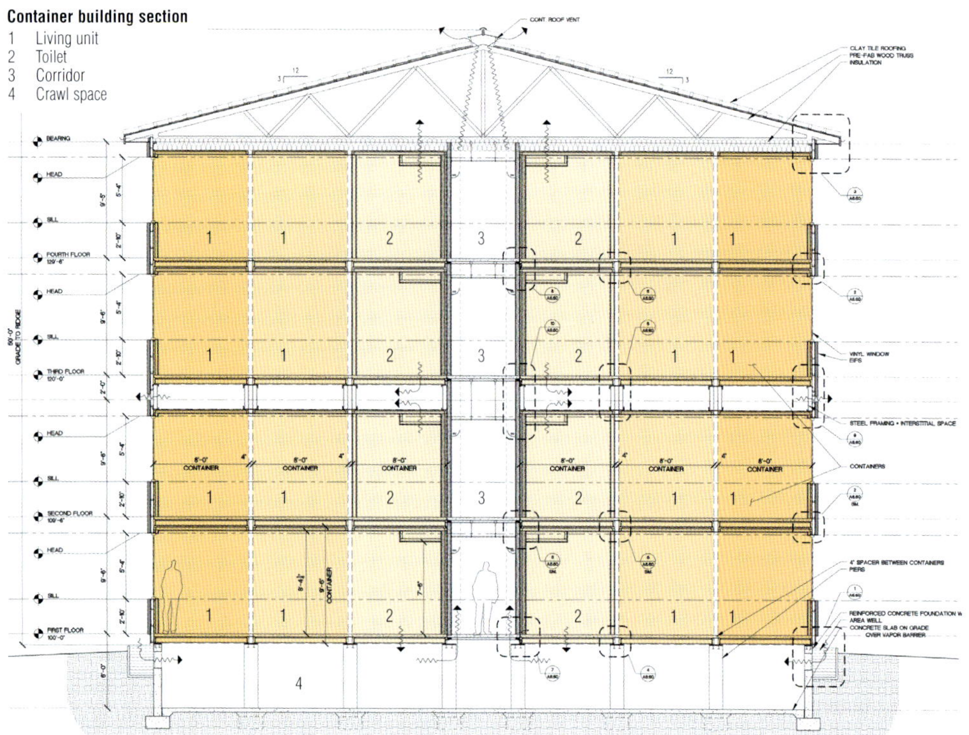

Container building section

1 Living unit
2 Toilet
3 Corridor
4 Crawl space

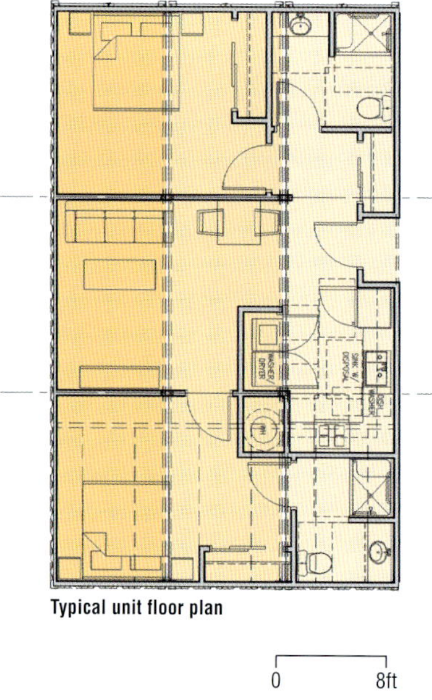

Typical unit floor plan

and street widening eastward to the Mission main entrance. Although the Villa's many services render a lot of offsite services unnecessary, the 'new' senior demands their independence and this project design and location supports those demands. For those who don't drive or are unable to walk, transportation will ensure access to offsite services to allow the senior a quality aging-in-place lifestyle.

Top trends

- Taking advantage of existing infrastructure: The project takes advantage of existing infrastructure and amenities in the surrounding neighborhood. The Mission captures not just a physical amenity, but also a psychological one. It was one of the very first significant economic, building, and religious institutions in the San Diego area. It is part of the history of California, its native tribes, and the current community of Oceanside. The entire community of Oceanside, from its streets to its businesses and infrastructure, has been influenced by the Mission. Taking advantage of this amenity and its history will provide the Villa with a unique position in the market and a special place for its residents to live.
- Addressing a holistic sense of wellness: The Villa, supported through programs, services, education, and physical plant, will provide all residents and staff with opportunities and encouragement to live a sustainable lifestyle. Senior communities have a great opportunity to become a catalyst for change because of the services and education they provide to their residents, creating a culture of sustainable and healthy living with their staff. From dining to activities, the Villa will create a program supported by a well-planned physical environment and education that will provide incentives and encouragement for both residents and staff to live life well.
- Being green/sustainable: When a modified container representing the structural system was brought to the Mission on Earth Day in 2008, it was clear that seniors understood the importance of sustainability. However, green certification does not seem to impress in the same way that something that is tangible and economically sensible does. The Villa is determined to meet the criteria of being green and leave as light a carbon footprint as possible with regard to construction and operations. A significant response to this trend

will be to utilize a sustainable structural system with the use of recycled shipping containers. They will be engineered to meet all codes and will provide strong, safe, and traditional living arrangements for the residents.

Sustainability: Does the project conserve energy, water, and other natural resources? Does it reuse existing material or buildings, or include recycled building materials? How will the project improve indoor air quality in operation?

- Over 75 percent of the facility's structural elements will be comprised of over 500 recycled shipping containers and will reduce the use of new materials substantially, thus lowering the impact on the environment through a reduced carbon output.

- High-efficiency operable windows for ventilation, an innovative water source heat pump system for energy efficient and effective climate control reduces energy consumption. Window placement enhances natural lighting, while utilizing LED.

- Low-VOC interior finishes include recycled content carpet. Rainwater is recaptured for use in a monitored irrigation system, reducing water use along with low-volume toilet design. There is also potential for a green roof and solar panels for LED lighting in the carport.

Community: How does the project advance the sense of community for residents, staff, families, and neighbors?

- The Villa's programming will be collaborating with the Mission to create senior volunteer and program support to their educational, botanical, and community outreach efforts. This Mission's 60,000 annual guests, including many schoolchildren, will provide many opportunities for interaction from residents should they choose to participate in either organized or individual efforts.

- The multitude of dining venues and resort-like gardens will enhance the number of visits from family and guests during meals and activities and provide interesting areas for entrainment for residents and the community.

- The Villa will serve as a community center that will cater to the many community groups residents have connections with that are looking for meeting and social places to gather. The beauty of the building, its courtyard gardens, and its Mission setting will make it a magnet for many small and large events.

Target market: What specific features/services/amenities were incorporated into the overall project to attract your target market?

- The target market continues to increase in age, so the facilities, programming, services, and organizations must accommodate this shift. The licensing of the facility as residential care will allow service offerings beyond that of a typical independent senior's apartment. The ability to enhance care to meet an individual's needs in their attractive and functional apartment home at any time during their residency will be an attractive market alternative.

- Full attention to utilizing the Southern California climate is a clear advantage for all markets because of the detail and planning of the outdoor amenities. Because most residents will come from within a 15-mile radius, there will be an expectation of easy access to the outdoors. For those from out of town in cold climates (there are several on the priority reservation list), the Villa will be a newfound climate, which will not been lost on them. Significant effort has been made to enhance this marketable feature of the community to the benefit of the residents with extensive outdoor courtyard amenities, programming, and landscaping.

- Because the Villa is on Mission San Luis Rey grounds, there is a special draw for Catholics. Although completely open to all, this is a niche market that naturally occurs in the Villa. The very presence of the Mission and its history and works provides not just a level of comfort but also the potential for Catholics and all other residents to volunteer and be part of something bigger.

Jury Comments

An interesting and unique concept. Kudos to the provider and designer for their truly unique, sustainable approach of using shipping containers as a building structure. Their reaching for LEED Gold illustrates how sustainability is becoming a mission statement for this provider in tangible terms. The Franciscans are caring for the environment as well as people. A sustainable strategy that is hidden from view, but speaks volumes about 'walking the talk.'

Lizard Rock Designs, LLC

Casitas on East Broadway Senior Housing

Tucson, Arizona // Casitas on East Broadway, an Arizona Non-Profit Corporation in care of Catholic Community Services of Southern Arizona, Inc. + Tucson Housing Foundation, Inc.

Facility type: Independent Senior Living

Target market: Low income/subsidized

Site location: Urban (city or town)

Capacity: 56 units

Total project cost: $5.5 million

Date of completion: August 2010

Green certification: Targeting LEED for Homes Gold certification

Below: Entrance
Opposite: Street elevation, facing south

Overall Project Goals

This Department of Housing & Urban Development (HUD) 202 project includes 56 apartments, a community meeting room, and new common areas on a site in Tucson, Arizona. Tucson Housing Foundation, Inc. and Catholic Community Services of Southern Arizona, Inc. are co-sponsors of the project. The design team assisted the non-profit corporation by applying for a HUD 202 grant, which was funded in 2006. At the request of the neighborhood, the non-profit agreed to LEED certify the building. Because of tight budget constraints, the design team made every effort to maximize sustainable design without adding cost; for example, the project received substantial LEED points for its density, use of an existing infill site, and compliance with City of Tucson low water use and native plant ordinances. The project will be one of the first HUD projects to achieve LEED certification, and although the Certified level was initially targeted, it now appears that Gold is feasible. The design is organized around four courtyards and a central parking area. Every apartment has either a corner window or a projecting bay, allowing greater connection for residents. The small courtyards also reduce the scale of the building – six apartments share each courtyard. Additionally, the central corridor opens north to allow for extensive daylighting. The project will include newly developed windows made from recycled materials, plumbing fixtures for low water use, and highly efficient mechanical units.

Provider's Statement

How did the provider plan to improve the residents' quality of life?

Every unit has a unique view and window (bay windows toward street or corner windows toward courtyards).

How did the provider want to improve workplace quality for employees?

The scale of the project is small enough to be manageable. Staff offices are easily accessible for residents.

Did the provider have specific goals for the project's staffing quantities, training, or distribution?

One unit is reserved for a 24-hour on-site manager. Offices are provided for a social worker and HUD manager.

Did the provider give specific direction about the style, materials, features, or other design aspects of the project? If so, what were those directives?

The provider stipulated that the project should integrate with the surrounding neighborhood and reflect traditional detailing and massing of regional architecture.

How did the provider's financial goals influence the project's organization, configuration, layout, or sizing of components?

Low construction cost allows for low rents. Energy efficiency keeps utility costs down.

Architect's Statement

Design goals

- The first design goal was to increase the amount of affordable housing for low-income seniors. Tucson is suffering a severe shortage of affordable senior housing, and this project will provide 56 new units. Once completed, the project will become one of several sites currently operated by Catholic Community Services of Southern Arizona, Inc. and benefit from existing supportive services provided by the agency.
- The second design goal was to demonstrate that sustainable design is achievable on a tight budget. Careful site selection contributed greatly to the green components of the design, and the owner, design team, and contractor worked together to identify affordable opportunities for sustainable design. Green design components include windows made of recycled materials, highly efficient water heaters and distribution, and landscaping for low water use. In addition, the site has been designed to minimize runoff and provide shaded outdoor courtyards.
- The third design goal was to create a project that fits well into the surrounding urban fabric. The site is in the historic Sam Hughes neighborhood of Tucson, and the building massing repeats existing block patterns (two stories at the perimeter, with a single-story

First floor plan

1 Lobby
2 Community room
3 Kitchen
4 Administrative office
5 Laundry
6 Unit type 1A
7 Unit type 1B
8 Unit type 1C
9 Unit type 1D
10 Patio
11 Stair
12 Seating alcove
13 Storage

mews building at the interior.) The site plan allows easy access to neighborhood streets for residents to walk, and the detailing of the building reflects the Territorial style architecture common to the southeastern part of Arizona.

Challenges: What were the most difficult challenges in designing the project?

- The project achieved a relatively high density on a tight infill site over two parcels with two different zoning densities. Because setbacks, access requirements, and density all impacted the form of the building, the first challenge was to achieve the massing suggested by the block structure of the neighborhood. The project respects the adjacent urban fabric while complying with the zoning – the two-story buildings face Broadway, the larger boulevard, while the single-story houses are located along the alley.

- The project's second challenge was to accommodate the City's requirements for parking and vehicle access, while respecting the neighborhood's desire to discourage shortcut traffic through neighborhood streets. This was accomplished by convincing the City to abandon an existing street that split the site, allowing the southern portion of this street to become access for the property.

- The project's third challenge was its proportions – the site is long in the east–west direction, and it was difficult to divide both the massing of the building and the interior access to break down the scale of the building. The design breaks the building into a series of shorter segments, and opens a portion of the interior corridor to the north to allow views of the gardens from the first floor and mountains from the second floor.

Innovations: Does the project offer its users unique opportunities or new features not typically available in previous similar projects?

- The plan and massing of the building are innovative in that they divide a very long building into a series of shorter, more compact buildings organized by courtyards. Each building is broken open at the center to allow natural light and views into the interior, instead of the more typical double-loaded corridor. This also allows the majority of the north-facing units to have corner windows and therefore diagonal views. The south-facing apartments along Broadway have bay windows to allow for similar diagonal views. Residents have a number of orientations and views to choose from, and every apartment has a good amount of natural light.

- The sustainable design approach of the building is innovative because of its affordability. The owner was determined to demonstrate that sustainable design need not be costly, and that smart choices during the early planning of the project can produce a good green design. The design team identified costs associated with every possible LEED point, and then worked with the owner to choose which points provided the biggest impact for the least cost.

- The apartment layout is innovative because the amount of circulation space is extremely minimal (the goal of the layout was to put as much space as possible into rooms and storage). Toilets, kitchens, and bedrooms all have built-in storage, and yet the bedroom and living room are spacious enough to be fully furnished. Toilets in the apartments are designed to maximize the clear floor area without forcing the apartment area to exceed HUD standards.

Form shapers: What factors had the most influence on the physical form of the project?

- Bedrooms and toilets are designed to be fully wheelchair accessible. In addition, the bathroom off the main bedroom has a shower and toilet in the widest area of the room to allow a home care attendant to assist a resident with bathing. This area is fully tiled and open enough to allow the care provider to assist the resident effectively.

- The rooms within each apartment are large enough to be furnished effectively, but small enough that a frail elder can manage the distances and obstructions. The kitchen is open to the main living space to allow ease of maneuvering and a central location to organize important items such as a telephone.

- This project qualifies at the top of the LEED density range, which means that it provides a larger number of units per acre than other comparable projects. Although the proportions of the site are long in the east–west direction, common amenities are located at the center, and the density of the project keeps travel distances within those manageable for an aging resident. The courtyard configuration breaks up the main corridor and provides multiple locations to enter each of the buildings. Perceived travel distances to the common spaces are less when the experience along the route changes, with views and natural light.

Top trends

- Being green/sustainable: The owner's commitment to sustainable design has greatly influenced the form of this project. The choice of an infill site, near existing infrastructure and community resources also makes this site an ideal one for seniors, because shopping, medical care, and recreational activities can be reached by walking or by bus, rather than driving. The desire to qualify for points in the Energy and Atmosphere section of LEED for Homes will produce a healthier building as a result of the elimination of materials that emit formaldehyde, wrapping of all ductwork, and a 48-hour flush of the building to eliminate construction dust. The same things that improve the performance of the building for LEED also make it a better, healthier building for seniors. Energy-saving measures such as compact distribution for ductwork and piping, high insulation values, and efficient mechanical units also save cost for the non-profit corporation that must operate the building on a limited budget. Many sustainable design goals also reinforce the goals of good design practice for the elderly.

Sustainability: Does the project conserve energy, water, and other natural resources? Does it reuse existing material or buildings, or include recycled building materials? How will the project improve indoor air quality in operation?

- The project is oriented east–west to minimize western exposures and to provide added glazing on the north face for daylighting. Shade structures and awnings will protect the south face from the sun.
- The project makes extensive use of recycled materials. Examples include recycled gypsum wallboard, cabinets made of FSC-certified cabinet board, and windows that are made of 100 percent recycled vinyl.
- The project is located in close proximity to existing community infrastructure (power, water, and sewer) and resources (parks, bus lines, hospitals). Residents will be able to access shopping, healthcare, and other needs on foot or by bus.

Community: How does the project advance the sense of community for residents, staff, families, and neighbors?

- The meeting room and lobby have been designed to provide a focal point for the building. Its central location and amenities (laundry, mail, and office functions) naturally draw groups of residents. The lobby will be furnished in a way that will encourage small conversations and social interaction, and thereby increase the sense of informal, naturally occurring communities.
- The project is organized around a set of four courtyards. For the majority of apartments, either their entry doors or corner windows open onto a courtyard, which gives a sense of belonging to a smaller community within the building-wide community. In contrast to other subsidized housing projects where hundreds of apartments open off one large courtyard, these smaller courtyards break down the scale of the project from 56 units to 6. Neighbors will be able to watch over neighbors, increasing the sense of security and safety within the community.
- The early and continued involvement of the Sam Hughes neighborhood in the design of this facility has led to a strong connection between the project and the neighborhood. The Sam Hughes Neighborhood Association plans to hold periodic meetings in the community room of this project, and there is an effort underway to obtain funds to landscape the parcel of land directly south of the site, which is owned by the City of Tucson. Neighborhood residents have been involved throughout design, they sit on the board of the housing project, and they have strongly supported the architecture and sustainable design strategies employed in the project.

Target market: What specific features/services/amenities were incorporated into the overall project to attract your target market?

- Both the owner and the neighborhood were concerned that the project have enough detail, massing relief, and quality materials to make it indiscernable as a residence for low-income seniors. The project has features not normally found in most market-rate apartments: landscaped courtyards, corner windows, corridors with natural light, and common areas that include a warming kitchen and a lobby with a fireplace.
- The location of the project was carefully chosen because of the amenities it offered seniors within walking distance of the site. There are two parks, a library, a grocery and a pharmacy within walking distance of the site. Downtown Tucson is a short bus ride away, as are two of the largest hospitals in southern Arizona. Finally, the adjacent historic neighborhood offers seniors a pleasant place to walk.

RLPS Architects

Hybrid Homes

Lititz, Pennsylvania // Landis Homes Retirement Community

Facility type: Independent Living

Target market: Middle/upper middle

Site location: Rural

Capacity (units): 75 homes

Date of completion: December 2010

Green Certification: USGBC Leadership in Energy and Environmental Design (LEED); Targeting Silver

Below: Perspective view of paired hybrid households

Overall Project Goals

The hybrid homes were designed to create a new choice in senior living, blending the benefits of patio homes and apartment living to provide an intentional community that can be tailored to special interests, educational development or economic need. To expand the range of campus housing options and continue to serve a diverse socioeconomic senior population, six hybrid homes and 59 patio homes are planned for an undeveloped parcel adjacent to the original 114-acre retirement community. The 140,000-square-foot hybrid households will accommodate up to 75 residents in a new housing concept that offers providers a higher density Independent Living model than a patio home and offers senior residents a more private, residential model than an apartment. Each hybrid home includes a private patio or balcony, multiple outdoor exposures and an open floor plan. The hybrid households will include under-building parking, hearth areas on each floor, an outdoor patio area and community room that can be shared between two households.

Provider's Statement

Provider goals for marketing and sales

The project meets the provider's goal of increasing the number of two-bedroom, two-bathroom homes with a higher density living option. The current mix of homes is heavy on studio and one-bedroom residences. In addition to responding to the market demand for larger residences, the sustainable features of the hybrid homes are also helping to generate interest. A priority program resulted in 55 members and after six weeks of sales, 20 members have reserved a home location.

How did the provider plan to improve the residents' quality of life?

The hybrid homes are designed to be accessible to residents, including those needing walkers or wheelchairs, in an appealing residence that combines the best features of apartments and cottages. Every hybrid home is essentially a corner residence providing private patios and multiple exposures.

Did the provider give specific direction about the style, materials, features, or other design aspects of the project? If so, what were those directives?

The designers were directed to provide a traditional design that coincides with the existing campus and avoids any kind of hierarchical distinctions that could contribute to an 'us versus them' mentality. Material selections focused on LEED guidelines as the provider was also most interested in stewardship of resources and making the best use of property with respect to future generations.

How did the provider's financial goals influence the project's organization, configuration, layout, or sizing of components?

Additional Independent Living homes improve operational performance as existing amenities and services can support the new homes. The new entrance fees and monthly fees improve financial performance as increases in costs relating to existing amenities and services are minimal.

Architect's Statement

Design goals

- To provide a higher density model that maintains the best features of a patio home while incorporating the advantages of apartment living, the three-story hybrid households are comprised of under-building parking on the first floor with two floors of six hybrid homes each on the floors above. The hybrid households are paired to share visitor and overflow parking and provide the option for a shared community room and a more moderately priced first-floor apartment in one of the households.
- To maximize outdoor connections, homes on each floor are positioned to function as corner units with multiple exposures for improved views and daylight connections. The patio for each hybrid home is positioned to provide privacy while a household patio area on the first floor affords opportunities for entertaining and socialization between household members.
- To reflect a community-wide commitment to sustainable design, a major focus of the design solution was achieving LEED Silver certification. From a geothermal mechanical system to recycled/regional/renewable materials, the hybrid homes are designed to provide a senior-friendly interior environment while achieving responsible stewardship and greater energy efficiency than a traditional building.

Challenges: What were the most difficult challenges in designing the project?

- The township regulatory process and selling the township on a new approach to storm-water management presented challenges. The Legacy Sediment Control Plan restores the adjacent stream to pre-development conditions and does not use conventional storm-water methods. The township was and still is very apprehensive concerning this approach.
- Designing affordable structured parking was also a major challenge. The cost of the parking garage and the associated support space such as the community room and off-season resident storage had to be absorbed into the cost of each home. The consumer, for obvious reasons, was accustomed to the cost of a traditional cottage with a one-car garage and ultimately compared the cost and perceived value of the new product before acceptance.
- The layout of each home and particularly the patio/balcony location, had to be carefully considered to provide privacy and

Site plan

1 Lobby
2 Vestibule
3 Mail room
4 Community room
5 Mechanical
6 Resident storage
7 Sprinkler/pump room
8 Patio
9 Parking
10 Bike parking
11 1 Bedroom home

0 20ft

independence while maintaining an open floor plan that offers appropriate interconnectivity of spaces allocated for living, dining, and food preparation.

Innovations: Does the project offer its users unique opportunities or new features not typically available in previous similar projects?

- By orienting the households in an L formation, each hybrid home benefits from multiple outdoor exposures and enhanced privacy, as well as a first-floor household patio/courtyard area defined by the building shape.
- Pairing hybrid households allows for shared resources such as overflow/visitor parking and a community room.
- As part of the project, the floodplain on the property will be restored through a legacy storm-water program. This involves measures to remove hundreds of years' worth of agricultural sediment that currently limits storm-water capacity and ultimately restoring campus stream channels and adjacent floodplains to historical elevations and locations to ultimately improve groundwater filtration and recharge.

Form shapers: What factors had the most influence on the physical form of the project?

- Accessibility, from door clearances to space templates, is designed into all homes. Kitchens and bathrooms are able to accommodate active residents, those who require assistance from a spouse or caregiver, and those who utilize wheelchairs or scooters to maintain independent mobility. The facilities are designed to allow equal access for all users without compromising the residential appearance.
- Residents can be monitored remotely and 'check in' with staff via wireless nurse call features without interrupting their daily routines.
- Discreetly supportive features such as shower grab rails, pocket doors, elevated commodes and vanities, and wheelchair-accessible doorways and bathrooms facilitate aging in place thereby enabling residents to maintain independence, control, and ultimately, a sense of well-being.

Top trends

- Helping aging adults stay in their homes longer: The facilities are designed to allow equal access to all users without losing the residential appearance. Discreetly supportive features such as shower grab rails, pocket doors, elevated commodes and vanities, and wheelchair accessible doorways and bathrooms facilitate aging in place.
- Being green/sustainable: The owner was most interested in being a good steward of the site's resources, based on a commitment to serve existing residents as well as future generations. The aim is to make the best use of the land while still providing the features that residents sought. Density was not to be gained at the expense of the residential character of the existing community. This directive was reflected via a geothermal mechanical system, gray water storage tanks, a tight thermal envelope and careful selection of building materials. The result is a project that is expected to achieve LEED Silver certification.
- Offering choice through a diversity of housing options: The hybrid homes provide seniors with a new housing option that combines the best of both worlds: patio homes and apartment living. Multiple exposures, sheltered parking, outdoor living and an absence of corridors are among the cottage-like benefits associated with this living option. Apartment-like features include indoor access to common and service areas and opportunities for social connections in a multi-story building that requires less site area. Hybrid homes foster a sense of community between occupants with up to 13 homes per household and shared living areas including a hearth room on each floor and a community room that is typically shared with a second hybrid household.

Sustainability: Does the project conserve energy, water, and other natural resources? Does it reuse existing material or buildings, or include recycled building materials? How will the project improve indoor air quality in operation?

- Geothermal mechanical system, high performance windows and increased insulation are projected to help earn eight out of ten points for energy efficiency. Preliminary modeling results indicate efficiency levels approximately 30 percent higher than the ASHRAE base model.
- The project utilizes ultra low-flow fixtures and rainwater harvesting for non-potable uses for water efficiency. A legacy storm-water initiative will restore stream channels and adjacent floodplains to historical conditions to improve groundwater filtration and recharge.
- Hybrid homes provide a more compact footprint than cottage homes, which helps to preserve open space, and the under-building resident parking reduces surface parking lots and the associated heat-island effects.

Community: How does the project advance the sense of community for residents, staff, families, and neighbors?

- Rather than a typical detached building with no indoor connection to other homes, hybrid households offer connection to occupants of up to 11 or 12 other homes with shared living areas including a hearth room on each floor and a community room, as well as service space associated with typical daily routines such as a mailroom or recycling area.

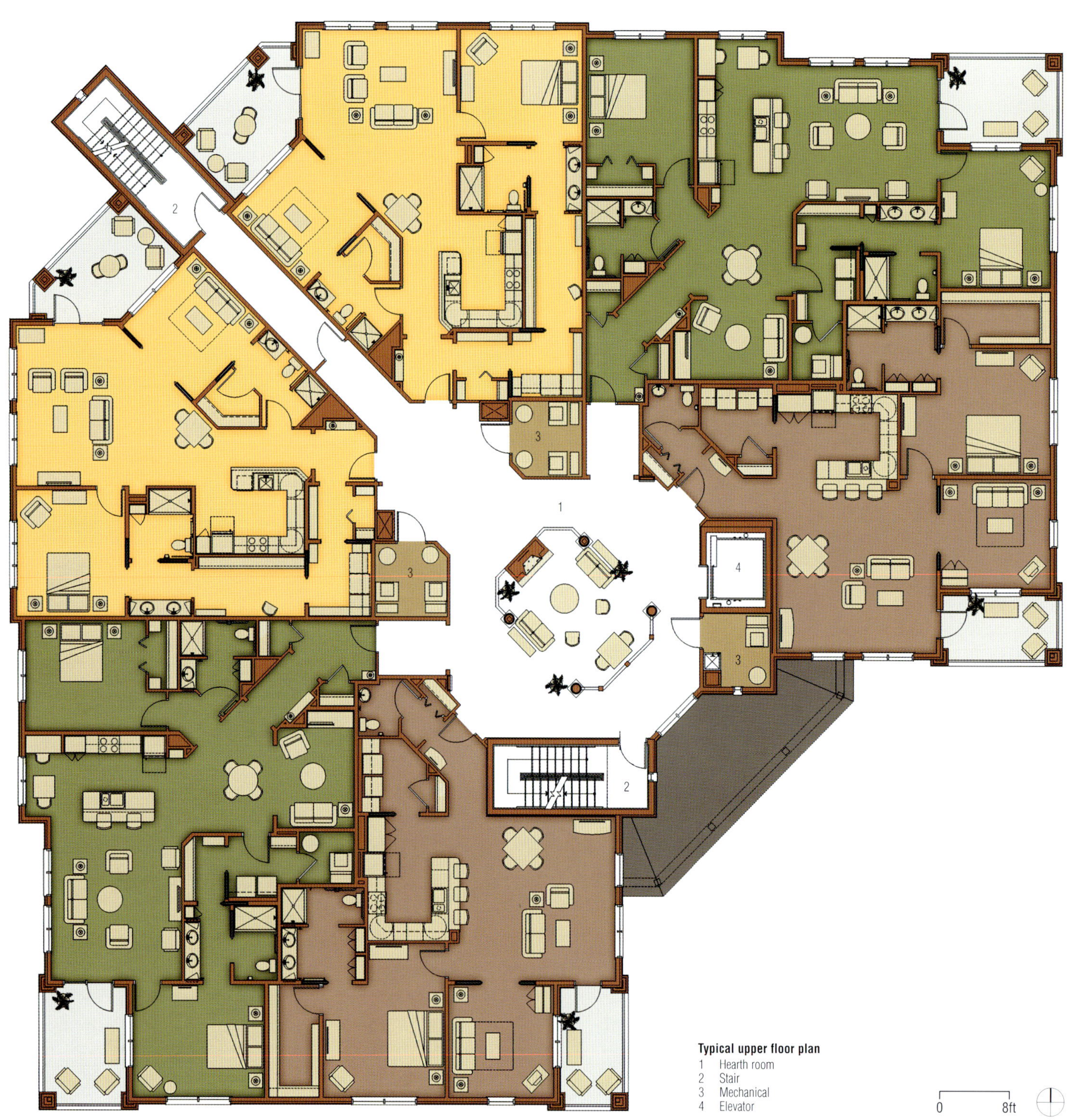

Typical upper floor plan

1 Hearth room
2 Stair
3 Mechanical
4 Elevator

- Hybrid homes provide opportunities for seniors with similar interests (for example, gardening, traveling, and learning in retirement) to live together in an intentional community with space for meetings, presentations, and/or activities.
- A first-floor patio/courtyard area, defined by the L-shaped household, further promotes social interaction between household members as well as visits between homes.

Target market: What specific features/services/ amenities were incorporated into the overall project to attract your target market?

- Covered parking is typically a key consideration for seniors considering a move to a retirement community and one of the benefits of patio homes. Placing parking on the first floor under the hybrid homes, offers the additional benefits of less surface space being needed.
- Today's elderly consumers expect direct assimilation of floor plan amenities that are available in private residences such as large walk-in closets, laundry centers, eat-in kitchens with daylight exposure, varied ceiling heights, access to a high-speed Internet service, convenient long-term storage, and a home office or den. Hybrid homes are designed to incorporate these amenities more cost effectively than a single patio home without losing the sense of community provided in an apartment setting.
- Full accessibility allows aging in place in a private residence that also offers indoor connections to other household members.

Top left: Each home will have multiple exposures
Above: The first-floor community room will accommodate meetings, family gatherings, and other social functions

Photography: istockphoto.com

McCormick Architecture

La Paloma - East Lubbock Regional MHMR

Lubbock, Texas

Facility type: Skilled Nursing, Dementia/Memory Support Unit, Wellness/Fitness Center, Hospice, Senior Community Center, Medical Services Care Facility, PACE Center

Target market: Low income/subsidized

Site location: Urban (city or town)

Date of completion: December 2011

Green certification: The building is not yet certified but is registered with the USGBC. Version 2.2 may be changed to 3.0 Silver with 36 points anticipated.

Below: Main entrance view
Opposite: Main entrance close-up view

Overall Project Goals

This 27,000-square-foot Program of All-inclusive Care for the Elderly (PACE) center will sit next to a flowing body of water perched in the southwest corner of what will become an 80-acre planned development for the provider. The project was planned to expand the PACE program in the State of Texas. The provider, a Mental Health and Mental Retardation (MHMR) center, has much experience in the service delivery system.

The provider possesses a strong belief in protecting the environment and sustainability and further believes in using regional materials for building, hence the brick, concrete, and plaster building with a strong expression of cultural significance in the use of color. The layered color configuration of the brick is reminiscent of serrations in the terrain of two favorite local weekend escapes. The building is very structured in terms of its major service components, which are the main activity, PT/OT/wellness, and outdoor participation area; the clinic/medical area; the staff and administration area; and the basic support areas for food preparation, mechanical, staff lounge, laundry, and storage, among others. All areas culminate in the central hub – a gathering space for purposeful interaction, informal meeting, and interplay between departments and services that promotes flow and function while minimizing travel distances.

Architect's Statement

Design goals

- To create a functional, efficient design minimizing walking distances for participants and specific staff with evidence-based knowledge gained from previous projects.
- To create a healthy environment for the well-being of staff and participants.
- To reflect the West Texas region and the population through color and use of materials. The participant population breaks down to 70 percent Hispanic, 15 percent Caucasian and 15 percent African American.

Challenges: What were the most difficult challenges in designing the project?

The most significant challenges were:

- Getting the land released from the City for purchase
- The flood plain zone as determined by FEMA
- Educating the contractors and subcontractors about the demands of a LEED project, which require a change in mindset.

Innovations: Does the project offer its users unique opportunities or new features not typically available in previous similar projects?

- The use of wind power coupled with solar panels certainly demonstrates innovation.
- Taking advantage of the local climate and West Texas plains vernacular gives the project a unique quality.
- The use of skylights to light all major pathways for a program that is in operation from 8 am

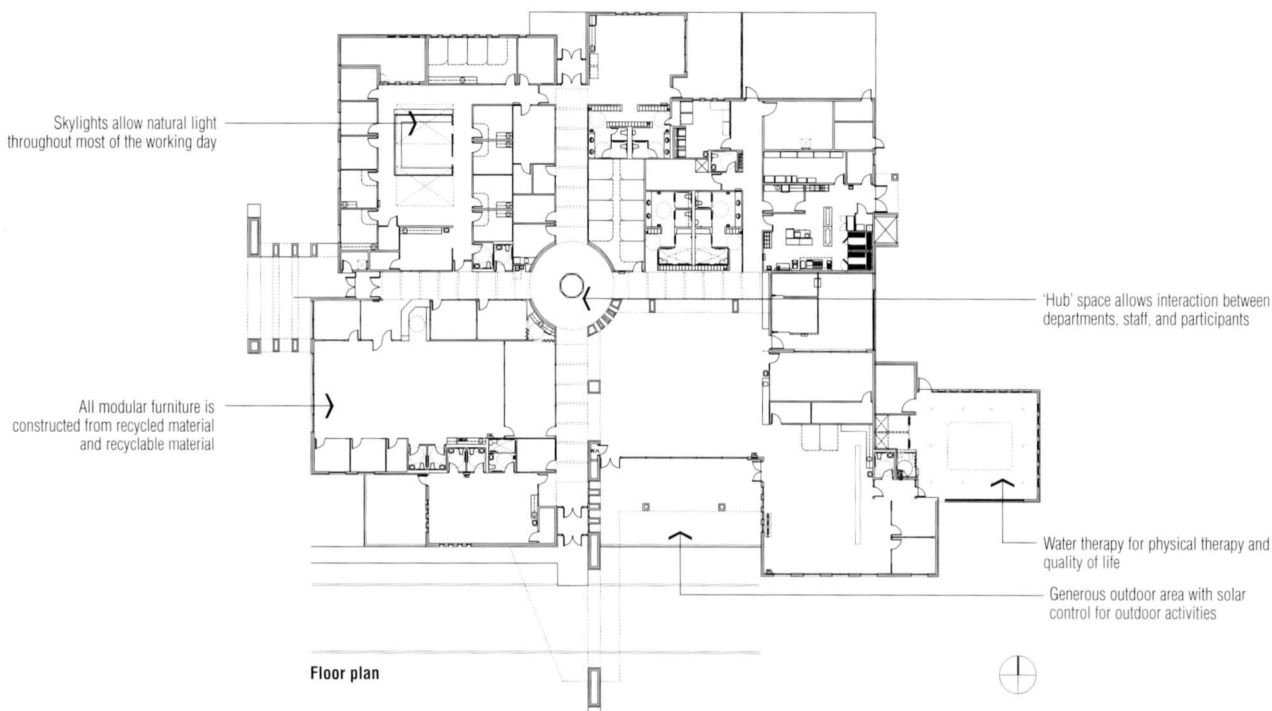

Floor plan

to 5 pm makes the need for lighting in these areas almost unnecessary.

Form shapers: What factors had the most influence on the physical form of the project?

- All participants' restroom entrances are designed without doors to facilitate maneuvering with less difficulty.
- Computer stations are set up for learning so that the participants are able to communicate with their grandchildren via the Internet.
- The PACE program is all about aging in place, giving the participants the ability to live at home as long as possible. The participants speak of going to the 'gym' – the physical therapy or wellness programs (which include water physical therapy).

Top trends

- Helping aging adults stay in their homes longer: PACE is about helping the aging population to stay in their homes for as long as they possibly can. In an effort to support the program the design continues to become more efficient in layout of functional relationships to perfect the service delivery system for participants and staff.
- Addressing a holistic sense of wellness: A holistic sense of wellness is derived from all aspects of the project coming together:
  a. The local culture is reflected in the building's color, form, materials, and site; the Hispanic elderly will readily identify the design as reflective of their culture and accept it as their home away from home
  b. The ecological approach to the building and its site
  c. The combination of natural and mechanical solutions for daylighting and fresh air; a comfortable environment that contributes to physical and mental healing
  d. The creation of a healthy and healing environment that parallels the healing of Mother Earth.
- Being green/sustainable: Being green/sustainable is fostered in the response to LEED specifications in the building and site – helping the elderly with quality of life while creating a healthier environment for the participants, staff, and the greater community.

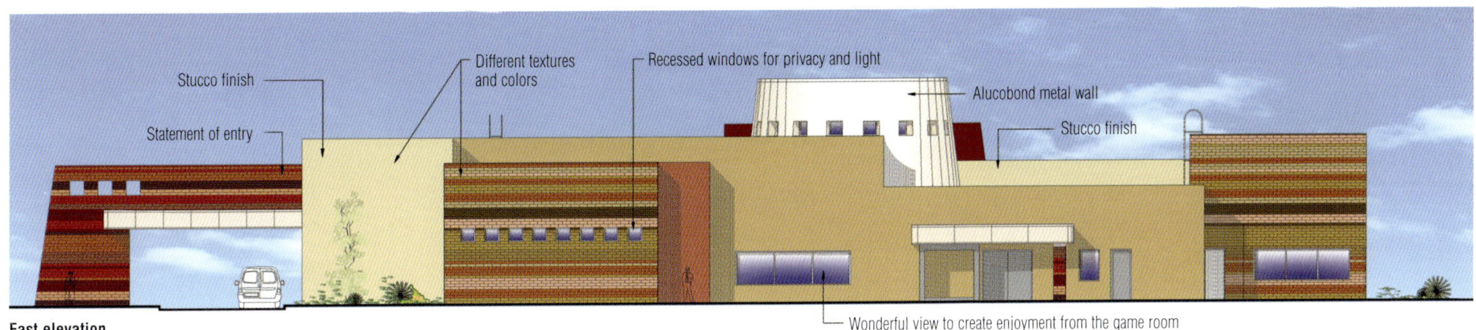

East elevation

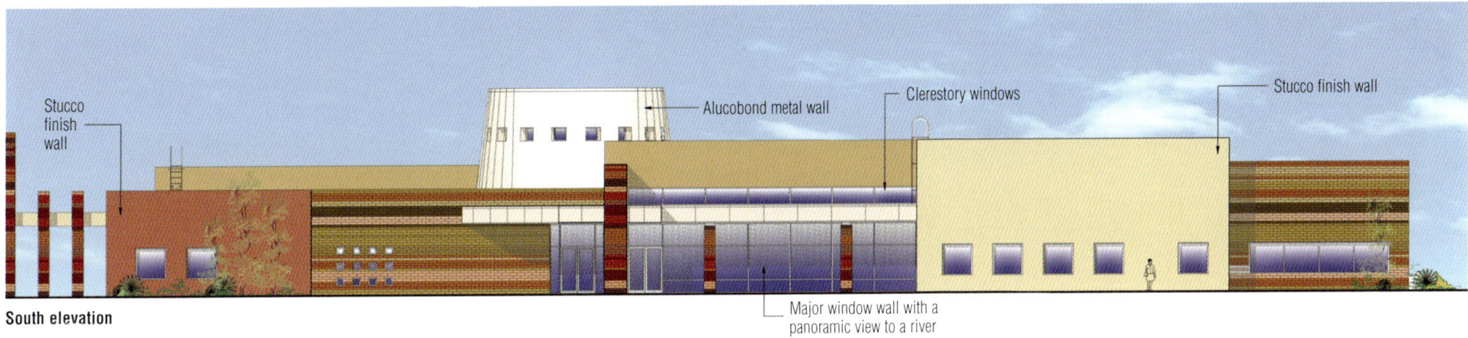

South elevation

Sustainability: Does the project conserve energy, water, and other natural resources? Does it reuse existing material or buildings, or include recycled building materials? How will the project improve indoor air quality in operation?

- Energy is conserved in several ways: one being an extensive skylighting system that crisscrosses the building, supplying most of the light during the standard 8 am to 5 pm day. The lighting system is also low-energy.
- The major materials are obtained within a 500-mile radius and many are recycled. All paints, adhesives, carpets, and composite wood and Agrifiber products are specified low-emitting materials.
- Wind turbines will produce a portion of the electricity requirement in conjunction with efficient HVAC systems.

Community: How does the project advance the sense of community for residents, staff, families, and neighbors?

- The project's site is largely a contribution from the City. The purchase price was greatly reduced in order for the program for the elderly to develop there as well as the use of green building and design. This provides a sense of community through the shared contributions of many.
- The staff being hired for this new facility is very proud to be a part of this project because of the LEED aspect as well as the vision for the future growth in this part of the city.
- Being an innovative thinker, the provider is creating a new PACE center in Texas (further evolving a good program) and introducing wind power and other green elements to create a community pride.

Target market: What specific features/services/ amenities were incorporated into the overall project to attract your target market?

- The natural skylit entrance and corridors are a definite selling point in the marketing of the project. The well-lit interior promotes a special sense of optimism.
- The therapy pool excites all new participants in the program.
- The beauty salon and game room (pool table and game tables) has been met with enthusiasm by new participants.

CJMW Architecture

Penick Village Garden Cottage

Southern Pines, North Carolina // Episcopal Diocese of North Carolina

Facility type: Assisted Living
Target market: Middle/upper middle
Site location: Suburban
Capacity: 10 rooms

Total project cost: $1.45 million
Date of completion: October 2009
Green certification: LEED for Homes, Silver (targeted)

Below: The cottage's exterior design complements its neighborhood
Opposite: Spacious resident bedrooms allow personalization

Overall Project Goals

The Garden Cottage is a one-story, 10-bedroom/10-bathroom single-family residence that will be licensed and operated as an Assisted Living facility. The Penick Village Board of Directors became dedicated to the Garden Cottage philosophy because they strongly believe it is the right way to provide life-enhancing care to elderly residents in both Assisted Living and Skilled Nursing settings. Until now, North Carolina's Department of Health Services Regulation (DHSR) has not permitted licensure of small homes like the Garden Cottage unless they contain all the institutional requirements of larger facilities. The project owners and architects asked the chief of DHSR to join the Design Team early on to explore how they might jointly interpret the governing regulations by use of 'equivalency measures' to remove barriers to single-family living in a licensed environment. The result of a year of cooperative efforts by the DHSR/Penick Village partnership, the Garden Cottage will be the very first licensed single-family Assisted Living home in North Carolina. In keeping with Penick Village's holistic philosophy, it will also be the first Assisted Living facility in North Carolina to be certified under the LEED for Homes program (LEED Silver targeted).

Provider's Statement

Provider goals for marketing and sales

How did the provider plan to improve the residents' quality of life?

The kitchen in the center of the house provides a place for people to enjoy the entire meal process; private bathrooms with private showers improve the protection of dignity; heated floors in the bathrooms make bathing a more comfortable experience; and easy access to outdoors gives the opportunity to experience many environments.

How did the provider want to improve workplace quality for employees?

The design of the building maximizes the opportunity for self-directed work teams, mastery of skills, variety in the job, and a sense of purpose in the big picture. Staff retention has been 100 percent in the first six months.

Did the provider have specific goals for the project's staffing quantities, training, or distribution?

Staffing quantities have been met with a little variance in order to deal with some additional training.

Did the provider give specific direction about the style, materials, features, or other design aspects of the project? If so, what were those directives?

The provider wanted a design that provided privacy, easy access to the outdoors, and space; and requested that anything not normally found in a person's home not be included in this building if at all possible.

How did the provider's financial goals influence the project's organization, configuration, layout, or sizing of components?

It provides an alternative to the traditional institutional model of care for Assisted Living and is meeting all budgetary goals that have been set.

Architect's Statement

Design goals

- To create a home for 10 Assisted Living residents – a real home, not a home-like environment. To completely deinstitutionalize Assisted Living.
- To build more Garden Cottages. The next one will be Licensed Skilled Nursing. The project team's goal was to use this cottage as a test case in working with the NC Division of Health Services Regulation to agree on interpretation of the rules governing licensing as Skilled Nursing, so the project team and governing authorities are in agreement about the next cottage's design criteria before beginning the design.

- To create a healthier living environment by designing and building to LEED certification requirements.

Challenges: What were the most difficult challenges in designing the project?

- Until now, NC's Department of Health Services Regulation (DHSR) has not permitted licensing as Assisted Living for a small, freestanding, 10-resident, single-family home. The project owners and architects asked the Chief of DHSR to join the design team early on to explore how to interpret the governing regulation by use of equivalency measures to remove barriers to single-family living in a licensed environment.
- Penick Village's Garden Cottage will be the first Assisted Living facility in North Carolina to be certified under the LEED for Homes program. LEED for Homes is a new program and the architect has worked closely with the USGBC during this pilot phase to help determine specifics of implementation and certification requirements.

Site plan
1 Phase 1, single-story cottages
2 CIL apartments
3 Village house
4 Existing cottages
5 South building
6 North building
7 Garden cottages
8 Maintenance building

Innovations: Does the project offer its users unique opportunities or new features not typically available in previous similar projects?

- The Penick Village Board became dedicated to the Garden Cottage philosophy because they strongly believe it is the right way to provide life-enhancing care to elderly residents. The board made the decision to develop Garden Cottages with the full realization of barriers such as higher construction costs and higher operational expenses presented by very small facilities. The board's mandate was, 'Build one and we'll learn how to run it at an agreeable cost.'
- At Penick Village's invitation, the chief of the DHSR took a personal interest in shepherding the Garden Cottage through the regulatory process, paving the way for North Carolina's first licensed Assisted Living Cottage and also the way for the next cottage – for licensed Skilled Nursing.

Form shapers: What factors had the most influence on the physical form of the project?

- The small, intimate size of the home reduces travel distances to the very minimum, increasing group interaction, reducing dependence on wheelchairs and walkers, and reducing the number of falls.
- The intimate, but open, design of the Garden Cottage affords residents the opportunity to see and hear what is going on around them, fostering the formation of real single-family behavior. Caring for others, even within the limits of one's infirmities, gives life meaning and importance.
- Universal design elements are employed throughout the Garden Cottage. Features such as lower kitchen counters to encourage

residents to participate in food preparation from a comfortable sitting position, a ceramic tile no-threshold shower in every resident bathroom, ample space for accessible travel indoors and out, and no-trip hazards all encourage mobility and participation.

Top trends

- Integrating with the surrounding community: Prior to schematic design, the architects researched the architectural history of Southern Pines from the early 1900s. The prevalent style in the area is Craftsman and this information inspired the design of the Garden Cottage. The goal was for the Cottage to complement its neighborhood.
- Addressing a holistic sense of wellness: The philosophy behind the Garden Cottage is to house 10 Assisted Living residents in a single-family setting attended by caregivers, the same people every day. The residents decide what to do and what to eat each day. Meal preparation, cleaning, and routine chores are all performed by the caregivers with as much involvement of residents as the residents themselves choose.
- Being green/sustainable: The Garden Cottage also promotes physical health because of its very good indoor air quality, ample daylighting and views to the outside, a sheltering roof structure, shading plants, outdoor gardens, and terraces.

Sustainability: Does the project conserve energy, water, and other natural resources? Does it reuse existing material or buildings, or include recycled building materials? How will the project improve indoor air quality in operation?

- The project has healthier buildings by enhancing outdoor air ventilation and combustion venting.
- The indoor environment is improved by the use of low-VOC materials for paint, carpet, and more.
- Energy Star appliances, lighting, and exhaust vents are used.

Cottage floor plan

1 Clean air systems
2 Low-flow fixtures
3 Energy-star appliances
4 Regional materials
5 Native plant varieties
6 Radiant flooring
7 Resident-provided furniture
8 Recycled materials
9 Natural daylighting
10 Entry
11 Den
12 Spa
13 Kitchen
14 Great room
15 Outdoor patio

Community: How does the project advance the sense of community for residents, staff, families, and neighbors?

- Residents and staff choose their meal menus together, prepare the food together, eat together at one big dining table, and clean up together. The kitchen is always open to the residents and food is available at any time. Food and its preparation are instrumental in bringing people together.
- The view of the great room from almost every resident's door affords awareness of group activities and residents can decide to participate fully or from the periphery. The short travel distance between any two points in the house encourages less-mobile residents to venture out.
- Studies are indicating that residents and staff living together in a home environment like the Garden Cottage begin to relate to each other as family. Those that are able to begin to give care to those who are less able. Lives are truly shared.

Target market: What specific features/services/amenities were incorporated into the overall project to attract your target market?

- The project provides single-family home living in an architecturally appropriate cottage.
- There is an abundance of storage space and display space in each resident room.
- Wireless communication components are utilized throughout, including Internet access.

Stantec Architecture (Toronto Office)

Residential Hospice for York Region

Newmarket, Ontario

Facility type: Assisted Living, Hospice

Target market: Mixed income

Site location: Suburban

Capacity: 10 Skilled Nursing Rooms

Date of completion: December 2011

Below: View of south entrance: conceptual rendering
Opposite top: North entrance view: scale model
Opposite bottom: Bird's eye view: scale model

North elevation

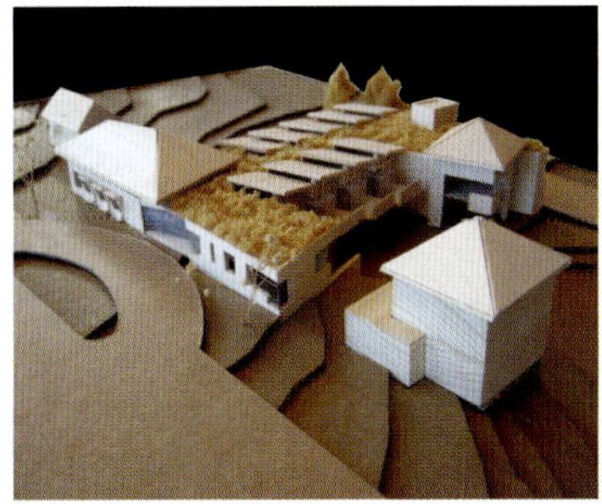

East elevation

Overall Project Goals

This design is a two-story hospice that aims to provide high-quality, 24-hour healthcare support for terminally ill patients and their families. Currently, the 19,000-square-foot building contains 10 resident rooms, each with its own balcony overlooking landscaped areas on the east and west side. The north side provides a direct connection to the Southlake Regional Health Center, while the south elevation is integrated into the surrounding residential area. In addition to the resident rooms, the building provides kitchen and dining space, volunteer work areas, a den, and multipurpose recreational spaces.

Provider's Statement

Provider goals for marketing and sales

The providers are able to represent the project as a fully integrated community space with residential character and neighborhood compatibility.

How did the provider plan to improve the residents' quality of life?

The green roof, skylight portals and bed access to an outside deck off each resident's room, the natural building materials and 'streetscape' hallways with an address for each resident demonstrate the facility's 'live until you die' approach to hospice care. The outdoor water feature and legacy garden walk will offer solace and serenity, as well as memorial opportunities for families.

How did the provider want to improve workplace quality for employees?

Employee facilities are naturally lit and spacious due to the split-level design.

Did the provider have specific goals for the project's staffing quantities, training, or distribution?

The split-level design offers maximum capacity for staff entrances, facilities, and activities separate from residential areas of the hospice.

Did the provider give specific direction about the style, materials, features, or other design aspects of the project? If so, what were those directives?

The hospice reflects the provider's philosophy of 'the circle of life,' or 'earth to earth.' Death is part of life. Light, air, plants, music, and water are integral to daily life in the hospice as people face the last weeks of their lives.

How did the provider's financial goals influence the project's organization, configuration, layout, or sizing of components?

The hospice is structurally efficient and green for sustainability in operating costs.

Architect's Statement

Design goals

- One of the most important goals for this project was to create a quiet and serene environment for each patient. Each room has

Second floor plan

1 Resident room
2 Den and library
3 Tub room
4 Clean linen
5 Shower room
6 Multipurpose room/ family room
7 Soiled utility
8 Kitchen/dining
9 Secretary
10 Vestibule
11 Executive director
12 Den
13 Tea room

Ground floor plan

1 Lobby/receptionist
2 Care coordinator
3 Entry vestibule
4 Laundry
5 Carport
6 Multipurpose room
7 Medical director
8 Director
9 Director of volunteers
10 Team room
11 Mechanical/electrical
12 Maintenance
13 Housekeeping
14 Lockers
15 Water feature
16 Wood deck

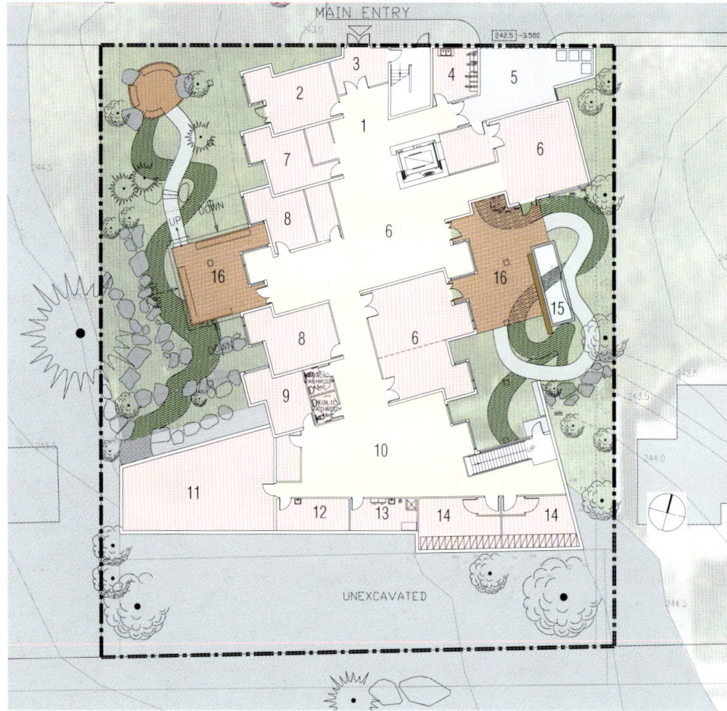

a balcony which beds can be wheeled onto, so that patients can still enjoy the outdoors despite limited mobility. Each balcony is also designed with planters for growing greenery while also providing a separation from neighboring balconies. The clerestory windows look onto the green roof. Beds can also be taken by elevator to the ground floor, where two landscaped areas are connected through a large multipurpose room. This allows for light to pass through unobstructed and provides comfortable spaces for patients and families to celebrate the holidays or enjoy the company of other families.

- The hospice was designed to be as home-like as possible. The angles of the rooms and tile patterns provide a street-like motif that turns each room into its own smaller home. A memory box located at the entrance allows for families to place important items on display to celebrate the life of each patient. Each residential room has a smaller, more intimate space with a couch for a family member to sleep on. The room is also constructed so that those coming into the room can spot family members first before seeing the patient, giving cues for privacy.
- Due to the special program of this building, a primary goal was to provide proper support for family members. It was important to consider what events occur when a patient passes away. The idea in this design was to create a ceremonious occasion. The deceased are wheeled from the elevator directly into the multipurpose room, where family members can say final goodbyes. The room overlooks a landscaped area that offers a dignified atmosphere for the event.

Challenges: What were the most difficult challenges in designing the project?

- The existing site slopes with a difference of approximately one level in the E15°N direction. As well, a children's playground is located within viewing distance to the east of the property. In order to address these issues, a split-level configuration provided two main entrances on two different levels. The rooms have been configured at a 15-degree angle to respond to the slope and also to optimize sun angles. This shift in angle also incorporates views to the children's playground on the east side, thus enhancing the psychological well-being of the residents. Family members can also have direct views into the playground, allowing them to observe the children while still caring for an elderly parent.

- The building is located in a residential area with historical houses dating back roughly 100 years. Many residents were concerned that the design would greatly overpower the space and decrease land values. The hospice is designed so that the south façade, which faces onto the street, would remain at a height that did not surpass adjacent buildings. What was originally a long, straight façade was broken up into two smaller façades that roughly match the size of an average house.

- The project is currently on a tight budget and relies mainly on donations. By providing a design that inspires passion and generates interest, the project becomes inclusive of the entire community and boosts fundraising efforts. The straightforward structure also keeps costs down, and the use of ready-made materials and repetition will create and deliver a custom, tailored look with an economical solution.

Innovations: Does the project offer its users unique opportunities or new features not typically available in previous similar projects?

- The project took advantage of the site's slope by orienting rooms and adjusting views. In doing so the rooms were able to follow the orientation of the sun.

- This project had the chance to explore a non-institutional design despite having an institutional program. In order to create a home-like atmosphere, the design incorporates local materials and focuses proportions and plan configurations. In doing so the hospice created a more fitting interpretation of the program requirements.

Top trends

- Addressing a holistic sense of wellness: To possess a holistic sense of wellness, a patient must become healthy physically, emotionally, and spiritually. While it is beyond an architect's power to give hospice patients the physical health they require, it remains important to enhance a patient's mentality. This project addresses those needs by providing a meditative and peaceful atmosphere, one that is reflective of a comfortable home.

- Integrating with the surrounding community: In order to promote the acceptance and support of this building type, it is important that the project's design can be integrated successfully with the surrounding community.

- Using an interdisciplinary approach to palliative care: With an interdisciplinary approach to palliative care, every profession plays a role as part of the healthcare team. With this approach, every person becomes passionate in the project's success. In doing so the hospice becomes the caring and dignified building that it needs to be.

Sustainability: Does the project conserve energy, water, and other natural resources? Does it reuse existing material or buildings, or include recycled building materials? How will the project improve indoor air quality in operation?

- A green roof will be installed to provide storm water management and landscaping. It will also act as heat control and improve air quality.

- The building will be constructed with local materials such as cedar and brick.

- The design will include operable shading devices to control and maintain thermal comfort.

Community: How does the project advance the sense of community for residents, staff, families, and neighbors?

- The hospice provides multiple spaces for family gatherings, including the kitchen, dining, den, and library areas. Multipurpose spaces allow families to celebrate during the holidays, and to connect with the outdoors. Neighboring homes can also share the landscape, which is adjacent to their lots.

- A green roof will provide an attractive view for residents of the four-story seniors' home on the north side of the site. At the same time, angled roofs are sloped to the south so that there is no visibility into the rooms from the four-story building. Room angles also allow for views into the children's playground, which contributes to a more positive outlook.

- The building connects directly with the Southlake Regional Health Centre, allowing for the larger community to become a part of the hospice.

Landon Bone Baker Architects

Roseland Senior Campus

Chicago, Illinois // Roseland Place Limited Partnership

Facility type: Wellness/Fitness Center, Independent Living, Senior Community Center, Grandfamily Housing for grandparents raising grandchildren

Target market: Low income/subsidized

Site location: Urban (city or town)

Capacity: 70 units

Total project cost: $16.4 million (estimated)

Date of completion: 2011

Green certification: City of Chicago Green Permit Program; State Energy Efficient Affordable Housing Program

Below: View of Roseland Place from Michigan Avenue

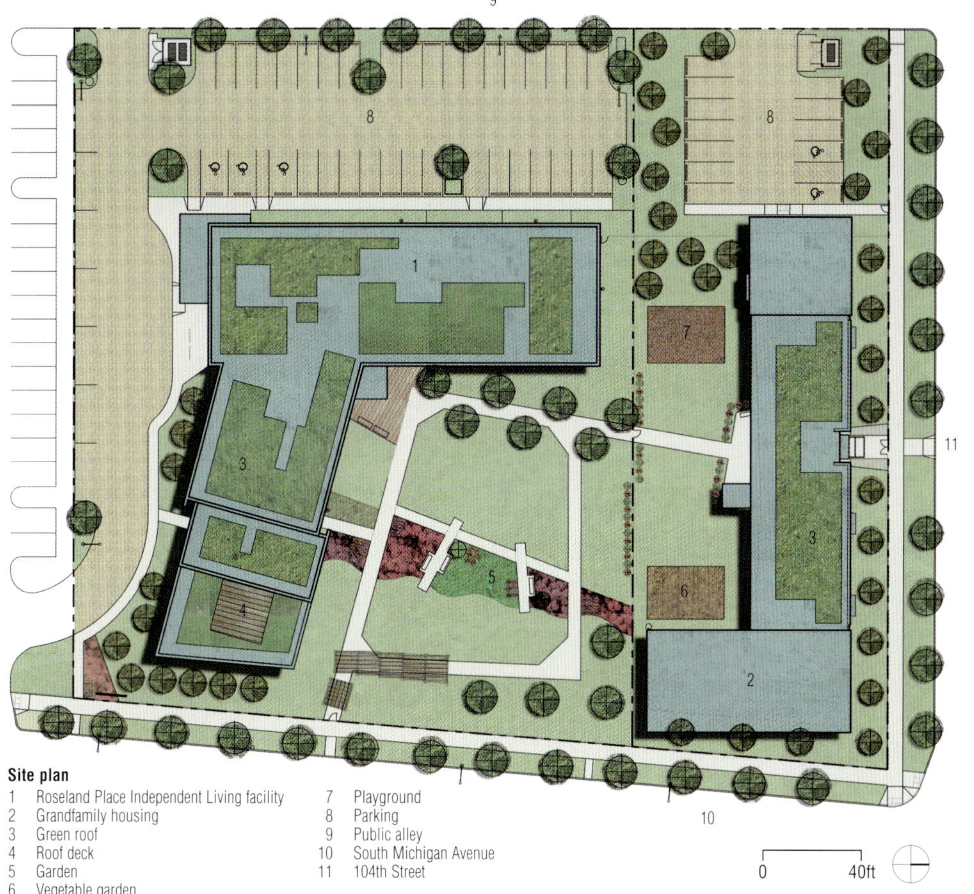

Site plan

1 Roseland Place Independent Living facility
2 Grandfamily housing
3 Green roof
4 Roof deck
5 Garden
6 Vegetable garden
7 Playground
8 Parking
9 Public alley
10 South Michigan Avenue
11 104th Street

Overall project goals

The Roseland Senior Campus is a project planned for a vacant 1.9-acre (84,000-square-foot) urban site and consists of a 60-unit Independent Living Residential (ILF) facility and a 10-unit grandfamily facility for grandparents raising grandchildren. The campus also includes a 124-unit Assisted Living building that was previously completed by another architect and is not part of this submission. All three buildings work together to provide a continuum of care for local seniors.

The five-story L-shaped ILF building is approximately 65,000 square feet and addresses the street while opening up onto a naturally landscaped garden and gazebo space. There will be a walking path through the garden area. A 36-car parking lot is concealed at the rear of the site, out of view from the street. In addition to the ILF lobby and accessed through a separate entry, the ground floor will also house a Senior Satellite Center of approximately 7,000 square feet. The Senior Center will be operated by the City of Chicago and will contain a large multipurpose room, library and craft space, computer lab, fitness and aerobics room, and warming kitchen. The smaller scale two-story, 14,600-square-foot grandfamily building is sited to the north of the ILF building and completes the courtyard. The building is one unit wide with an exterior protected corridor, which allows natural light and ventilation to penetrate two sides of each unit. Each unit overlooks the garden and play space so grandparents can keep an eye on their grandchildren.

Provider's Statement

Provider goals for marketing and sales

The project provides generous public and private space for the prospective tenant. The amenities provided (beauty shop, game room/solarium, computer room, and exercise space, among others) exceed what is typically expected in this market. The large public outdoor space and garden is also a major positive element for marketing.

How did the provider plan to improve the residents' quality of life?

In general, the provider aimed to create a safe, affordable, comfortable place for seniors to live. The Grandfamily Apartments also allow for grandparents to provide a safe and affordable haven for their grandchildren. Other project amenities contribute to quality of life as well, including the exercise facilities, computers, public dining and classes, outdoor garden space, and more.

How did the provider want to improve workplace quality for employees?

The office and meeting spaces are all connected to both the public spaces and the building exterior. The spaces are appropriately sized and provide all of the necessary technology and storage required.

Fifth floor plan and Grandfamily second floor plan

1 Solarium
2 Elevator lobby
3 Green roof
4 Rooftop deck
5 Community room
6 Three-bedroom unit
7 Secure lobby
8 Four-bedroom unit

First floor plan

1 Main entry
2 ILF entry/lobby
3 SSC entry/lobby
4 Recreation and dining room
5 Computer lab
6 Aerobics room
7 Fitness room
8 Beauty shop
9 Community room
10 Garden entry
11 Three-bedroom unit
12 Secure lobby
13 Four-bedroom unit

0 40ft

Did the provider have specific goals for the project's staffing quantities, training, or distribution?

The provider and designer worked together to program the staff and training spaces. The office, meeting, and office storage spaces are appropriately located and sized for the project functions. The community room space could also be used for any meeting larger than 10 people.

Did the provider give specific direction about the style, materials, features, or other design aspects of the project? If so, what were those directives?

The provider first and foremost wanted to avoid an institutional feel for the buildings. The provider wanted lots of natural light, while maintaining warmth and comfort in the interior spaces. Some of the directions were more specific: for example, providing a public shelf or marker at the unit entries to allow for some personalization or flair, and providing breaks and turns in the residential hallways to avoid a monotonous institutional feel. The provider wanted to provide a generous outdoor garden space for socializing, exercise, and relaxation. They also pushed hard to make the building as green and energy efficient as possible within the given budget constraints.

How did the provider's financial goals influence the project's organization, configuration, layout, or sizing of components?

The project was designed with significant focus on energy and water efficiency, which will aid financial performance for the provider and tenant. The project was also designed with an eye towards long-term durability with its interior and exterior material choices.

Architect's Statement

Challenges: What were the most difficult challenges in designing the project?

- Addressing and coordinating the various funding and local agency requirements such as US Department of Housing and Urban Development (HUD) and the City of Chicago's Department of Housing and Department of Planning.
- Providing many green/energy efficient features, interior and exterior social spaces and amenities for the residents while working with a modest budget.
- Developing a site strategy and physical layout that would allow the two separate buildings to interact together while defining an exterior common space; and at the same time allowing each to be functionally individually secure.

Innovations: Does the project offer its users unique opportunities or new features not typically available in previous similar projects?

- The L-shaped building design is set back from the street, which allows the public face of the building to be a green landscaped garden while simultaneously allowing the required parking to be concealed behind the building.
- The unique program, which incorporates an Independent Living Facility, senior café, and grandfamily housing, encourages many opportunities for multi-generational interaction and activities.
- The many green and energy-efficient features incorporated into the design will result in low operating costs for the building's owner and a healthy living and working environment for the residents and staff.

Form shapers: What factors had the most influence on the physical form of the project?

- The project includes many amenities that are not typically found in senior residences. There is a satellite senior center in the Independent Living Facility that will give residents the opportunity to attend fitness and craft classes, use computer facilities, and socialize with other seniors who live outside the building. For building residents there are two recreation rooms with lounge and dining areas. Residents also have access to a hair salon located on the first floor of the building.
- The project was designed so the Independent Living Facility and grandfamily apartments create an edge around the sides of the large open space between the two buildings. Shared views of the garden space and play areas will enable the residents of the two buildings to interact with each other more than if the buildings were designed with more private open spaces. This interaction between the children and residents of the Independent Living Facility will help to enliven the garden space and provide residents with greater opportunities to be more active.

Sustainability: Does the project conserve energy, water, and other natural resources? Does it reuse existing material or buildings, or include recycled building materials? How will the project improve indoor air quality in operation?

- The project's total energy use will be minimized by installing high-efficiency furnaces, boilers, and chillers. Super-insulated walls and roofs, air sealing, and full slab insulation will further reduce the energy load on the building.
- Building occupants will benefit directly from the project's sustainable design features. Energy Star appliances and lighting, low-flow plumbing fixtures, and high-efficiency furnaces will help limit tenant utility costs.
- The site has been designed for maximum permeability. Over 50 percent of roof areas will have a green roof system, permeable pavers will be used in a large portion of the parking area, and a majority of the site will be covered in landscape planting.

Community: How does the project advance the sense of community for residents, staff, families, and neighbors?

- The senior café is available for use by the residents and the public alike. It is located close to the street and public sidewalk to encourage the immediate community to come in and use the facility and mix with the residents.
- The central garden space located at the front of the building provides a naturally landscaped garden and sitting area for the multi-generational residents of both buildings to use and share. A walking path and gardening plots encourage a mix of multi-generational activities.
- The ground-floor spaces of the Independent Living Facility such as the lobby, community room, and beauty shop were designed to be inviting and encourage resident interaction and to allow the residents to see the building's comings and goings. Additionally, the fifth-floor solarium space provides a more casual multipurpose room with comfortable seating and pool tables for the residents to get together and socialize in a less public setting.

Mithun

The Sterling of Pasadena

Pasadena, California // Sunrise Senior Living

Facility type: Independent Living, Assisted Living, Dementia/Memory Support Unit, Wellness/Fitness Center

Target market: Upper

Site location: Urban (city or town)

Capacity (units): 200 Independent Living condominiums; 22 Assisted Living apartments; 26 Memory Care apartments

Green certification: LEED and City Building Department; LEED Silver

Below: Entrance
Opposite: Dining

Overall Project Goals

The provider saw the opportunity to create a superior retirement community on a beautiful site in the heart of a vibrant and prosperous city. The location was a perfect match for their aspirations to create a luxury senior-living community that demonstrates their new 'Condo for Life' concept. The Sterling of Pasadena is two blocks from downtown Pasadena. Within a prestigious historic neighborhood, the site contains a mix of mansions and gardens constructed in the early 1900s along with buildings and mature park-like open spaces created by a private college in the 1960s. Several obsolete college buildings will be torn down. One existing 1910 mansion and its two gardens (walled and formal Italian) are integrated into the project. New construction will consist of five- and six-story buildings connected by a bridge at one level. Nearly all parking will be subterranean in order to preserve open space. The neighborhood's love for this site resulted in a zoning district with specific guidelines. This zoning diverts density and new development from the southwest to the northeast corner where The Sterling is located. The provider and the designers worked with the City of Pasadena and neighborhood groups to preserve and promote connections throughout the entire site. Following a full environmental impact report, numerous meetings and a City council hearing and vote, the project has the full support of its neighbors and the City.

Architect's Statement

Design goals

- Maximize location: The Sterling is located within an historic neighborhood on a former private college campus containing a mix of mansions and gardens constructed in the early 1900s, along with buildings and mature park-like open spaces created by the college in the 1960s. In this setting, The Sterling demonstrates the possibility of incorporating senior living into the existing fabric, which is so valued by local citizens that they organized with the City of Pasadena to create zoning to preserve it.
- Incorporate the 'Condos For Life' concept: The Sterling explores the potential of Sunrise's new retirement concept, 'Condos for Life,' in which a senior purchases a condominium and receives supportive services at home according to changing needs over time. All units are designed to conform to universal design principles and to be easily adaptable to the residents' evolving needs. All living spaces are larger than average allowing more maneuvering room. These features include enough space and clearance for wheelchair access to all primary living spaces, kitchens, master bathrooms, guest powder rooms, and utility rooms. The larger size also facilitates in-unit home healthcare delivery.
- Marketability: The key to setting The Sterling apart from its competition was through unit design. Making the units larger in area than is typical allows for elegant and gracious spaces. These larger areas are not being used to add more dens or bedrooms. Additionally every condominium has a large deck or patio. With the integration of site design, The Sterling is ideally situated for marketability with maximum opportunities for seniors to live as active, engaged members of a larger community – enjoying the beautiful, uplifting surroundings of an historic neighborhood.

Challenges: What were the most difficult challenges in designing the project?

- The design concept was to fit the site like a fine glove, respecting context and the neighborhood's concerns about the project's potential bulk. In consultation with many concerned neighbors and preservation groups, schemes to mitigate size while achieving Sunrise's goals were developed. The building façade along the street was broken into smaller segments and significant portions

Standard Pacific
Parcel 3
Standard Pacific - Parcel 5
Standard Pacific
Parcel 9
NOT A PART
NOT A PART
Standard Pacific
Parcel 16

Site plan

of the top floor were set back to prevent a continuous roof profile. Also, the exterior elevations are differentiated in ways to diminish their scale and size.

- The City issued strong directives to protect public access to the internal park and to preserve open space, mature trees, the mansion, and its gardens. The design goal went beyond these requirements to connect physically, visually, and emotionally with the site's existing elements. The building's footprint avoids trees, increases the setback on St. John Street, and widens the public access on Green Street to make it a gateway rather than a simple gap between two buildings. The mansion's walled garden is preserved, but aligns new building access points with various existing gates and openings in the walls. This provides direct visual access from interior spaces to the existing garden.
- Of all the existing campus structures, the public was most sensitive about the auditorium and its plaza. It was important to preserve their urban formality while distinguishing a separate identity. The new building's elevation was modified to create a distinctive monolithic element on axis with the plaza fountain. The need to match the auditorium's height was resolved by developing a flat roof with a cantilevered overhang, creating a continuous multi-story glass window for part of the façade. To avoid competing with the auditorium on St. John Street (the public side), the building is separated into two smaller parts and pushed back so that drivers can see it more easily. The top floor is also pushed back for more visibility.

Innovations: Does the project offer its users unique opportunities or new features not typically available in previous similar projects?

- The historic 1910 Merritt mansion on the site is important to the project. It's a well-known icon in Pasadena and serves as a connection to the city and its history. The Merritt Mansion is connected and incorporated into the whole community. The main floor and daylit lower level are in pristine original state with large spaces, graduated stairway, ornate wood and outside terraces. The original spaces on these floors will be converted to a variety of common areas for the whole project, such as meeting/club rooms, reception/party spaces with adjacent catering kitchen, and arts and crafts rooms. The second floor will be converted into two large condominiums. The design provides for a direct, enclosed accessible link between the mansion and new buildings.
- The mansion gardens and Ambassador West College open spaces are primary visual and accessible features of the project. The design provides direct access to them from the mansion and the new buildings.

Form shapers: What factors had the most influence on the physical form of the project?

- 'Condos for Life' precipitated all residential units being designed to conform to universal design principles and to be easily adaptable to the residents' evolving needs. These features include enough space and clearance for wheelchair access to all primary living spaces, kitchens, master bathrooms, guest powder rooms, and utility rooms. Also, all living spaces are larger than average allowing more maneuvering room.
- Kitchens, master bathrooms and powder rooms are easily adaptable to meet specific accessibility needs. Kitchens have raised wall ovens, removable cabinets to create some lower counter tops or open 'knee space' below the counter. Bathrooms have removable cabinets to facilitate lowering counter heights and open space below counters, and extensive wall blocking to allow for the installation of individual customized grab bars and other equipment. These unit adjustments will be accomplished with the help of on-site facility staff.
- Besides the customary social and exercise programs, The Sterling will have onsite 'wellness' staff and facilities that provide healthcare monitoring, advice, and services associated with managing outside healthcare; and in-unit home healthcare services customized to residents' needs.

Top trends

- Offering diversity of housing options: The Sterling of Pasadena is an example of a new model of senior living that allows seniors to age in community. Service-enriched 'Condos for Life' are emerging as a niche in seniors housing. Many seniors feel that homeownership is important. For some, moving to a rental apartment is not an option for them. The Sterling fills this niche through condominiums with facilitated homecare services. The condos are designed to be adaptable, accommodating live-in support if necessary. Residents interested in this model are making a lifestyle decision, one that anticipates aging needs down the road.
- Being green/sustainable: Registered for LEED Silver, the sustainable design strategies have multiple benefits, including increased resident health and satisfaction, decreased operating costs, reduced environmental impact, heightened community support, and compliance with the City's green building ordinance.

Sustainability: Does the project conserve energy, water, and other natural resources? Does it reuse existing material or buildings, or include recycled building materials? How will the project improve indoor air quality in operation?

- The site design increases community connectivity, development density, and alternative transportation options; it also

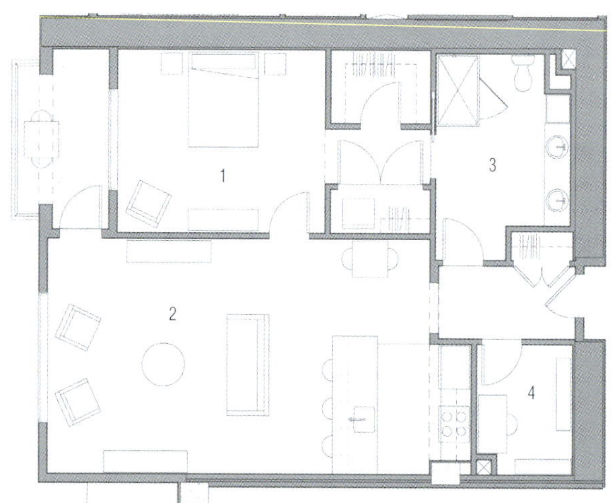

Floor plan – one-bedroom plus study

1 Master bedroom
2 Living/dining
3 Bathroom
4 Study

0 8ft

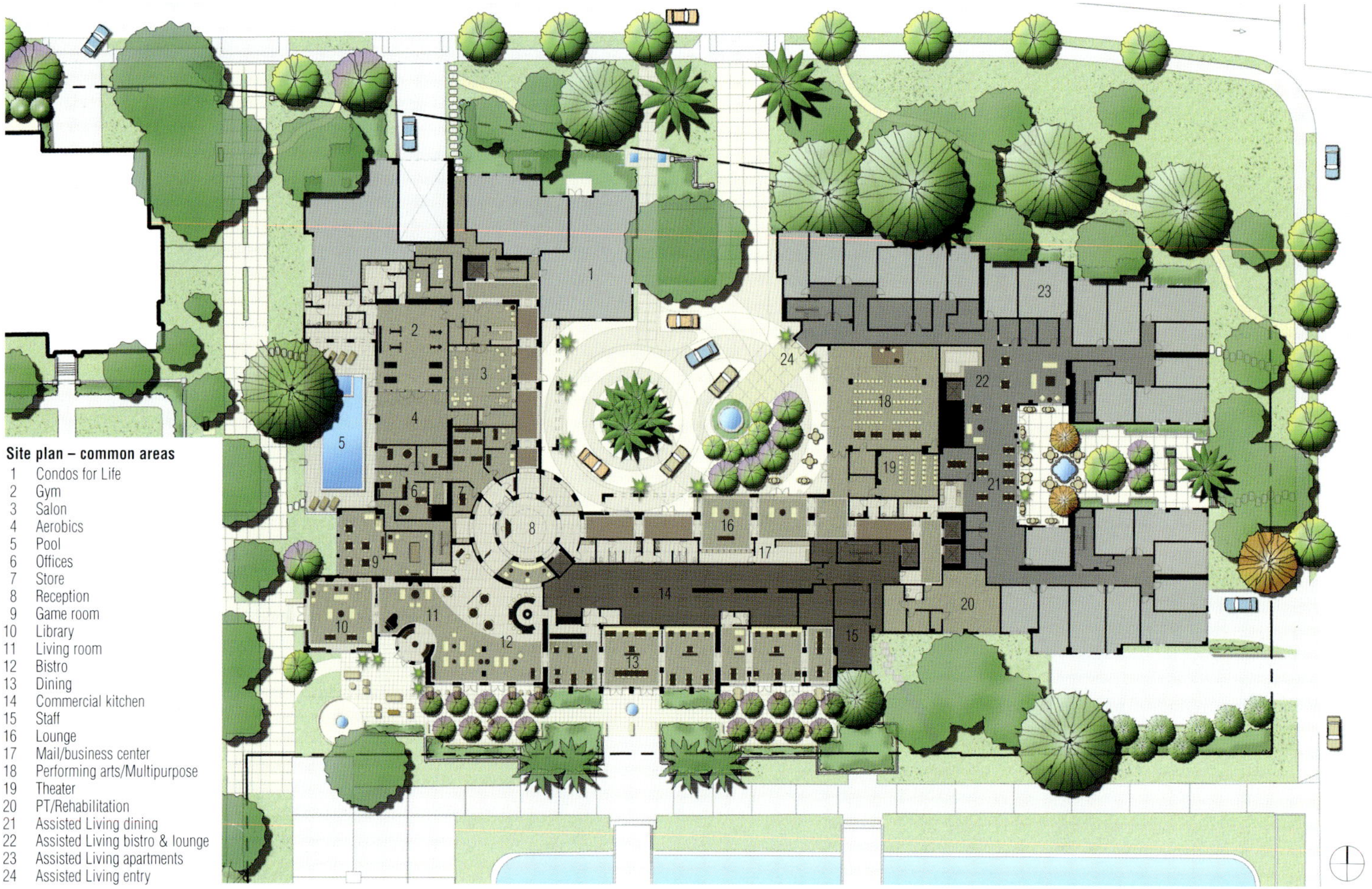

Site plan – common areas

1 Condos for Life
2 Gym
3 Salon
4 Aerobics
5 Pool
6 Offices
7 Store
8 Reception
9 Game room
10 Library
11 Living room
12 Bistro
13 Dining
14 Commercial kitchen
15 Staff
16 Lounge
17 Mail/business center
18 Performing arts/Multipurpose
19 Theater
20 PT/Rehabilitation
21 Assisted Living dining
22 Assisted Living bistro & lounge
23 Assisted Living apartments
24 Assisted Living entry

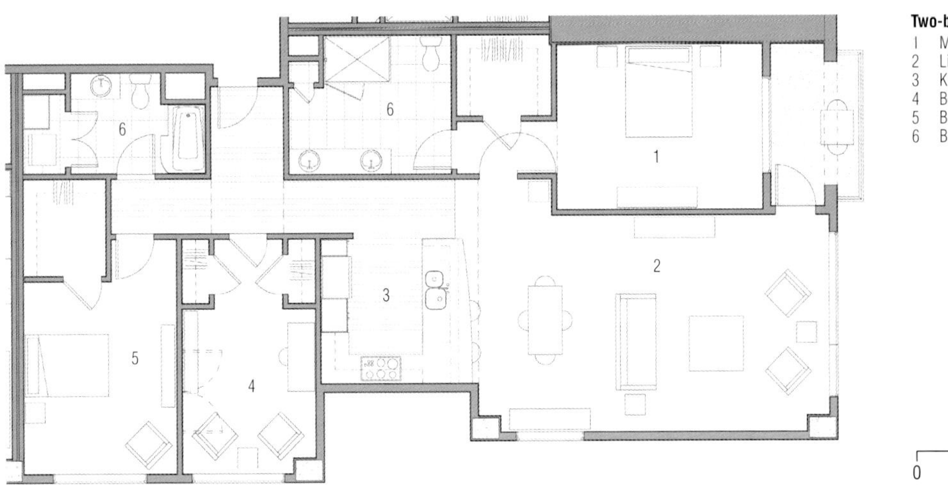

Two-bedroom plus den plan
1 Master bedroom
2 Living/dining
3 Kitchen
4 Bedroom three/den option
5 Bedroom two
6 Bathroom

0 8ft

Opposite top left: Merritt Mansion stairs

protects and restores existing historic landscaping and lowers the heat-island effect with reflective roofs and parking below grade.

- Low-VOC materials (carpet, coatings, adhesives/sealants, composite wood); the careful monitoring of construction practices; windows maximizing daylight and views for 90 percent of spaces; and individual control of lighting/HVAC systems all improve indoor environmental quality.
- The historic Merritt Mansion's building and garden were conserved and restored; demolition and construction waste was recycled; and the materials used included 10 percent recycled content while others were extracted, processed, and manufactured regionally.

Community: How does the project advance the sense of community for residents, staff, families, and neighbors?

- All Independent Living common areas are either on the first floor of the lower campus building or in the Merritt Mansion. These areas are concentrated to encourage a higher level of human energy and interaction.
- The primary common areas and main entrance are in the best part of the site with its visual and pedestrian access to the campus plaza and park-like environment. The first floor of the southwest corner of the lower campus building is the natural hub of the community – a place that residents naturally gravitate to.
- The next most natural spot for people to gather is the mansion, also due to its setting near the campus plaza and park. It's an obvious landmark, in terms of the historic building and gardens, and naturally draws visitors and encourages community interaction.

Target market: What specific features/services/amenities were incorporated into the overall project to attract your target market?

- The 'Condo for Life' concept and the high-end targeted market have precipitated many features specifically associated with the unit designs. The unit sizes are larger in area than their competitors. Besides averaging 1,450 square feet, there was an early decision to make the spaces within the units larger and more elegant and gracious than is typical in the marketplace. Additionally every Independent Living unit has a large deck or patio (of a 60-square-foot minimum size).
- The larger condo size also facilitates in-unit home healthcare delivery. The 'Condo for Life' concept saw all units conform to universal design principles and be easily adaptable to the residents' evolving needs. These features include enough space and clearance for wheelchair access to all primary living spaces, kitchens, master bathrooms, guest powder rooms, and utility rooms. Also, all living spaces are larger than average allowing more room for maneuvering.
- The project's common areas, design, and location on the site are intended to address the Southern California inside/outside lifestyle. From the beginning, all primary common areas were to have visual and direct access to The Sterling's park-like setting. Furthermore, interior dining spaces, exterior dining patios, living rooms, outside lounging spaces, bar, library, exercise rooms, and the pool are located to take maximum advantage of views and access to the adjacent open spaces at the center of the overall development.

RLPS Architect

The Houses on Bayberry

Winston-Salem, North Carolina // Arbor Acres Retirement Community

Facility type: Independent Living
Target market: Mixed income
Site location: Urban (city or town)
Capacity: 8 cottages
Total project cost: $1.5 million
Date of completion: January 2010

Below: Perspective view of a Bayberry courtyard housing cluster

Phase I site plan
1 Bayberry Homes
2 Courtyard Apartments
3 McPherson Apartments
4 Administrative Offices
5 Duplex Cottages

Overall Project Goals

This new neighborhood of up to five small house clusters responds to a need for affordable, moderately sized, higher density homes that will be inserted near the center of a retirement community over several phases of construction. Each cluster consists of two one-bedroom-with-den patio homes of 950 square feet joined as a duplex and two two-bedroom patio homes of 1,187 square feet. To fulfill the client's mission of providing affordable housing for seniors, the homes reflect a high level of thoughtfulness and detailing in a relatively small square footage at a modest price point.

Provider's Statement

Provider goals for marketing and sales

The project sold out in less than a month's time, and attracted applicants not on the waiting list by virtue of the affordability of this residency option. Demand for these accommodations is growing and waiting lists are accumulating, encouraging consideration of building additional clusters.

How did the provider plan to improve the residents' quality of life?

Connectivity among houses, and the clustering of houses around a courtyard enhances community. Covered walkway connection to the congregate buildings further enhances community. Dormers and vaulted ceilings create a sense of openness and furnish natural light, which improves mood and enhances visibility. Storage is ample. Covered porches, part of the interconnecting walkway system, are sufficiently wide to accommodate furniture, replicating the front porch way of life so beloved in the past. Carefully placed trash and recycling receptacles promote cleanliness and good environmental habits.

Did the provider give specific direction about the style, materials, features, or other design aspects of the project? If so, what were those directives?

The provider's directions were to:

- Keep the entrance fee low
- Create as much sense of openness and space as is possible within small square footage
- Provide one- and two-bedroom options
- Create connectivity among the houses, and between the house and congregate buildings via a covered walkway system
- Use traditional architectural detailing to complement existing campus residences
- Use siding and roofing to create interesting color contrasts and to generate an identity for each cluster

How did the provider's financial goals influence the project's organization, configuration, layout, or sizing of components?

The project delivers to the product continuum a price point that did not previously exist. Entrance fees are considered low and affordable in today's housing market. Monthly fees are comparable to existing apartment options, meaning that the project is generating revenue sufficient to refund the required initial investment within five years.

Architect's Statement

Design goals

- To design an attractive affordable home that would not visually compromise the adjacent market rate housing. The Houses on Bayberry feature carefully detailed, compact one and two-bedroom floor plans. The clusters are positioned with two one-bedroom apartments joined as duplex, flanked by two two-bedroom plans to create a common garden courtyard. A cathedral ceiling and dormers create volume within a small living space to allow for the infusion of natural light, create an overall feeling of openness, and ultimately achieve a sense of spaciousness within limited square footage.
- To develop a phasing strategy that permitted the owner to build new replacement homes over a five-year period of time. The multi-phased plan will

introduce the first phase of new housing cluster without requiring demolition of any existing homes. Later phases will incrementally replace the existing stock with the new cluster homes.

- To manage costs by controlling building complexity while maximizing visual impact via creative use of color and familiar materials. A distinctive color palette, appropriate to the regional vernacular, was selected for each housing cluster to provide a unique sense of identity and visual interest.

Challenges: What were the most difficult challenges in designing the project?

- The first challenge was disciplining the team to stay small to control costs. The tendency to increase square footage was a constant challenge. The final plans reflect a high level of thoughtfulness and detailing to ultimately deliver an open floor plan incorporating marketable amenities in a compact footprint. The design solution reflects traditional detailing evident elsewhere on campus and offers universal accessibility and interconnectivity to common areas and courtyard gardens that are highly valued by residents.

- Another challenge was achieving sufficient resident acceptance to increase owner confidence in moving forward. This involved convincing existing residents that the features they loved about the existing homes would not be lost in the new designs. The covered porches and courtyard flower gardens were a critical component of the new housing clusters. The plan layout and façades highlight the courtyards while providing equal appeal in a more supportive, marketable setting.

- The Phase 1 cluster ended up being on the most aggressive of the site allocations because its location did not require removal of any existing homes. The owner paid a premium for site development costs associated with the aggressive terrain.

Innovations: Does the project offer its users unique opportunities or new features not typically available in previous similar projects?

- The project turned limited room size into an advantage and compensated for the shading effect of porches through the use of cathedral ceilings and dormer skylights for abundant natural light while reinforcing volume and spaciousness.

- The project elaborated on an existing concept of courtyard gardens with a new interpretation of building placement and wraparound porches that expand a sense of ownership while proving community connectivity.

- The house clusters utilize highly disciplined color palettes to identify community and control costs.

Left: A distinctive color palette for each housing cluster provides a unique identity and visual interest
Right: Dormers and vaulted ceilings create a sense of openness and furnish natural light

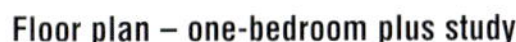
Floor plan – one-bedroom plus study

1 Living/dining
2 Study
3 Kitchen
4 Bedroom
5 Bedroom two/den option
6 Bathroom
7 Walk-in closet
8 Laundry
9 Mechanical

0 6ft

Floor plan – one-bedroom plus den

Form shapers: What factors had the most influence on the physical form of the project?

- Universal accessibility was designed in all aspects from door clearance to space templates.
- The covered walkway access to common areas permits residents to give up driving without fear of separation from community.
- Discreetly supportive features such as shower grab rails, pocket doors, elevated commodes and vanities and wheelchair accessible doorways and bathrooms facilitate aging in place thereby enabling residents to maintain independence, control and ultimately, a sense of well-being.

Top trends

- Helping aging adults stay in their homes longer: The design provides full accessibility to allow aging in place in a desirable open floor plan.
- Offering choice through a diversity of housing options: Aimed at residents who require less space but prefer living in a house rather than an apartment, the Houses on Bayberry feature efficient, marketable floor plans. The project achieved the owner's affordability goals without compromising design integrity.
- Integrating with the surrounding community: Attractive affordable homes that do not visually compromise the adjacent market rate housing. The Houses on Bayberry feature an economical interpretation of the traditional architectural forms and detailing of historic Winston-Salem, North Carolina.

Sustainability: Does the project conserve energy, water, and other natural resources? Does it reuse existing material or buildings, or include recycled building materials? How will the project improve indoor air quality in operation?

- The new homes replace outdated, inefficient 25-year-old dwellings with an updated, higher density living option without expanding the footprint.
- The footprint is compact and shares a parking area with the campus infill project.
- The project used low-VOC materials/adhesives.

Community: How does the project advance the sense of community for residents, staff, families, and neighbors?

- The space between the buildings gives the structures a sense of freedom and independence while deep porches and a system of covered walkways offer residents a safe, weather-protected connection to the commons areas at the heart of the community.
- Each Bayberry cluster features its own color palette and small-scale garden commons to promote a sense of identity and commonality between residents. The housing clusters allow for seniors with similar interests (gardening, traveling, learning in retirement) to live together in an intentional community.
- The covered front porches serve as a catalyst for neighbors to connect with each other and the shared gardens encourage community among the residents living around them.

Target market: What specific features/services/amenities were incorporated into the overall project to attract your target market?

- The Houses on Bayberry incorporate features routinely found in a traditional home within a compact floor plan. This includes walk-in closets, a laundry area, a den/office, and outdoor living areas. Upscale amenities, such as cathedral ceilings and dormer 'skylights' are also included.
- Full accessibility to allow aging in place in an open floor plan considered desirable within the market provides interconnectivity of spaces allocated for living, dining, and food preparation.
- The architectural character and amenities belie the price.

Lizard Rock Designs, LLC

Tohono O'odham Elder Homes

Sells, Arizona // Tohono O'odham Nursing Care Authority

Facility type: Assisted Living

Target market: Low income/subsidized

Site location: Rural

Capacity: 12 Assisted Living Apartments

Total project cost: $8 million

Date of completion: September 2010

Below: Pedestrian pathway
Opposite: Exterior elevation

Overall Project Goals

This project is a cluster of four 12-bedroom Elder Homes located adjacent to the Archie Hendricks Skilled Nursing Facility on the Tohono O'odham Indian Reservation. Each residence contains 12 private bedrooms with bathrooms, as well as common kitchen, dining, living, and social areas. The homes are based on the Green House® model of care, although the model has been adapted to work within the culture of the Tohono O'odham. Each house opens to important views (sacred mountains to the east and west) and outdoor patios, cooking areas, walkways, and seating areas surround the homes.

Each home is a place where elders can receive assistance with the activities of daily living without the assistance becoming the focus of their existence. Elders each enjoy a private room with access to all areas of the house, including the kitchen, living, and outdoor patios. The elders are free from a rigid institutional schedule and live a comfortable daily life – sleeping, eating, and engaging in activities as they choose to. Staff members prepare meals in the open kitchen and serve them at a large dining table where residents, visitors, and staff enjoy pleasant dining and good conversation. The living space is focused on the hearth, with high levels of natural light, views, and several easily accessible patios. Separate covered controlled outdoor areas are provided for each house. Staff offices and other areas are provided in each unit. Houses will be connected to the main building by exterior walks.

Provider's Statement

Provider goals for marketing and sales

The project provides a small-scale model for extending Assisted Living facilities to all 15 districts across the Tohono O'odham Nation.

How did the provider plan to improve the residents' quality of life?

The scale and access to the exterior was given priority, as residents have lived the majority of their lives outdoors.

How did the provider want to improve workplace quality for employees?

Employees develop strong bonds with residents because they are caring for only 12 people at a time instead of a much larger number. Employees understand residents' preferences and schedules better in a small home model.

Did the provider have specific goals for the project's staffing quantities, training, or distribution?

The amount of staff required for models like this is less than for traditional Assisted Living facilities, which makes this a more feasible model for a rural senior-care system.

Did the provider give specific direction about the style, materials, features, or other design aspects of the project? If so, what were those directives?

The project was to reflect materials and stone used by Tohono O'odham in traditional buildings (for example, rough-sawn wood framing, wood floors, and volcanic stone veneer).

How did the provider's financial goals influence the project's organization, configuration, layout, or sizing of components?

The project shares services and staff with the local nursing home, eliminating the need for subsidy by the tribe.

Architect's Statement

Design goals

- After an extensive survey of senior-care needs by a Native-owned health-planning firm, the Tohono O'odham Nation determined that there is a significant need for Assisted Living services on the reservation. These homes are an effort to meet that need. Seniors are often faced with a choice between extended stays in the existing nursing home or returning to home environments that are unsafe. However, traditional Assisted Living models do not work in dispersed rural environments. This project attempts to provide Assisted Living in small clusters that could later be spread throughout the reservation.
- The owner's second goal was to rethink the Green Home® model of elder care to adapt it to the Tohono O'odham culture. Many focus groups were held with residents, family members, staff, and the Board of the Archie Hendrix Skilled Nursing Facility to shape the design of the homes. Two key priorities emerged: maximize outdoor views, access, and living space; and provide layers of privacy between individual suites and common areas. The floor plan reflects both priorities: providing multiple ways to live and be connected to nature, and locating a den space outside resident rooms to separate them from the main common room.
- The owner's third goal was to create a project that could be replicated in each of the 15 districts on the reservation. Long travel distances and a dispersed population present unusual challenges, and traditional methods of providing home care, meals assistance, and Assisted Living must be adapted to work in this environment. The Tohono O'odham Nursing Care Authority hopes to create a network of Elder Homes to anchor other services such as home care, wound care for seniors with diabetes, and assistance with meals.

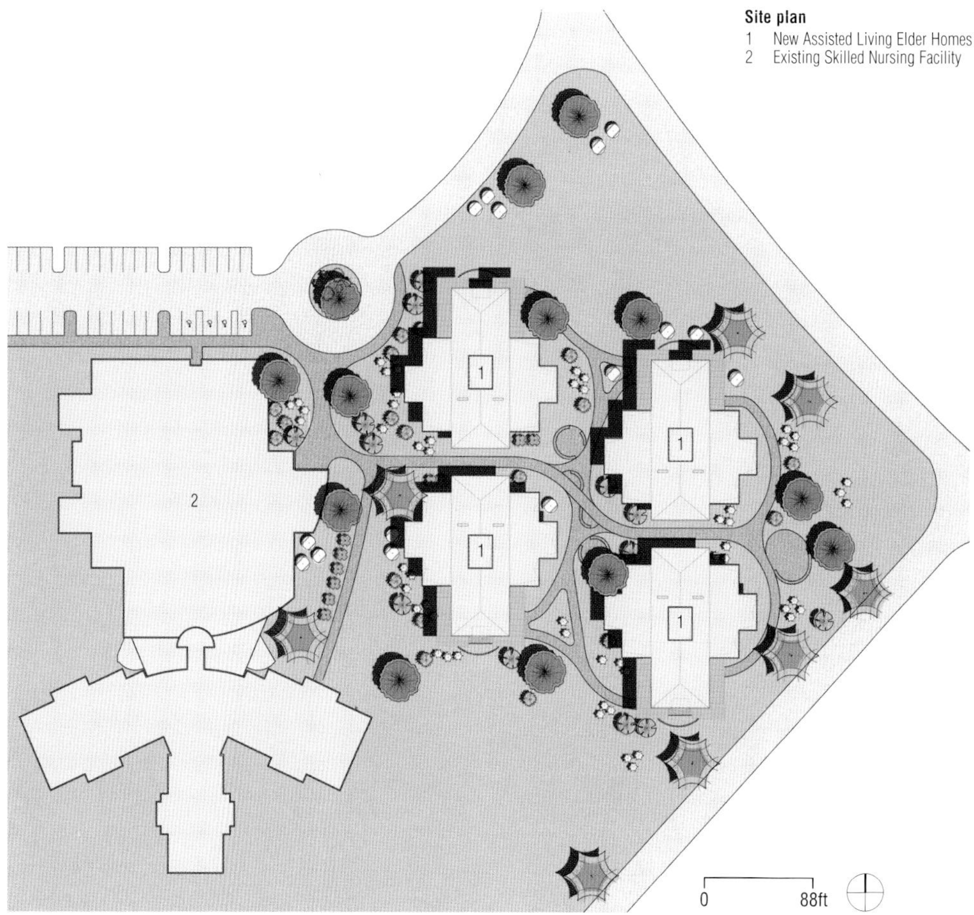

Site plan
1 New Assisted Living Elder Homes
2 Existing Skilled Nursing Facility

Challenges: What were the most difficult challenges in designing the project?

- The first challenge for the project was to find a model for Assisted Living that would be both affordable to operate and appropriate to the Tohono O'odham culture. The owner chose to adapt a model of care in the style of Green Home®, but faced the challenge of convincing residents that they would be comfortable in a group living situation. (Most residents live in single-family homes at a great distance from each other.) This was achieved by adapting the model to provide den spaces outside each resident room to offer an additional layer of privacy between the most public areas and the residents' rooms.
- The second challenge for the project was to create a cluster of homes that fit the operational model the owner wished to begin with (that is, a series of independently staffed homes that are supported by the infrastructure of the adjacent

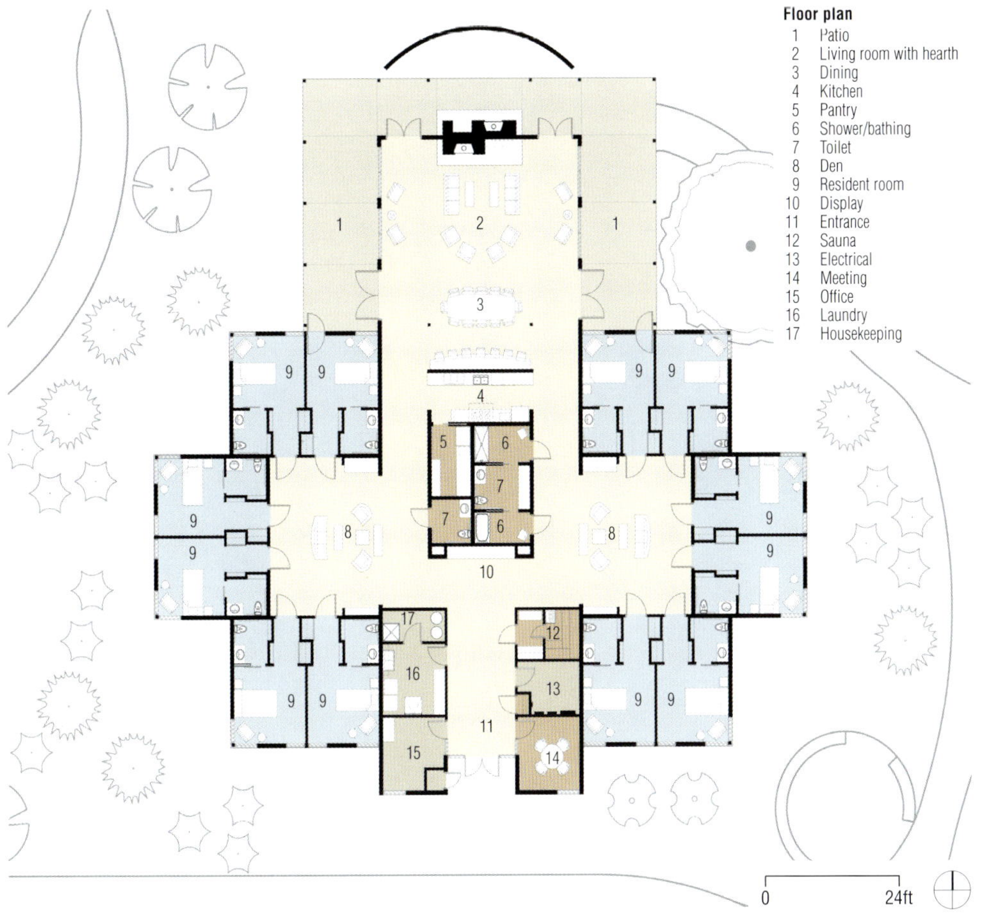

nursing facility). The goal is to demonstrate that this model of Assisted Living can work on the reservation before extending it to the remaining 14 districts throughout the reservation.

- The final challenge was to relate the new homes to the existing Skilled Care facility in such a way that they feel residential and take advantage of important views and connections with nature. Both views and access to nature were listed as residents' top priorities, and there were concerns that too close an association with the nursing home facility could compromise the residential character of the Elder Homes.

Innovations: Does the project offer its users unique opportunities or new features not typically available in previous similar projects?

- The project is innovative because it adapts the Green Home model to a different culture. The Tohono O'odham place great value on respect for nature, and many of the residents interviewed stated that they have lived most of their lives outside. The design reflects this by opening the common areas and surrounding patios completely to the exterior, and orienting them to focus on important landmarks, including Baboquivari Peak and a mine that many residents worked in. In addition, spaces between resident rooms and the main common room reflect the fact that most residents are accustomed to more privacy, having lived dispersed from their neighbors across the reservation.

- The site design is innovative because homes can either stand alone or be grouped in twos or fours. This was created to support a model where the nursing care authority seeks to provide Assisted Living services across a widely dispersed area (15 separate districts).

- The project provides both interior and exterior cooking areas as requested by residents. Many residents spent most of their adult lives cooking outside over mesquite fires, and the residents requested the facilities to continue this practice in the Elder Homes.

Form shapers: What factors had the most influence on the physical form of the project?

- Bedrooms and toilets are designed to be fully wheelchair accessible. In addition, two bathing areas are provided to allow a home care attendant to assist a resident with bathing or showering at the resident's preference. One of the homes will also have an indoor sauna area to accommodate customary healing rituals.

- Because it is located on the same campus as a Skilled Care facility, the project provides a version of a continuum of care that responds to conditions on the Tohono O'odham Reservation. The project provides an intermediate level of care between being discharged and an extended stay in the nursing facility. Residents who need more intensive care can move to the nursing facility when necessary, then return to the more residential care provided in the Elder Homes.

- One of the biggest challenges to providing elder care services on the Tohono O'odham Reservation are the extensive distances residents must travel to receive care. This project attempts to co-locate several services needed by seniors (Assisted

Living, Skilled Nursing, and wound care) so that seniors do not have to travel via bus to multiple locations across great distances.

Top trends

- Offering choice through a diversity of housing options: Many Native American communities face the challenge of an aging population with few options between traditional Skilled Nursing care and no care whatsoever. Because of rural conditions and long travel distances, traditional models of Assisted Living and home care have not worked in Native American communities. This project seeks to adapt the Green House® model to the particular conditions and cultural influences of the Tohono O'odham community. If successful, the model will be extended across the reservation, providing not only Assisted Living, but other senior care services such as adult care and wound care for diabetics.

Sustainability: Does the project conserve energy, water, and other natural resources? Does it reuse existing material or buildings, or include recycled building materials? How will the project improve indoor air quality in operation?

- The project is surrounded by shade structures, landscaping, and awnings to protect south and west exposures from sun. To protect against heat gain, but allow for a strong connection to the outdoors, roofs are extended to shade exposed glass.
- The entire site is served by a natural wastewater treatment system, which uses settling ponds and plants to break down solids while liquids are evaporated or consumed by the plants.
- The project has been designed for future connection of solar power panels, and combines an evaporative cooling system with high-efficiency heat pump units for heating and cooling.

Community: How does the project advance the sense of community for residents, staff, families, and neighbors?

- Community and a sense of belonging start around the hearth in the great room of this project. The Tohono O'odham have a long tradition of sharing oral traditions around a fire, and hearths have great symbolic value in their culture. This project provides a two-way hearth to honor resident requests that they have a

place to be outside close to nature, and to cook with traditional mesquite wood.

- The homes are separate and distinct, but organized in a way to create a cluster with shared outdoor spaces. Many of the local male residents worked in a mine, which is visible in the distance from the campus of the Skilled Nursing facility, and the men tend to gather in locations with a view of the mine to talk and share company. The gardens are all visible from the common rooms of the Elder Homes, increasing the sense of security and safety within the community, in case a resident has difficulty outside.
- Members of the Tohono O'odham Nursing Care Authority Board, staff of the nursing home, residents and their families have contributed to the design from the outset. One resident has suggested that the Elder Homes each include 'story sticks' – carved sticks, which tell the story of who came before in the development of the place. Tohono O'odham community members have been involved throughout design, they sit on the board of the nursing authority, and they have enthusiastically supported the architecture and design strategies employed in the project.

Target market: What specific features/services/ amenities were incorporated into the overall project to attract your target market?

- The project includes many elements requested by residents and family, including the ability to cook outdoors, extensive connections to nature, appropriate landscaping, and multiple ways for families to gather with residents in the homes.
- Residents and family members helped choose the finishes and building systems throughout. As a result, there is extensive use of natural materials (exposed wood structure and roof deck, natural stone at the fireplaces, and natural stone in limited areas on the floor). The building's mechanical system includes both evaporative cooling (an effective and sustainable system in a dry desert climate) and highly efficient heat pumps for individual control.
- One of the key features is that this project will provide care for family members on the reservation itself. Too often, family members are forced to relocate off reservation to Phoenix to receive appropriate care.

Opposite: Living room/hearth
Above: Dining room/kitchen

The 10-Year Award

The Design for Aging 10-Year award, now in its second cycle, was created to recognize projects that:

- have been completed and occupied for more than 10 years
- incorporate innovative, high-quality designs
- have survived the test of time
- offer lessons still valuable to today's consumers and competitive environment.

Instead of a singular project, the Jury elected to recognize Paul and Teresa Klaassen who we feel unanimously have significantly impacted the design direction of the field. Their work has fundamentally shaped the underlying notion of what senior living can and should be.

This year's Jury, comprised of past Design for Aging Knowledge Community Chairs, including Glen Tipton, Jeffrey Anderzhon and Leslie Moldow, chose this direction for the award after only brief consideration of the criteria. Founded in 1981 by the Klaassens, Sunrise Senior Living built many projects that became award winners of the Design for Aging Review (DFAR). Over the many cycles of the DFAR awards, several of Sunrise Senior Living's projects have received citations or other recognition. While the emeritus jury could have selected numerous single projects as models, the Klaassen's concept of residential-care settings has changed the standards of design for aging so we wanted to honor the entire scope of their influence on senior-living design within both the care and design professions.

The Klaassens became familiar with the model of senior-living design in Holland where both of Paul's grandmothers lived. There, both care and assistance were brought to the elders in a residential environment. Frustrated by the predominant institutional, medical-model of long-term care in the United States, Paul and Terry Klaassen renovated a building in Oakton, Virginia in 1981. Sunrise Terrace opened to their first community of residents and later gave its name to the business: Sunrise Senior Living Inc. Within a year, they opened a second building followed by a third within a year after that. Paul said that he 'always envisioned it as a growth company.' Since nursing homes were caring for some people who really didn't need nursing, the Klaassens felt there was a better model for long-term care that focused more on the resident and the family, a model with a more attractive physical setting.

They learned many lessons from that early experience. They understood that the environment matters and that the physical manifestation of the nursing home may not be the most suited for care of less acute seniors. They saw that the residential model brings pleasure to residents and with this knowledge they set out to build the first Sunrise prototype that could be placed on three acres anywhere in the country. According to Paul Klaassen, 'It had to be reproducible; it had to have timeless appeal.'

The first prototype home, located in Arlington, Virginia, was built in 1988. The project, located high on a hill with a view of the Washington Monument, drew hundreds of industry and policy leaders in long-term care who came to tour the community. The interiors featured large areas dedicated to shared spaces, residential-quality corridors, and apartments with kitchens and private bathrooms. The building's furnishings added the touches of home. Most people caught the excitement and understood the significance of the vision. Although William Shields recollects that 'when some people toured they commented, "it was too small … too homey … not medical enough."' Paul and Terry listened, thanked the visitors, and moved on with their vision, continuing to make modifications for the next 23 years. Paul Klaassen explains, 'That building changed everything. It was the first really purpose-built, Assisted Living community of its type.'

As the old nursing home paradigm changed, the vocabulary changed along with it. Rather than facilities filled with patients, their business and the industry was now comprised of communities where staff provided senior residents with assistance in the activities of daily living.

The prototype sported an iconic bay tower, a wrap-around front porch, and a grand internal staircase, which were incorporated into subsequent projects. As the business developed in different regions of the country, the prototypes were adapted to suit the vernacular architecture and address varied consumer preferences and expectations. The first project on the west coast, Sunrise Mercer Island in Washington State, adapted to a challenging hillside site. A later Washington State project, Sunrise Bellevue, integrated the Craftsman vernacular in its façade. Other sites acquired, such as the one in Victoria Canada, worked around the preservation of large trees. Northern California projects, such as Sunrise San Mateo, began to take on a more Mission-style architectural feeling, while in Southern California, a Spanish Revival vocabulary was most suitable for Sunrise Pacific Palisades. The designers did not shy away from sites with historically significant landmark buildings and managed to integrate them into the new context, such as Sunrise Claremont, which adaptively reused a historic 1912 Arts and Crafts house for offices and resident activities.

The prototypes established a large amount of quality common areas as a ratio to resident apartments in order to encourage more time spent socializing and participating in shared activities. They included both formal and informal sitting areas similar to a home's living room and family room, a pre-function ice-cream parlor for snacks and activities, and an intimate dining space. The kitchens were designed to serve three meals a day although the residents did have the option of making a simple meal for themselves using apartment kitchenettes.

The buildings support residents who have a higher acuity. Rather than institutional-looking grab rails in the corridor, there are leaning rails reminiscent of wainscoting; large bathrooms allow better mobility and have support rails. Increased lighting levels aid the seniors' vision and care is taken with the selection of the furnishings to provide elements that are appropriately scaled and easy to move and clean. The overall effect is of a comfortable country inn where you feel you can put up your feet: a place that is your own.

The Klaassens recognized that to create a major change in the United States' system of senior care, they needed to do more than develop their own properties; they coined the term 'Assisted Living' and in 1990 Paul Klaassen helped found the Assisted Living Federation of America (ALFA) and served as its founding chairman until 1994. For 20 years ALFA has helped champion the concept of Assisted Living by defining it, educating the public and lobbying for regulatory change. This new model enhanced elder consumer choice and quality of life and began to influence for-profit and not-for-profit development alike. People were continually surprised and impressed with Paul's generosity in sharing what he had learned; if you cared about what you were doing for seniors, he would help.

Paul and Terry were never satisfied simply to rest on the success of a particular project. Having served residents with dementia and Alzheimer's disease since the company's founding, they formalized a care program in 1995 called Sunrise Reminiscence Program. The environment they crafted was comfortable, safe, and secure and allowed residents to participate in familiar, meaningful everyday activities. All programs included outdoor gardens or terraces, activity spaces, and residential-style kitchens. Bathing occurred in non-threatening 'spa' spaces and they tried new concepts such as snoezelen rooms, which provide controlled multisensory stimulation in a soothing space.

In the early part of the new century, Sunrise began to include Independent Living alongside its Assisted Living communities and, with the acquisition of Marriott Senior Living, expanded into the Continuing Care Retirement Communities (CCRC) market. Their next expansion tapped urban and international markets with their first foray into the United Kingdom and Germany.

Throughout all these new directions, Paul and Teresa Klaassen continued to embody the culture that focused on taking care of special people – the elders. If you worked for Sunrise, you caught the spirit of the organization that they set in place. They have a passion for making senior care better and will say, when asked, that the best community has not yet been built. However, this award recognizes that the first community and the waves of influence that followed in their expansions compelled others to adapt to a new idea of Assisted Living. The body of work is more than worthy of this 10-Year Award.

Leslie G. Moldow, FAIA

Data Mining Findings

Perkins Eastman

Research study description

In September 2007, the organizer of a design competition conducted its first web-based submission process for their ninth biennial design competition. Applicants were required to complete an online submission form, in any of the four submission categories: Planning, Concept Design, Building, or Research/POE. Seventy-two projects were submitted by architects and providers. With the data now in hand, the organizer recognized an opportunity: A great deal of information had been collected from architectural firms and service providers. If this information could be systematically analyzed, the results could be shared so that others could learn from the best projects in the country. In March 2008, the organizer submitted a grant request for the organization and analysis of the data collected in the 2007 design competition. The Data Mining Findings report is the culmination of this research study.

What facilities were involved in the research?

The study analyzed data from 72 different submissions to the design competition, with an emphasis on the 36 award-winning projects. The submissions represented a broad cross-section of the senior-living industry in terms of facility type, context, and geographic location. The submissions consisted of nine building types: Independent Living, Assisted Living, Skilled Nursing, Special Care Unit, Wellness/Fitness Center, Hospice, Senior Community Center, Other Medical Services Care Facility, and Other. Several Research/POE submissions were also analyzed. The analyzed projects are spread fairly evenly throughout the United States, excluding the northwest region; and several are located in Japan. The projects range in size from small chapels to large Continuing Care Retirement Communities (CCRCs). Total project costs for 80 percent of the submissions ranged from $1.93 million to $92.3 million. Almost three-quarters of the submissions were new construction, with the remainder being additions or renovations/modernizations.

Who funded the research?

The study had two funding sources: the AIA generously provided a grant to the organizer of the design competition to have the data collected by the design competition analyzed; and these funds were then matched by the submitting architect.

What was the purpose of the research?

The primary goals of the study were to: enable designers and providers to learn about various design approaches to senior living in order to better serve their clients; promote a better understanding of the range of design goals and approaches, sharing lessons learned among peers; provide a more comprehensive look at statistics, patterns, and innovations impacting the senior-living industry and design community; establish a data bank that will offer members the opportunity for future 'longitudinal' perspectives; and provide a benchmark from leading-edge, state-of-the-art design submissions that can help the design community to raise the bar on the quality of design solutions provided to the industry as a whole. A second part of the study was performed to assess the questions included in the design competition submission forms and the quality of the data received to determine how to improve the submittal process to produce more usable and informative data in the future.

Hypothesis

Unlike conventional research, data mining does not impose the structure of pre-determined hypotheses, but rather elicits questions from the data that may offer insights into underlying patterns and evolving trends. As with any data mining study, there were an infinite number of questions that could be asked and answered. But because of the scope of this study, we chose to analyze and present the findings that were the most interesting to the senior-living industry and that would have the most value to architects, providers, and the organizer of the design competition. Some of the questions that we explored included: What were the common design objectives? What were the innovative ideas and strategies? Based on intent and project size, could the various projects be grouped into 'types' of communities, and if so, how did the types compare in terms of space breakdowns (for example the ratio of common area to resident area) and the typical sizes and distributions of units?

Methodology

The data mining study was conducted between June and October in 2008. The study took into account all 72 projects submitted to the design competition, though particular attention was paid to the 36 award winners at different times during the analysis. The study consisted of both quantitative and qualitative evaluations of four types of submission forms, which included 202 questions, and garnered 9,804 responses, plus charts of project metrics. Primary data mining included a question-by-question analysis of responses, correlations between questions, and a comparison of the award winners to the other submissions. Secondary data mining consisted of further inquiry into the award-winning projects, where several project groupings were established based on project descriptions and size (as defined by project costs). We also provided feedback on the design competition submission forms so that future cycles could have a streamlined submittal process, which could result in better-quality data.

Findings

We found a number of key themes or patterns that characterize today's award-winning senior-living projects, such as the idea of 'integration' – of communities with their surroundings, of interior and exterior settings, and of residents with each other in a natural aging process. Another important theme was 'wellness,' which is driving new facilities across market sectors, from affordable to luxury. We also noted significant differences between 'campus-centered' and 'greater-community-focused' developments. Campus-centered communities typically allocate 11 percent more building area to private residential space. In contrast, greater-community-focused developments build a higher proportion of common space with more diverse and specialized functions, often providing amenities that the general public is encouraged to use.

Applicability

The mission of the organizer of the design competition, for whom this study was performed, is to foster design innovation and disseminate knowledge necessary to enhance the built environment and quality of life for an aging society. Accordingly, the themes and patterns described in the data mining study were intended to inform both senior-living architects and providers. The Data Mining Findings report has been made available to the public on the AIA's website, where it can be viewed by anyone interested in the results.

Form of communication

The report includes a lot of information, so it was organized with clear sections and hierarchies of information to assist comprehension. The report has four parts. Section One, 'Methodology,' explains how we approached the study. Section Two, 'Data Mining Findings,' summarizes the information that was derived directly from the submissions, which comprises the primary data analysis. Section Three, 'Reflections on the Data,' describes patterns or concepts that emerged from the secondary analysis. Section Four, 'Quality of the Data,' examines the submission form questions that produced the data and recommends ways to improve data collection in future submission processes. The submission forms from the design competition and detailed reports were provided as appendices. Wherever possible, photographs and charts were included to visually convey information; and throughout, portions of the text are highlighted so that someone skimming the report can easily pull out the key ideas.

Relationship to recent studies

Before embarking on the study, we explored precedent data mining research studies to understand how best to elicit useful information in an efficient way. We found that data mining is generally applied to very large sets of numerical or quantifiable data for the purpose of building predictive models. Such research studies demand both sophisticated analytical tools and rigorous statistical parameters. By comparison, the data collected by the design competition was drawn from a very small sample and consists of a mix of both quantitative and qualitative data. The research techniques we used, therefore, rely on much simpler methods of finding commonalities and comparisons. It was because of our precedent research that we were able to develop a methodology suited to this particular study and the types of data that were available for analysis.

What questions does this research or POE raise?

The data collected by the submission forms for the design competition adds to the information that has been collected in the eight previous cycles of the design competition conducted by the organizer. However, only data from the ninth cycle was analyzed in this study. Though this study yielded interesting findings, it is a snapshot of patterns instead of an indication of trends. The value of this data is going to be truly realized only when data mining can be conducted on the information collected from the past eight cycles and/or from future design competitions. The greatest advantage of this data mining process will be seen when the findings can be compared to other years, which will enable the organizer of the design competition to start tracking trends. Also, the addition of submissions from other years would increase the pool of projects being compared, which would improve the validity of the findings.

Other points

Analyzing the data collected by the design competition was complicated for several reasons. There were 72 submissions in four categories: eight Planning submissions, four Concept Design submissions, 56 Building submissions, and four Research/POE submissions; and each category included different sets of questions. The submitted projects consisted of any of nine building types; and varied from a single building to an entire campus. The scope of the submitted projects included new construction, additions and/or renovations. And during analysis, even after all of the submissions were divided into groups based on project similarities, in some cases there were more than 10 comparable projects, but in others less than three. However, even with these obstacles, we were able to develop findings that could inform future senior-living projects, provide a benchmark against which to compare a project, and provide a basis for comparison and trends development with future cycles of the design competition.

Final Thoughts

The full Data Mining Research Project – Design for Aging Review 9 Data Mining Findings – can be found at www.aia.org/dfa. This report as well as a new DFAR10 Research Report are located in the 'Research' section.

Project Data

Buena Vista Terrace

Provider: Citizens Housing Corporation

Architect: HKIT Architects

Contractor: Cahill Contractors, Inc.

Interior designer: Marie Fisher Interior Design

Landscape architect: Orsee Design Associates, Inc.

Structural engineer: OLMM Consulting Engineers

Mechanical engineer: Tommy Siu & Associates

Electrical engineer: Bhatia Associates, Inc.

Civil engineer: Luk and Associates

Independent Living Building Data			
Unit type	Number of units	Size range (NSF)	Typical size (NSF)
Studio apartment	33	319 to 371	334
One-bedroom apartment	7	501 to 528	501
Total (all Units)	40		
Total NSF			19,313

DeVries Place Senior Apartments

Provider: Mid-Peninsula Housing Coalition

Architect: HKIT Architects

Collaborating architect: Rothschild Schwartz Architects

Role of collaborating architect: DeVries Home Restoration

Contractor: J.H. Fitzmaurice, Inc.

Interior designer: Mimi Evans, Interior Concepts (owner's consultant)

Landscape architect: LaRocca & Associates

Structural engineer: H.D. Rueb Structural Engineers (wood frame); FBA, Inc. (concrete podium consultant)

Mechanical engineer: Tommy Siu & Associates

Electrical engineer: BWF Consulting Engineers

Civil engineer: Kier & Wright

Independent Living Building Data			
Unit type	Number of units	Size range (NSF)	Typical size (NSF)
Studio apartment	1	455 to 455	455
One-bedroom apartment	92	559 to 579	579
Two-bedroom apartment	10	802 to 858	858
Total (all Units)	103		
Total NSF			60,524

Silver Sage Village Senior Cohousing

Arhcitect: McCamant & Durrett Architects

Collaborating architect: Bryan Bowen Architects

Role of collaborating architect: Construction documents

Contractor: Wonderland Hill Development Company

Landscape architect: Ciofalo & Associates, Landscape Architect

Structural engineer: Boulder Association of Structural Engineers

Mechanical engineer: Silvertip Integrated Engineering Consultants

Electrical engineer: Johnson & Robertson, Inc.

Civil engineer: Charles Kiem & Associates

Independent Living Building Data			
Unit type	Number of units	Size range (NSF)	Typical size (NSF)
One-bedroom apartment	2	-	1100
Two-bedroom apartment	8	-	860 or 1060
Two-bedroom plus den apartment*	6	-	1520–2794
Total (all Units)	16		
Total NSF			21,330

*Note: 'Two-bedroom plus den' does not accurately describe the 'two-bedroom plus' units in this project. There are three types of 'two-bedroom plus' apartments that have one or two offices and additional spaces, which were designed in conjunction with the residents.

SKY55

Provider: Forest City Residential Group

Architect: Solomon Cordwell Buenz

Contractor: McHugh Construction

Interior designer: SCB

Landscape architect: Daniel Weinbach & Partners

Structural engineer: Chris Stefanos Associates

Mechanical engineer: WMA Consulting Engineers

Electrical engineer: WMA Consulting Engineers

Independent Living Building Data			
Unit type	Number of units	Size range (NSF)	Typical size (NSF)
Studio apartment	6	-	710
One-bedroom apartment	85	544 to 621	522
Total (all Units)	91		
Total NSF			-

Hospice of Lancaster County

Provider: Hospice of Lancaster County
Architect: RLPS Architects
Contractor: Benchmark Construction Company, Inc.
Interior designer: Interior Planning Group
Structural engineer: O'Donnell, Naccarato & MacIntosh
Mechanical engineer: Reese Engineering, Inc.
Electrical engineer: Reese Engineering, Inc.
Civil engineer: Derck & Edson Associates

Skilled Nursing Building Data			
Unit type	Number of units	Size range (NSF)	Typical size (NSF)
Single-occupancy room	24	460 to 460	460
Total (all Units)	24		
Total NSF			11,404

Lenbrook

Provider: Lenbrook Square Foundation, Inc.
Architect: THW Design
Contractor: Bovis Lend Lease, Inc.
Interior designer: Interior Design Associates, Inc.
Landscape architect: THW Design
Structural engineer: Uzun & Case
Mechanical engineer: Barrett, Woodyard & Associates, Inc.
Electrical engineer: Barrett, Woodyard & Associates, Inc.
Civil engineer: Long Engineering, Inc.
Developer/marketer: Spectrum Marketing, Inc.
Irrigation design: Irrigation Consultant Services, Inc.
Low-voltage systems design: Reese Engineering
Culinary service: Culinary Design Service
Wellness design: Montague, Eippert & Associates
Conveyance consultant: Lerch, Bates & Associates, Inc.
Fountain design: Hobbs Architectural Fountains
Pool design: Water Technology, Inc.

Independent Living Building Data			
Unit type	Number of units	Size range (NSF)	Typical size (NSF)
One-bedroom apartment	18	Up to 1097	1097
Two-bedroom apartment	96	Up to 2915	N/A
Two-bedroom plus den apartment	28	Up to 2674	N/A
Total (all Units)	142*		
Total NSF			233,994

*Note: does not include the 225 pre-existing units

Lenbrook continued

Assisted Living Building Data			
Unit type	Number of units	Size range (NSF)	Typical size (NSF)
One-bedroom apartment	16	533 to 724	N/A
Total (all Units)	16		
Total NSF			10,242

Skilled Nursing Building Data			
Unit type	Number of units	Size range (NSF)	Typical size (NSF)
Single-occupancy room	40	260 to 390	338
Total (all Beds)	40		
Total NSF			12,932

Dementia/Memory Support Building Data			
Unit type	Number of units	Size range (NSF)	Typical size (NSF)
Single-occupancy room	20	260 to 390	338
Total (all Beds)	20		
Total NSF			6,466

NewBridge on the Charles

Provider: Hebrew SeniorLife

Architect: Perkins Eastman

Collaborating architect: Chan Krieger & Associates

Role of collaborating architect: Associate architect

Contractor: Suffolk Construction

Interior designer: Perkins Eastman

Landscape architect: Stantec

Structural engineer: LeMessurier Consultants

Mechanical engineer: Richard D. Kimball Company, Inc.

Electrical engineer: Richard D. Kimball Company, Inc.

Civil engineer: Stantec

Food Service: Food Facilities Concepts Inc.

Low Voltage: ART Engineering Corporation

Independent Living
Building Data

Unit type	Number of units	Size range (NSF)	Typical size (NSF)
One-bedroom apartment	9	825 to 999	825
One-bedroom plus den apartment	36	1,041 to 1,078	1,041
Two-bedroom apartment	69	1,146 to 1,134	1,076
Two-bedroom plus den apartment	68	1,374 to 1,595	1,374
Two-bedroom cottage	12	1,476	1,476
Two-bedroom plus den cottage	38	1,799 to 2,741	1,799
Two-bedroom villas	24	-	-
Total (all Units)	256		
Total NSF			314,351

Assisted Living
Building Data

Unit type	Number of units	Size range (NSF)	Typical size (NSF)
One-bedroom apartment	22	469 to 544	544
One-bedroom deluxe	26	642 to 700	675
Two-bedroom apartment	3	985	985
Total (all Units)	51		
Total NSF			43,076

Skilled Nursing (includes 48 sub-acute beds)
Building Data

Unit type	Number of units	Size range (NSF)	Typical size (NSF)
Single-occupancy room	185	230 to 257	257
Double-occupancy room	36 (72 Residents)	435	435
Seclusion	1	257	257
Isolation Room	6	257	257
Total (all Units)	268		
Total NSF			163,987

NewBridge on the Charles continued

Dementia/Memory Support Unit
Building Data

Unit type	Number of units	Size range (NSF)	Typical size (NSF)
Single-occupancy room	32	281 to 257	300
Double-occupancy room	4 (8 Residents)	548	548
Total (all Units)	40		
Total NSF			18,874

Sun City Palace Tsukaguchi

Provider: Half Century More

Architect: BAR Architects

Collaborating architect: Ken Asai Architectural Research, Inc.

Role of collaborating architect: Architect of record

Contractor: Okamura Corporation

Interior designer: BAMO (Independent Living), Yokomizo Associates (Nursing Care)

Landscape architect: SWA Group

Structural engineer: Ken Asai Architectural Research, Inc.

Mechanical engineer: Ken Asai Architectural Research, Inc.

Electrical engineer: Ken Asai Architectural Research, Inc.

Civil engineer: Ken Asai Architectural Research, Inc.

Coordinating Architect: M.D.A. Associates

Independent Living
Building Data

Unit type	Number of units	Size range (NSF)	Typical size (NSF)
Studio apartment	390	660 to 735	690
One-bedroom apartment	90	735 to 810	765
Two-bedroom apartment	90	810 to 835	840
Two-bedroom plus den apartment	30	885 to 960	915
Total (all Units)	600		
Total NSF			440,000

Skilled Nursing
Building Data*

Unit type	Number of units	Size range (NSF)	Typical size (NSF)
Single-occupancy room	120	-	190
Double-occupancy room	40	-	430
Total (all Units)	160		
Total NSF			40,000**

*Note: the numbers for Assisted Living, Skilled Nursing and Dementia/Memory Support are assumptions. At the time of completion, it was not determined which rooms would be single or double occupancy, or which would be allocated to skilled nursing, assisted care or dementia care.

**This is a very approximate area for the living units only, and does not include public space.

Sun City Palace Tsukaguchi continued

Dementia/Memory Support Unit Building Data***			
Unit type	Number of units	Size range (NSF)	Typical size (NSF)
Single-occupancy room	40	-	190
Total (all Units)	40		
Total NSF			7600

***The precise measurement is not yet available. At the time of completion, it was approximated that one secure floor would be dedicated to dementia patients – approximately 40 units and 40 beds, all single-occupancy.

The Point at C.C. Young

Provider: C.C. Young

Architect: Perkins Eastman

Contractor: Bovis Lend Lease

Interior designer: Perkins Eastman

Landscape architect: David C. Baldwin

Structural engineer: Raymond L. Goodson, Jr.

Mechanical engineer: Blum Consulting Engineers

Electrical engineer: Blum Consulting Engineers

Civil engineer: Raymond L. Goodson, Jr.

Zoning consultant: Masterplan

Accessibility consultant: Access by Design

Acoustics consultant: Wrightson, Johnson, Haddon, and Williams, Inc.

Owner's representative: Morris Company

Westminster Village Town Center

Provider: Westminster Village

Architect: Perkins Eastman

Contractor: Sundt Construction

Interior designer: Perkins Eastman

Landscape architect: Waibel & Associates Landscape Architecture

Structural engineer: GRAEF

Mechanical engineer: GRAEF

Electrical engineer: GRAEF

Civil engineer: David Evans & Associates

Assisted Living Building Data			
Unit type	Number of units	Size range (NSF)	Typical size (NSF)
One-bedroom apartment	23	650	650
Total (all Units)	23		
Total NSF			-

The Legacy at Willow Bend

Provider: Legacy Senior Communities, Inc.

Architect: DiMella Shaffer

Contractor: Andres Construction Services

Interior designer: Studio Six5 & DiMella Shaffer

Landscape architect: MESA Design Group

Structural engineer: L.A. Fuess Partners

Mechanical engineer: Purdy McGuire

Electrical engineer: Purdy McGuire

Civil engineer: Walter P. Moore & Associates

Geotech: Reed Engineering Group

Food Service: Systems Design International

Lighting: Lang Lighting Design, Inc.

Acoustical: PMK Consultants

Independent Living Building Data			
Unit type	Number of units	Size range (NSF)	Typical size (NSF)
One-bedroom apartment	62	-	1135
Two-bedroom apartment	25	-	1375
Two-bedroom plus den apartment	28	-	1870
Total (all Units)	-		
Total NSF			-

The Legacy at Willow Bend continued

Assisted Living Building Data			
Unit type	Number of units	Size range (NSF)	Typical size (NSF)
One-bedroom apartment	36	-	520
Two-bedroom apartment	4	-	860
Total (all Units)	-		
Total NSF			-

Skilled Nursing Building Data			
Unit type	Number of units	Size range (NSF)	Typical size (NSF)
Single-occupancy room	60	-	-
Total (all Units)	-		
Total NSF			-

Dementia/Memory Support Unit Building Data			
Unit type	Number of units	Size range (NSF)	Typical size (NSF)
Double-occupancy room	18	-	360
Total (all Units)	-		
Total NSF			-

Three Links Care Center Lodging Facility

Provider: Pat Vincent

Architect: Architects Inc

Contractor: College City Homes, Lakeville, Minnesota

Interior designer: Interiors By Design, Minnetonka, Minnesota

Structural engineer: Larson Engineering

Mechanical engineer: Design Build

Electrical engineer: Design Build

Civil engineer: Mcghie and Betts

Dementia/Memory Support Unit Building Data			
Unit type	Number of units	Size range (NSF)	Typical size (NSF)
Single-occupancy room	18	-	211
Double-occupancy room	2	-	275
Total (all Units)	20		
Total NSF			4,348

Bloomfield Township Senior Center

Provider: Charter Township of Bloomfield & Bloomfield Township Senior Services

Architect: Fusco, Shaffer, & Pappas, Inc.

Contractor: George W. Auch Company

Interior designer: Fusco, Shaffer & Pappas, Inc., Architects & Planners

Landscape architect: James C. Scott & Associates, Inc.

Structural engineer: L & A, Inc.

Mechanical engineer: EAM Engineers, Inc.

Electrical engineer: EAM Engineers, Inc.

Civil engineer: Hubbell, Roth & Clark, Inc.

Boutwells Landing Care Center

Architect: InSite Architects

Contractor: Adolfson and Peterson Construction

Interior designer: Senior Lifestyle Designs

Landscape architect: Savanna Designs

Structural engineer: Mattson Macdonald Young

Mechanical engineer: Steen Engineering

Electrical engineer: Steen Engineering

Civil engineer: Folz Freeman Erickson

Skilled Nursing Building Data			
Unit type	Number of units	Size range (NSF)	Typical size (NSF)
Single-occupancy room	77	320 to 850	340
Double-occupancy room	2	500 to 500	500
Total (all Units)	81		
Total NSF			-

Dementia/Memory Support Unit Building Data			
Unit type	Number of units	Size range (NSF)	Typical size (NSF)
Single-occupancy room	25	320 to 400	340
Double-occupancy room	1	500	500
Total (all Units)	27		
Total NSF			-

Episcopal Home Church St. Luke's Chapel

Architect: K. Norman Berry Associates Architects
Contractor: F.W.Owens Co., Inc.
Landscape architect: Sabak Wilson Lingo, Inc.
Structural engineer: Tetra Tech
Mechanical engineer: Kerr-Greulich Engineers Inc.
Electrical engineer: Kerr-Greulich Engineers Inc.
Civil engineer: Sabak Wilson Lingo, Inc.
Acoustical engineering: Acoustical Design Group Inc.
Special inspections: GEM Engineering, Inc.
Code review: Arcodect Code Consulting, PLLC
Cost estimating: Robert Pass & Associates Inc.

Fox Hill

Architect: DiMella Shaffer
Lighting Designer: Collaborative Lighting
A/V: Acentech Incorporated
Food Service Consultant: Savoy/Brown Consultants

Independent Living
Building Data

Unit type	Number of units	Size range (NSF)	Typical size (NSF)
One-bedroom apartment	52	786 to 1142	926
Two-bedroom apartment	104	1175 to 1697	1380
Two-bedroom plus den apartment	66	1422 to 1919	1700
Three-bedroom plus apartment	18	1756 to 1976	1818
Total (all Units)	240		
Total NSF			333,736

Assisted Living
Building Data

Unit type	Number of units	Size range (NSF)	Typical size (NSF)
One-bedroom apartment	14	250 to 600	349
Two-bedroom apartment	15	412 to 635	582
Total (all Units)	29		
Total NSF			12,127

Dementia/Memory Support Unit
Building Data

Unit type	Number of units	Size range (NSF)	Typical size (NSF)
Single-occupancy room	43	245 to 540	295
Double-occupancy room	11	412 to 625	437
Total (all Units)	65		
Total NSF			17,512

Mennonite Home Skilled Care Reinvention

Architect: RLPS Architects

Skilled Nursing
Building Data

Unit type	Number of units	Size range (NSF)	Typical size (NSF)
Single-occupancy room	15	237 to 314	279
Double-occupancy room	59	285 to 441	285
Total (all Units)	133		
Total NSF			61,233

Dementia/Memory Support Unit
Building Data

Unit type	Number of units	Size range (NSF)	Typical size (NSF)
Single-occupancy room	10	277 to 277	277
Double-occupancy room	9	345 to 370	370
Total (all Units)	28		
Total NSF			12,000

Montgomery Place

Provider: Montgomery Place Retirement Community
Architect: Dorsky Hodgson Parrish Yue
Contractor: Benchmark Construction Company, Inc.
Interior designer: RLPS Architects
Structural engineer: Zug & Associates, Ltd.
Mechanical engineer: Reese Engineering, Inc.
Electrical engineer: Reese Engineering, Inc.
Civil engineer: Derck & Edson Associates, LLP

Assisted Living
Building Data

Unit type	Number of units	Size range (NSF)	Typical size (NSF)
Studio apartment	10	307 to 407	-
One-bedroom apartment	2	474 to 539	-
Total (all Units)	12 (14 beds)		
Total NSF			Approx. 4,510

Skilled Nursing
Building Data

Unit type	Number of units	Size range (NSF)	Typical size (NSF)
Single-occupancy room	4	240 to 250	-
Double-occupancy room	18	268 to 420	-
Total (all Units)	40		
Total NSF			Approx. 6,255

Montgomery Place continued

Dementia/Memory Support Unit Building Data			
Unit type	Number of units	Size range (NSF)	Typical size (NSF)
Single-occupancy room	4	290 to 450	-
Double-occupancy room	2	476 to 564	-
Total (all Units)	8		
Total NSF			Approx. 2,270

Porter Hills GREEN HOUSE® Homes

Provider: Porter Hills Retirement Communities & Services

Architect: Dorsky Hodgson Parrish Yue

Contractor: Elzinga-Volkers Construction

Interior designer: Dorsky Hodgson Parrish Yue

Landscape architect: Hitchcock Design Group

Structural engineer: Thorson Baker & Associates

Mechanical engineer: Integrated Engineering Consultants, Inc.

Electrical engineer: Integrated Engineering Consultants, Inc.

Civil engineer: Exxel Engineering, Inc.

Furniture Selection and Procurement: Progressive A/E

Skilled Nursing Building Data			
Unit type	Number of units	Size range (NSF)	Typical size (NSF)
Single-occupancy room	20	280 to 325	300 (average)
Total (all Units)	20		
Total NSF			6,000

Sharon S. Richardson Community Hospice

Provider: Sharon S. Richardson, C.H.

Architect: Engberg Anderson, Inc.

Contractor: Quasius Construction, Inc.

Interior designer: Engberg Anderson, Inc.

Landscape architect: Kelly's Landscape Design

Structural engineer: KompGilomen Engineering, Inc.

Mechanical engineer: Engineering Concepts, Inc.

Electrical engineer: Leddy & Petzold Associates, LLC

Civil engineer: Short Elliot Hendrickson, Inc.

Food service: Stewart Design

Skilled Nursing Building Data			
Unit type	Number of units	Size range (NSF)	Typical size (NSF)
Single-occupancy room	16	-	400
Double-occupancy room	2	-	530
Total (all Units)	20		
Total NSF			7,460

Signature Apartments

Provider: Martins Run

Architect: RLPS Architects

Interior designer firm name: RLPS Architects

Structural engineer firm name: Joseph Barbato Associates, LLC

Mechanical engineer firm name: Reese Engineering, Inc.

Electrical engineer firm name: Reese Engineering, Inc.

Independent Living Building Data			
Unit type	Number of units	Size range (NSF)	Typical size (NSF)
Studio apartment	8	467 to 467	467
One-bedroom apartment	30	598 to 897	598
Two-bedroom apartment	22	956 to 1209	1082
Total (all Units)	60		
Total NSF			49,033

Hope House at Hope Meadows

Provider: Generations of Hope

Architect: Mithun

Collaborating architect: JSR Associates, Inc

Role of collaborating architect: Programming and predesign

Interior designer: Design Concepts Unlimited

Landscape architect: Mithun

Independent Living Building Data			
Unit type	Number of units	Size range (NSF)	Typical size (NSF)
One-bedroom apartment Two-bedroom apartment	4 4	730 to 730 1100 to 1100	730 1100
Total (all Units)	8		
Total NSF			7320

Taube Koret Campus for Jewish Life

Provider: Taube Koret Campus for Jewish Life

Architect: Steinberg Architects

Contractor: Webcor Builders, Inc.

Interior designer: Steinberg Architects

Landscape architect: Conger Moss Guillard

Structural engineer: Forell Elsesser

Mechanical engineer: Flack & Kurtz/Acco.

Electrical engineer: Flack & Kurtz/Cupertino Electric

Civil engineer: Brian Kangas Foulk

Plumbing: Flack + Kurtz/ACCO

Food Service: The Marshall and Associates

Acoustics & Audiovisual: Charles Salter Associates

Waterproofing: Simpson, Gumpertz & Hager, Inc.

Environmental: Geosyntec Consultants

Geotechnical: Engeo Inc.

Independent Living Building Data			
Unit type	Number of units	Size range (NSF)	Typical size (NSF)
One-bedroom apartment Two-bedroom apartment Two-bedroom plus apartment	42 116 12	680 to 973 1016 to 1280 1750 to 1750	865 1220 1750
Total (all Units)	170		
Total NSF			164,812

Taube Koret Campus for Jewish Life continued

Assisted Living Building Data			
Unit type	Number of units	Size range (NSF)	Typical size (NSF)
One-bedroom apartment	12	621 to 679	650
Total (all Units)	12		
Total NSF			7,800

Dementia/Memory Support Unit Building Data			
Unit type	Number of units	Size range (NSF)	Typical size (NSF)
Single-occupancy room	11	308 to 308	308
Total (all Units)	11		
Total NSF			3,388

The Ridge and Boulders of RiverWoods at Exeter

Provider: Exeter, NH

Architect: JSA Inc.

Contractor: LeCesse Construction

Interior designer: Bridget Bohacz & Associates

Landscape architect: Stantec

Structural engineer: JSN

Mechanical engineer: RDK

Electrical engineer: RDK

Civil engineer: Altus Engineering, Inc.

Development consultant: Greystone Communities

Independent Living Building Data			
Unit type	Number of units	Size range (NSF)	Typical size (NSF)
One-bedroom apartment Two-bedroom apartment Two-bedroom cottage	51 106 35	815 to 975 1,160 to 1,441 1,920 to 2,350	975 1,334 2,080
Total (all Units)	192		
Total NSF			238,158

Assisted Living Building Data			
Unit type	Number of units	Size range (NSF)	Typical size (NSF)
One-bedroom apartment Two-bedroom apartment	47 4	533 to 550 800 to 837	533 800
Total (all Units)	51		
Total NSF			28,663

The Ridge and Boulders of RiverWoods at Exeter continued

Skilled Nursing Building Data			
Unit type	Number of units	Size range (NSF)	Typical size (NSF)
Single-occupancy room	31	261 to 275	275
Total (all Units)	31		
Total NSF			8,315

Dementia/Memory Support Unit Building Data			
Unit type	Number of units	Size range (NSF)	Typical size (NSF)
Single-occupancy room	8	261 to 261	261
Total (all Units)	8		
Total NSF			2,088

Villa at San Luis Rey

Provider: Senior Partners West LLC

Architect: Lawrence Group

Contractor: Ledcor Construction

Interior designer: Lawrence Group

Landscape architect: The Lightfoot Planning Group

Structural engineer: KPFF Structural Engineers

Mechanical engineer: BCER Engineering

Electrical engineer: BCER Engineering

Civil engineer: O'Day Consultants

Assisted Living Building Data			
Unit type	Number of units	Size range (NSF)	Typical size (NSF)
One-bedroom apartment	28	643 to 855	18,028
Two-bedroom apartment	108	970 to 1,641	106,817
Three-bedroom plus apartment	44	1,300 to 1,341	59,580
Total (all Units)	180		
Total NSF			184,425

Skilled Nursing Building Data			
Unit type	Number of units	Size range (NSF)	Typical size (NSF)
Single-occupancy room	40	568 to 638	36,006
Total (all Units)	40		
Total NSF			36,006

Villa at San Luis Rey continued

Dementia/Memory Support Unit Building Data			
Unit type	Number of units	Size range (NSF)	Typical size (NSF)
Single-occupancy room	15	568 to 638	10,375
Total (all Units)	15		
Total NSF			10,375

Hybrid Homes

Provider: Landis Homes Retirement Community

Architect: RLPS Architects

Contractor: Benchmark Construction Company, Inc.

Interior designer: RLPS Architects

Structural engineer: Zug & Associates

Mechanical engineer: Reese Engineering, Inc.

Electrical engineer: Reese Engineering, Inc.

Civil engineer: RGS Associates

Independent Living Building Data			
Unit type	Number of units	Size range (NSF)	Typical size (NSF)
One-bedroom apartment	3	875 to 875	875
Two-bedroom apartment	48	1315 to 1370	1342
Three-bedroom plus apartment	24	1620 to 1620	1620
Total (all Units)	75		
Total NSF			12,060 per floor

La Paloma - East Lubbock Regional MHMR

Architect: McCormick Architecture

Interior designer: McCormick Architecture, LLC

Landscape architect: KDC Design

Structural engineer: Allied and Associates

Mechanical engineer: Allied and Associates

Electrical engineer: Allied and Associates

Civil engineer: Allied and Associates

Penick Village Garden Cottage

Provider: Episcopal Diocese of North Carolina
Architect: CJMW, PA
Contractor: Pinnacle Development Corporation
Interior designer: CJMW, PA
Landscape architect: Lappas & Havener, PA
Structural engineer: Arrowood & Arrowood, PC
Mechanical engineer: CJMW, PA
Electrical engineer: CJMW, PA
Civil engineer: Mulkey Engineers & Consultants
LEED for homes provider: NC Solar Center
Energy rater: Commissioning WorCx

Assisted Living Building Data			
Unit type	Number of units	Size range (NSF)	Typical size (NSF)
Studio apartment	10	303 to 337	307
Total (all Units)	10		
Total NSF			3080

Residential Hospice for York Region

Architect: Stantec Architecture (Toronto Office)
Interior designer: Stantec Architecture
Landscape architect: Shirley den Houdyker
Structural engineer: Halcrow Yolles
Mechanical engineer: HH Angus & Associates Limited
Electrical engineer: HH Angus & Associates Limited

Assisted Living Building Data			
Unit type	Number of units	Size range (NSF)	Typical size (NSF)
Single-occupancy room	10	-	Approx. 350
Total (all Units)	-		
Total NSF			-

Roseland Senior Campus

Provider: Roseland Place Limited Partnership
Architect: Landon Bone Baker Architects
Contractor: Linn – Mathes Inc.
Landscape architect: McKay Landscape Architects
Structural engineer: Klein and Hoffman, Inc.
Mechanical engineer: Calor Design Group, Ltd.
Electrical engineer: Calor Design Group, Ltd.
Civil engineer: Prism Engineering, Inc.

Independent Living Building Data			
Unit type	Number of units	Size range (NSF)	Typical size (NSF)
One-bedroom apartment (Independent Living Facility)	60	527 to 663	555
Three-bedroom plus apartment (Grandfamily Apartments)	10	1,115 to 1,540	1,270
Total (all Units)	70		
Total NSF			46,025

The Houses on Bayberry

Provider: Arbor Acres Retirement Community
Architect: RLPS Architect
Collaborating architect: Lambert Architecture + Interiors
Role of collaborating architect: Construction Observation
Contractor: I.L. Long Construction Company, Inc.
Mechanical engineer: Reese Engineering, Inc.
Electrical engineer: Reese Engineering, Inc.
Civil engineer: Allied Civil Engineering & Land Surveying

Independent Living Building Data			
Unit type	Number of units	Size range (NSF)	Typical size (NSF)
Two-bedroom cottage	4	1082 to 1082	1082
One-bedroom cottage	4	957 to 957	977
Total (all Units)	8		
Total NSF			8,156

The Sterling of Pasadena

Provider: Sunrise Senior Living

Architect: Mithun, Seattle, Washington

Local architect: ONYX Architects, Pasadena, California

Landscape architect: EDAW, Irvine, California

Interior designer: Mithun, Seattle, Washington; Martha Child Interiors, McLean, Virginia

Civil: Adams-Streeter, Irvine, California

Structural: KPFF, Seattle, Washington

Mechanical: The Rice Group, Lynnwood, Washington

Electrical: AWA Electrical, Lynnwood, Washington

Renderings: Mike Kowalski

THF/CCS Casitas on East Broadway Senior Housing

Provider: Casitas on East Broadway, an Arizona Non-Profit Corp in care of Catholic Community Services of Southern Arizona + Tucson Housing Foundation

Architect: Lizard Rock Designs, LLC

Contractor: Tofel Construction

Structural engineer: Schneider & Associates, Inc.

Mechanical engineer: KC Mechanical Engineering, LLC

Electrical engineer: McGetrick & Associates

Civil engineer: Dowl

Cost: Compusult

Independent Living Building Data			
Unit type	Number of units	Size range (NSF)	Typical size (NSF)
One-bedroom apartment	56	497 to 519	519
Total (all Units)	-		
Total NSF			-

Tohono O'odham Elder Homes

Provider: Tohono O'odham Nursing Care Authority

Architect: Lizard Rock Designs, LLC

Landscape architect: Logan Simpson Design, Inc.

Structural engineer: Schneider & Associates, Inc.

Mechanical engineer: KC Mechanical Engineering, LLC

Electrical engineer: Matthews Consulting and Design

Civil engineer: Cornerstone Environmental Group, LLC

Surveying: Full Circle Engineering

Assisted Living Building Data			
Unit type	Number of units	Size range (NSF)	Typical size (NSF)
Studio apartment	12	230	230
Total (all Units)	-		
Total NSF			-

Index of Architects

Index of Projects